Reading from the South depicts the vast complexity of Africa in the Indian Ocean world, presenting evidence and arguments that render the continent an open space of mobility on land and sea. A very satisfying intellectual odyssey.

—RILA MUKHERJEE, maritime historian and author of
*India in the Indian Ocean World: From the
Earliest Times to 1800 CE*

An immersive intellectual portrait of a scholar whose capacious itineraries model what it means to widen the horizons of our scholarly practice. A rewarding read.

—GRACE A. MUSILA, Associate Professor,
Department of African Literature, University
of the Witwatersrand, Johannesburg

Reading from the South

African print cultures and oceanic turns in Isabel Hofmeyr's work

Edited by

CHARNE LAVERY & SARAH NUTTALL

WITS UNIVERSITY PRESS

Published in South Africa by:
Wits University Press
1 Jan Smuts Avenue
Johannesburg 2001

www.witspress.co.za

First published 2023

http://dx.doi.org.10.18772/22023088363

978-1-77614-836-3 (Paperback)
978-1-77614-837-0 (Hardback)
978-1-77614-838-7 (Web PDF)
978-1-77614-839-4 (EPUB)

Project manager: Lisa Compton
Copyeditor: Lisa Compton
Proofreader: Alison Paulin
Indexer: Sanet le Roux
Cover design: Hybrid Creative
Typeset in 11 point Minion Pro

CONTENTS

FIGURES

ACKNOWLEDGEMENTS

The editors would like to express their warm appreciation to all the contributors to this volume – for their astute, beautiful and deeply meaningful writing, and for their willingness to offer their chapters at some speed for the timeous making of this book.

Thanks to artist and designer Joni Brenner, the Marigold beadwork co-operative, and photographer Liz Whitter for our cover image; to Adrienne van Eeden-Wharton for image assistance; and to Isabelle Delvare for early editing help. We are thrilled to publish this book with Wits University Press, Southern book publisher par excellence – and to have drawn the book to life in the Press's centenary year. Roshan Cader and Veronica Klipp have been highly engaged, tipping the book towards the best title and the right cover, and offering always crucial feedback along the way. They also connected us with Lisa Compton, an editor's dream editor. We express our thanks to each other, for a process of intellectual collaboration that has been formative, fast and fun in the midst of so much else. Our tremendous debt to, and admiration for, Isabel Hofmeyr, her scholarship and her person, is suffused throughout this book: we offer it to her and to so many others who will read it in the spirit of profound thanks.

Southern Lodestar:
Isabel Hofmeyr's Life and Work

Sarah Nuttall and Charne Lavery

This book draws together reflective and analytical essays by renowned intellectuals from around the world who critically engage with the work of one of the global South's leading scholars of African print cultures and the oceanic humanities. Isabel Hofmeyr's scholarship spans more than four decades, and its sustained and long-term influence on her discipline and beyond is formidable. Her contributions range from her early work in orality and feminist critical engagement, to transnational histories of the book, to Mohandas Gandhi's conceptualisation of print culture and its potentialities in his philosophy of satyagraha, to 'dockside reading', hydrocolonialism, and the 'landing' of books and settler subjects on African shores.

If the history of print cultures has been written primarily from the North, Isabel Hofmeyr is one of the leading thinkers producing new knowledge in this area from Africa, the Indian Ocean world and the South. Her major contribution to print histories encompasses the history of the book as well as newspapers, pamphlets, extracts, multiple editions, anthologised textual segments, excised books and abridged iterations of canonical works such as John Bunyan's *The Pilgrim's Progress*. Hofmeyr has pioneered archival research on the ways in which such printed matter moves across the globe, focusing on intra-African trajectories and circulations as well as movements across land and sea, port and shore. The essays gathered here are written in a blend of intellectual and personal modes, and mostly by scholars of Indian and African descent. They in turn elaborate and contribute to, via an engagement with Hofmeyr's path-breaking work, studies of the history of the book as well as critical oceanic studies, consolidating these fields from the point of view of Southern historical contexts and textual practices.

Hofmeyr has published four major monographs, all highly influential: *'We Spend Our Years as a Tale That is Told': Oral Historical Narrative in a South African Chiefdom* (Wits University Press/Heinemann/James Currey, 1993); *The Portable Bunyan: A Transnational History of 'The Pilgrim's Progress'* (Wits University Press/Princeton University Press, 2004); *Gandhi's Printing Press: Experiments in Slow Reading* (Harvard University Press, 2013); and *Dockside Reading: Hydrocolonialism and the Custom House* (Wits University Press/Duke University Press, 2022). A wide array of her writing has also circulated and percolated between, around and beyond these books. These articles and book chapters address, variously, the book in Africa, histories of the book in South Africa, African popular literature and its publics, African literatures and transnationalism, cultures of circulation in the Indian Ocean, South–South cultural connections between India and South Africa, print cultures, nationalism and publics along Indian Ocean routes, and literary ecologies of the Indian Ocean. Her very early work – on the mining novel in South Africa, orality and literacy, and feminist literary criticism – remains influential, while current work

Figure 0.1: Isabel Hofmeyr on the library lawns in front of the Great Hall at Wits University, 1976

includes writing on port cities such as Durban and Cape Town and their histories of harbour engineering; on censorship and intellectual copyright; and on thinking through the challenge of climate change to humanities scholarship by such new methods as 'going below the waterline' and 'reading in Antarctica'. This incomplete overview demonstrates the range of Hofmeyr's innovative scholarship and far-reaching influence, which, we suggest, is inextricably linked to the Southern- and African-centredness of her biography.

Therefore, in this introduction we begin with a focus on Hofmeyr's life, focusing on key moments that shaped her intellectual trajectory and the networks that feed and are fed by her conceptual contributions. We first outline her education and early career, before interleaving descriptions of her monographs and key papers with the political, creative and institution-building activities that are bound up with her intellectual work. Hofmeyr describes herself as a 'swot' (British/South

African schoolyard slang for someone who studies hard), but this is only a way of saying that her core work has always been in reading and finding new ways of reading. Of equal significance is that her life, archives and intellectual investments are deeply rooted in place – the Department of African Literature, Wits, Johannesburg, Africa, the global South – while reaching far and wide across the world. Those far-reaching impacts are registered and elaborated in the chapters that follow, breaking new ground in reading from the South while guided by the lodestar of Hofmeyr's work.

SETTING SAIL

There is a lost photograph of Isabel Hofmeyr from around 1979, which is so full of portent, young charisma and a tone of feminist rebellion that we begin by describing our memory of it: Hofmeyr, with her feet up on a desk at the front of a classroom, smoking a cigarette and laughing. It was taken at the University of Durban-Westville (UDW), which at the time was, by apartheid law, an Indians-only offshoot campus from the University of Natal. One of her best students that year was Jay Pather, who recalls the campus then: 'It was the late seventies and the complexities and circumstances around attending such a university in the wake of so much political activity and repression is difficult to adequately describe.' Students, he recalls, would both attend their classes and burst regularly into protest action. Hofmeyr taught him African literature with 'uncompromising candour': not only did she 'break rank and regale us with acerbic, intellectually refreshing and astonishingly honest critique', but she 'threw out all pretensions around propriety and the lecturer-student space and engaged us with the immediacy of the literature, yes, but most especially of that specific moment'. She made 'the learning and the critique not just more real, but necessary'.[1]

Hofmeyr's post at UDW was her first lecturing position, teaching literature to undergraduates. She had her honours and MA degrees behind her, having been part of a dynamic honours class at the University of the Witwatersrand, Johannesburg (Wits), that would produce well-known Marxist literary scholars and left-wing and anti-apartheid journalists and newspaper editors (see figure 0.1). If UDW gave impetus to her nascent political and professional self, Johannesburg had already opened the lid on that liberating project. When the temporary lectureship ended, the new decade of the 1980s found her back in the big city, working at the leftist adult education non-governmental organisation known as the South African Committee for Higher Education (SACHED) and on two small literary magazines. The latter would be the first of many 'out-of-office' activities she would be involved in, which ran alongside what she considered her core work: literary and cultural studies. One of these literary magazines was *Donga*, which, after a short run, was banned in perpetuity by the apartheid government. A second was *Inspan*, which started in the late 1970s and of which she became an editor. It, too, was banned and Hofmeyr was charged with producing an undesirable publication under the Suppression of Communism Act. SACHED covered her legal fees and, with excellent anti-apartheid legal representation, she was ultimately acquitted. The caption to a photograph of her in the *Rand Daily Mail* at the time of the trial reads 'Miss Christine Isabel Hofmeyr outside court yesterday'; next to it is a handwritten label, 'The Angel of Yeoville' (see figures 0.2 and 0.3). Hofmeyr, referred to by her full birth name, lived in the alternative, mixed-race suburb of Yeoville at the time.

By 1982 Hofmeyr had arrived at the School of Oriental and African Studies (SOAS) at the University of London to work on a second MA degree under the supervision of renowned southern African historian Shula Marks. This was an experience she later said equipped her with the interdisciplinary skills needed to calibrate history and literature in meaningful ways – a crucial aspect of the History Workshop/ history-from-below movement she would subsequently join at Wits.

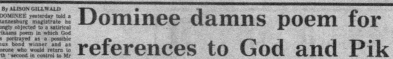

Dominee damns poem for references to God and Pik

By ALISON GILLWALD

A DOMINEE yesterday told a Johannesburg magistrate he strongly objected to a satirical Afrikaans poem in which God was portrayed as a possible bonus bond winner and as someone who would return to earth "second in control to Mr Pik Botha".

Dominee Jacobus Botha, chairman of the Nederduitse Gereformeerde Kerk's (NGK) Doctrine and Current Affairs Commission, was giving evidence for the State in the case against Miss Christine Isabel Hofmeyr, editor of the now banned literary magazine, Inspan.

Miss Hofmeyr, 27, of Yeoville, pleaded not guilty in the Johannesburg Magistrate's Court to charges under the Publications Act, of having produced an undesirable magazine.

Inspan (October 1978) was banned in January 1979, after poems and prose printed in it were found by the Publications Board to be blasphemous, indecent and a danger to the security of the State.

Mr Botha said a poem based on the Lord's prayer, by Andre le Roux du Toit, was "despicable and offensive".

Cross-examined by Mr Dennis Kuny, for Miss Hofmeyr, Mr Botha conceded the poem might not be disrespectful and could, in fact, have been written by a devout man who was criticising people who had replaced God with a materialistic form.

He said he had been particularly offended by the lines referring to the possibility of God winning bonus bonds, and coming down to earth to "be second in control to Pik Botha".

"My church forbids the buying of bonus bonds as it is a form of gambling and the poem makes God look like a gambler.

"The poem relegates the Almighty God to a position below Mr Pik Botha," he said.

But he agreed with Mr Kuny that the poem could be interpreted as referring to a distortion of values that had crept into society.

This was symbolised by references to a God in Lynnwood or Groenkloof, upper-middle class suburbs in Pretoria, and Cabinet Ministers, models and boxers who became gods for the corrupted population.

References to Morne du Plessis, Glenda Kemp, Kallie Knoetze and "Adrenalien" Kriel, could have shown that these people were elevated to God-like positions, Mr Botha said.

The "Angel of Yeoville". Miss Christine Isabel Hofmeyr outside court yesterday.

And he added the poet might have meant in his poem that in order to maintain materialistic values it was necessary to resort to violence and oppression.

He also agreed with Mr Kuny that references to people who "wore combs in their socks" and complained of having to pay sales tax, when they only had three cars and two "garden boys", were, in fact, typifying those whites who were content with their superior position in society and were intent on maintaining it.

Mr Kuny said: "This poem is highly critical of a group of people with distorted values and in fact has a moral mes-

sage as opposed to an immoral message."

Mr Botha agreed the poet might be saying the NGK upheld the present South African system and performed a role to ensure the maintenance of apartheid.

"If that is how you see it, that's fine, but it is not true," Mr Botha said.

If the man was a devout Christian he should have used another form, not the Lord's Prayer, he said.

"The poem was intended to offend certain people in society with misplaced values, but not a religious section of society," Mr Kuny said when applying for a discharge, after Mr

Botha's evidence had been heard.

The application for a discharge on the grounds that no evidence was led to prove the accused intended to offend a religious section of the population was overruled.

In refusing the application, the magistrate, Mr A C Allcock, said besides the evidence heard, other material in the publication, such as the poem "Sara — die Hoer van Rundu", was indecent.

Miss Hofmeyr, who has a Masters degree in South African literature, and who lectured at the University of Durban-Westville and University of the Witwatersrand before be-

coming a course writer for the South African Council for Higher Education (Sached), told the court she saw none of the material as undesirable, indecent or threatening State security.

"In fact, I was very surprised when the publication was banned," she said.

Professor Elise Botha, literary critic of the University of Pretoria, had even written in the banned issue encouraging the establishment of an "avant garde" magazine, stressing its important role — not to provide enduring literature, but work that was contemporary, holding a certain interest, Miss Hofmeyr said.

The hearing continues today.

Figure 0.2: 'The Angel of Yeoville', *Rand Daily Mail*, 27 January 1981. Isabel Hofmeyr smiling outside the Johannesburg Magistrate's Court after being acquitted of charges under the Publications Act of producing an undesirable magazine. (Arena Holdings Archives)

Prof praises banned poems in court

Staff Reporter

PROFESSOR Ampie Coetzee — a well-known Afrikaans poet, writer and academic — praised a banned magazine for its high standard when he gave evidence in the Johannesburg Magistrate's Court yesterday.

He was giving evidence for the defence at the trial of the editor of the now-banned Inspan, Miss Christine Hofmeyr, 27, of Yeoville, who has pleaded not guilty to a charge under the Publications Act of producing an undesirable magazine.

The October 1978 issue of Inspan was banned in January, 1979, after poems and prose printed in it were found by the Publications Board to be blasphemous, indecent and a danger to State security.

Yesterday Prof Coetzee, a lecturer at the University of the Witwatersrand, poet and writer, praised the "high standard" of works in both Afrikaans and English which were published in the magazine.

He said the magazine was a "literary laboratory" for poets wishing to experiment in literature and also an attempt to overcome the "stiffness" of works before the sixties.

Referring to an alleged "despicable and offensive" poem based on the Lord's Prayer, Prof Coetzee said the poem satirised the Afrikaner's power struggle in which he — the Afrikaner — relegates Almighty God to a position below himself. This could be the intention of the poet, Mr Andre le Roux du Toit.

An intelligent reader with a broad frame of reference would not be offended, but would understand the satire, Prof Coetzee said.

The case continues today.

Editor of the now-banned Inspan literary magazine, Miss Christine Hofmeyr, outside court yesterday. *Picture: TREVOR SAMSON*

Figure 0.3: 'Editor of the now-banned *Inspan* literary magazine, Miss Christine Hofmeyr, outside court yesterday', *Rand Daily Mail*, 27 January 1981. Hofmeyr stands outside the courthouse during her trial for editing a magazine whose content was found by the Publications Board to be 'blasphemous, indecent, and a danger to State security'. (Arena Holdings Archives)

Figure 0.4: Isabel Hofmeyr (*centre left*), walks alongside other protestors at an anti-nuclear demonstration in London, 1982

When out of office, she can be seen in photographs from the time 'sitting in' at Greenham Common in the cold and wet and participating in anti-nuclear marches through London (see figure 0.4). By 1984 she was back home, with a job in the newly established Department of African Literature at Wits, where she found herself right inside the cauldron of late anti-apartheid politics, with Johannesburg as its vital political nerve centre.

'HARDLY ENGLISH 1, MISS HOFMEYR'

In the 1980s, teaching literature at university in South Africa involved teaching students in prison. During the apartheid regime's punitive state of emergency, increasing numbers of students were detained. Hofmeyr, along with Debra Nails (then a philosophy lecturer), set up a group at Wits to ensure that students continued to study. As Hofmeyr explains, this involved 'setting up structures across all Faculties to gather lecture material and readings for students, take these to prisons, collect essays, deliver exam papers, collect scripts, arrange support for students' families and so on'. In quite typical manner, she remembers not just her tasks but also the 'occasional light moments' that the work produced. For instance, as lecturers dealt with the same warder over some time, the checking of the study material brought in by lecturers became more cursory. Inevitably, comrades of the students secreted banned material between the academic texts. One day Hofmeyr encountered a new warder, who checked everything carefully. As she recalls: 'Very soon he came across photocopies of Fanon, Marx and the like. "Hardly English 1, Miss Hofmeyr," he said.'[2]

Several significant decades later, in 2009, Hofmeyr could be found doing out-of-office work of a different kind, this time in a post-apartheid setting, delivering lectures on trains travelling between Johannesburg and Soweto. This was part of a project developed by Molemo Moiloa and Nare Mokgotho in the Wits School of Arts. They wanted to see how public one could make a public lecture and what a university-style lecture would look like in a truly public domain. Hofmeyr was asked to give a lecture on a packed commuter train as it journeyed from Park Station to Phomolong in Soweto and back again. She chose to speak about the importance of the Indian Ocean. Photographs from the time show that she had a ready audience, even if one more used to 'train sermons' of a different kind (see figure 0.5).

These out-of-office activities map interestingly and with a gendered slant onto a much earlier moment in her life. Hofmeyr was a new arrival at Jeppe High School, an all-girls school in Johannesburg, where she had moved with her parents, both teachers, from the small town of Potchefstroom in what is now South Africa's North West province. The school gave her early clues to how one might go about being a professional woman and having a writing career. In an interview with Cynthia Kros, she talks about the things that made a lasting impression on her: the importance of seeing women in authority when 'outside [the school] it was different'; the 'sense that you could be a professional person if that's what you wanted to

Figure 0.5: Hofmeyr with microphone lecturing to passengers on the commuter train from central Johannesburg to Phumulong in Soweto, 2009. (Sermon on the Train, courtesy of MADEYOULOOK; photograph by Stacey Vorster)

be'; and, significantly, 'a stress on the craft of writing, reinforced, for example, by the idea that writing was selected for publication in the school magazine'.[3] Yet she wasn't always so preoccupied – she sometimes filled school suitcases with bricks and put them in the way of teachers marching up and down classrooms during lessons so that they would stub their toes, an activity for which she was roundly punished. Moving from school in Potch to Jeppe in Johannesburg was, she said once, like going from 'Mary Poppins to Mary Quant' – from a fictional and somewhat angelic character to a modern urban woman (with short hair and hot pants, either by fact or imagination), building what would be her brilliant career.

THE DEPARTMENT OF AFRICAN LITERATURE

At Wits in 1984, a key figure for Hofmeyr was Tim Couzens, who had been teaching African literature in the Department of English since the late 1960s. The English department was then still very focused on teaching 'the Great Tradition' and was, like most English departments around the world, not especially interested in African literature. At the same time, the iconic South African writer Es'kia Mphahlele had returned to Johannesburg from exile. Keen to attract him to the university, and on the back of increasing frustration with the intractability of the English department regarding the literature of its own continent, a group of breakaway academics including Hofmeyr established the Department of African Literature as a separate unit. The department opened its doors in late 1983 and almost immediately drew in the young Hofmeyr. She also rotated to the History Workshop, which was doing pioneering work on 'history from below'. Intellectually, the history-from-below movement, South Africa's version of subaltern studies, was dominated by historians and social scientists, with literary studies as something of an outlier. Hofmeyr learned to conduct thinking and research across these two sometimes competing terrains. By that stage, having levelled some strong challenges to historians in a series of critiques which would gain ground in her first monograph, she took on her own discipline in no uncertain terms.

In a scathing and still influential essay from the late 1970s, as described by Khwezi Mkhize in the opening chapter of this book, Hofmeyr considers the state of South African literary studies as 'singularly lacklustre', a 'sorry battology' repeating similarly angled analyses of the same few texts – those classed as 'high literature' (Hofmeyr 1976, 39). In so doing, it 'ignores all working class literature, both African and Afrikaans, and it shuns large chunks of white popular literature with vehemence. In total, then, this "tradition" which claims to represent South African Literature, quite staggeringly ignores the culture and literary endeavours of the majority of people in this country' (39–40). Hofmeyr's is an argument that necessarily shifts from the question of the canon, what is worthy of study, to a theory of literature itself. What is required is a conception of literature that is resolutely anti-elitist and not confined only to the upper classes – which, she argues, requires rejecting 'the distinction between "high" and "low" culture, and begin[ning] instead to explain the complexities of a dynamic society and its culture' (44). At the heart of and entangled with these questions, which would percolate through Hofmeyr's work over the coming decades, was her growing interest and expertise in oral historical narratives as texts.

A decade in the making, Hofmeyr's 'We Spend Our Years as a Tale That is Told': Oral Historical Narrative in a South African Chiefdom insists on placing historical and social change and transformation at the centre of critical analysis, thus 'forcing [literary] scholars to lift their eyes from the page' and to confront anew 'the complex links that unite producer, text, audience and the world in which they exist' (Hofmeyr 1993, 181). In turn, oral literature and historical narrative cannot, she tells historians, be mined for 'facts' but compel a reconnection with 'the ordering force of language in society' and an understanding of narrative 'which encodes political ideas and historical thinking in particularly effective ways' (181). Anyone wishing to come to terms with popular consciousness, she continues, would do well to 'pay close attention to words and stories', granting them an independence that 'is not inevitably yoked to a material base' (181). How did men and women tell historical stories differently? What were the influences of a literacy purveyed by missions and what was the impact of literate bureaucracies on oral modes of operation? What did forced removals do to traditions of male storytelling? How did the two 'technologies of the intellect' (12), the oral and the literate, interlace and in what unexpected permutations?

Based on her fieldwork in Valtyn, a chiefdom in the former Transvaal province close to Potgietersrus (now Mokopane), Hofmeyr read for the thresholds of change and transition that characterise 'tradition' rather than the stasis that coloniality and also at times scholarly analysis sought to impose (see figure 0.6). Out of this came what Carolyn Hamilton describes in her chapter as the methodological openings of 'fluidity'. Crucial to Hofmeyr's work in 'We Spend Our Years' was the scholarship of Karin Barber, who, working on Nigerian oral literatures and cultures, insisted on

Figure 0.6: Hofmeyr talking to two interlocutors during a meal while conducting PhD fieldwork in Valtyn, 1990

the simultaneous acknowledgement of 'the historicity and the textuality of texts' (cited in Hofmeyr 1993, 2). In her chapter in this book, Barber extends Hofmeyr's work in the then Transvaal to rethink how orality in fact transformed literacy more than the other way round, in the different but linked context of early Yoruba-medium Lagosian newspapers.

More widely, Hofmeyr's work in bringing popular cultural forms into the purview of serious study had the effect of avoiding a binary model of opposition and resistance. As James Ogude describes in his chapter, postcolonial theory on this model 'strait-jackets African readers and writers by assuming that everyone is obsessed with Western imperialism'. Instead, he suggests, Hofmeyr's emphasis provides a different way forward by focusing on the 'complex and layered fears, desires and aspirations of African readers, which are embedded in their everyday lives'. These were never purely academic debates. As Ogude goes on to detail, Hofmeyr proceeded to radically reimagine the curriculum of the

Wits Department of African Literature in collaboration with Bhekizizwe Peterson, who was, throughout Hofmeyr's career, a close colleague, ally, interlocutor and friend (see figure 0.7).

'We Spend Our Years' appeared a year before South Africa's political transition to democracy in 1994, and these curricular changes occurred in the context of other transformations in the department and university. University committees proliferated and Hofmeyr was very much in the thick of things as Wits began to engage with the prospect and possibility of a post-apartheid future. For much of her first decade and more of work at Wits, Hofmeyr was the only female academic in the Department of African Literature (see figure 0.8). Pumla Dineo Gqola joined the department in 2007, with more women scholars – notably Danai Mupotsa and Grace Musila – and avowedly feminist agendas – soon to follow. The department later added new courses on East African literary and cultural studies, through James Ogude and Dan Ojwang's scholarship and

Figure 0.7: Hofmeyr (*right*) in conversation with James Ogude (*left*) and Bheki Peterson (*centre*) at a celebratory event after her inaugural lecture, 2000

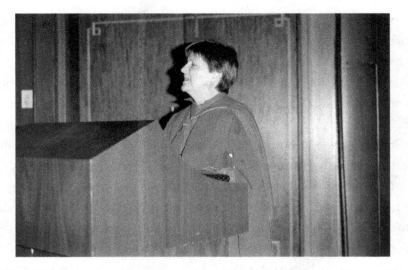

Figure 0.8: Hofmeyr at the podium during her inaugural lecture, University of the Witwatersrand, 2000

networks, and the work of students such as Tom Odhiambo, Grace Musila, Dina Ligaga and Joyce Nyairo. Amid all this change and intellectual proliferation, Hofmeyr's new and outward-looking book project was forming.

HIGH SEAS

As if South Africa's opening up to the world at large shifted the bow to a new set of latitudes, Hofmeyr set afloat her new major work on the shipboards, surfaces and cross-continental travels of the Protestant Atlantic. In *The Portable Bunyan: A Transnational History of 'The Pilgrim's Progress'* (Hofmeyr 2004), she chose to tell the historical narrative and social life of a book that had a rambunctious transnational and multi-tongued history but had been confined, purified and stultified by an ideological apparatus: Englishness. John Bunyan's *The Pilgrim's Progress* (written in two parts, published in 1678 and 1684) was a translingual mass text, an early world best-seller, which had been translated into two hundred languages.[4] Eighty of these were African and an important focus for Hofmeyr – but in her work the African continent is 'understood as part of a broader diasporic and imperial history in the Protestant Atlantic' (Hofmeyr 2004, 3). How were methods of textual creation stretched across time and space, unfolding in different places often at the same time? What forms of publicness did translated texts bring into being? What was it about the generic, episodic and eminently abridgeable features of the text that won it such wide audiences everywhere?

True to form, Hofmeyr insisted that we could only really answer any of these questions via a serious and sustained engagement with the African intellectual formations into which the book, or segments of it, arrived. 'Popular judgement' (Hofmeyr 2004, 21) had a decisive effect on whether translated forms became 'portable' or not. Furthermore, translations that took place at missions were at times 'less about technologies of colonial domination than about widening space for manoeuvre' (22). Kele-speaking Protestants, a religious community on the Upper Congo, excised tracts on original sin in *The Pilgrim's Progress*, while African and African American editions showed black characters such that the book acquired 'new personnel' (23) on its travels. Existing Kongo narrative traditions could make Bunyan's story seem 'a bit of a yawn' (29).[5] In short, the imperial arena was 'a complex forcefield in which circuits of influence travel in more than one direction' (24). *The Portable Bunyan* has proven highly portable itself, both building on and extending out into new debates, research platforms and publications. These range from 'The Book in Africa' (special issue of *Current Writing*, 2001) to Ranka Primorac's chapter in this volume on Zambian literary histories. Primorac draws on portability as method, especially the idea that as a text circulates, it functions as a 'compendium of generic possibilities', 'merging with local forms and adapting to local agendas'.

TRANSOCEANIC TILTS

But what about processes of transnationalism and textuality that happen without (much) reference to Europe at all? With Pamila Gupta, an anthropologist and historian of Goa and Portuguese colonialism, and Michael Pearson, who wrote on littoral societies on the Indian Ocean, Hofmeyr produced the important collection *Eyes Across the Water: Navigating the Indian Ocean* (Gupta, Hofmeyr and Pearson 2010), bringing together nascent Southern scholarship on the Indian Ocean. With a foreword by Amitav Ghosh and emerging from a conference of the same title and organised by Gupta and Hofmeyr, the book tackled the Indian Ocean, including its islands, as 'idea'. Debates had begun by the early 2000s at Wits, and especially at the Wits Institute for Social and Economic Research (WiSER), about what Françoise Vergès, Sarah Nuttall and Adboumaliq Simone had called 'the African South Indian Ocean'.[6] Gupta, based at WiSER, would go on, in strong interface, to write extensively on decolonisation processes across lusophone India and southern Africa, focusing on Goa, Mozambique, Angola and South Africa (e.g. Gupta 2018).

Eyes Across the Water marked Hofmeyr and her colleagues' pivot 'away from a singular oceanic frame of reference', as Christopher Ouma puts it in his essay in this volume. Invoking Dipesh Chakrabarty's call for a process of 'provincialising Europe' and Ngũgĩ wa Thiong'o's for scholars to 'move the centre', Ouma situates Hofmeyr's work in relation to Brent Hayes Edwards's work on diaspora, pointing away from a 'calcified' intellectual discourse overdetermined by the Atlantic seaboard. Hofmeyr's article 'The Complicating Sea: The Indian Ocean as Method' (2012) shows how the Indian Ocean draws out a complexity that takes us beyond received notions of nation, race, class and gender, as well as the 'black Atlantic' and 'diaspora', among many other things. Ouma, Sunil Amrith, Lakshmi Subramanian and others in this volume point to this article as vital to both the wider field and their own work within it.

Much of this work at Wits was underpinned by the establishment of the Centre for Indian Studies in Africa (CISA), envisaged by Hofmeyr. Beginning as a Mellon-funded research thrust which she led, it soon became a lively centre under the directorship of Dilip Menon, who joined from Delhi. Emerging and established Indian Ocean scholars found CISA to be a vital institutional nexus for the research agendas they were themselves calling into being at the time. Both Subramanian and Amrith write in this book about the vital role that exchanges at CISA played in refining their method, revisiting the Indian Ocean rim from new perspectives and, most significantly, drawing in and on occluded African histories and perspectives in the making of this oceanic world. Amrith describes how coming to CISA had the effect of 'blow[ing] open . . . an Indian-centred parochialism' in Indian Ocean studies. Both CISA and WiSER offered him, he writes, a post-area studies framework and 'diverse intellectual ecosystem' which shaped his own work.

As most of the essays in this volume make clear, Hofmeyr's writing and her institution- and network-building work have always gone hand in hand, just as her intellectual curiosity and innovation are inextricable from her hospitality, conversation and humour. In editing and launching *South Africa and India: Shaping the Global South* (2011) with Michelle Williams, for instance, Hofmeyr demonstrated her love of irony, seren-dipity and the unexpected. The Mr Bones series of South African films, she notes, were a runaway success in India, translated into a range of Indian languages and circulated widely in cinemas and on television. These slapstick films, in which a white comedian plays a traditional healer, were wildly popular first in South Africa, where they sold more tickets than *The Titanic* despite, or as a result of, playing on reverse racial stereo-types and relying on scatological comedy (Smith 2009). The strangeness of this locally rooted comedy's popularity in India is, for Hofmeyr, both an amusing story and the basis for a wide-ranging set of arguments about the many layers of connectedness that link postcolonial nations across the global South. Just as she had done earlier in the context of South African literary studies, Hofmeyr argued that attention should be paid to the full range of cultural trajectories, including the 'high, low and in-between' (Hofmeyr 2015, 99). In this and other work, Hofmeyr demonstrates the ways in which popular cultures (whether of film, fashion or cricket) connect just as clearly across South–South networks as literary fiction or political resistance networks such as the Non-Aligned Movement. Her work is thus attentive to the 'unexpected, bizarre, and jagged alignments (or non-alignments) that the Indian Ocean Global South throws up' (105). Tina Steiner (2021), in her theorisation of alternative modes of connection modelled in African Indian Ocean narratives, highlights the importance of the everyday, humour and hospitality in forging moments of what she terms 'conviviality' – which also aptly describes Hofmeyr's work and life in similar regions.

DIVING IN

If Hofmeyr's work in the Indian Ocean provides a way of thinking trans-nationalism and globalisation within and across the South, her 2013 book, *Gandhi's Printing Press: Experiments in Slow Reading*, dives more deeply into elaborating it, situating the larger-than-life figure of Gandhi not only within South Asian political history but within his long South African sojourn as well. Although this sojourn is largely thought of as a digression from the main part of Gandhi's life's work, Hofmeyr shows his years in South Africa to be central, a key setting for the emergence of his most important ideas. There is no way of thinking from the South, she shows, without thinking across it.

There is a pair of stories at the start of the book, about a 'phantom printing press'. One story is that Gandhi's printing press was on a ship stopped by protest in the harbour from entering the port of Durban, and the other is that Gandhi's press sank when the ship wrecked off the coast of India on its return from South Africa (Hofmeyr 2013). The images invoked by these stories are arresting, centring the printing press and the sea as key to Gandhi's biography. *Gandhi's Printing Press* effectively puts aside the question of Gandhi as an ethical icon, as Madhumita Lahiri observes in her chapter, 'situating him instead as a person of print cul-ture' on a transoceanic scale. Since the Gandhian approach to self-rule 'territorialises sovereignty in the individual rather than in a territory', as Lahiri elaborates from Hofmeyr's text, proper reading practices could instantiate how self-rule and satyagraha (passive resistance/soul force) should operate and unfold. Reading could, Hofmeyr argues, create 'small moments of intellectual independence' through 'pausing industrial speed' (Hofmeyr 2013, 4). These moments in turn enabled a point from which to theorise Gandhi's best-known ideas. Hofmeyr tracks how Gandhi experimented with *Indian Opinion*, an 'anti-commodity, copyright-free, slow motion newspaper' (40) which operated like an 'ethical anthology' (5) for a greater India. Gandhi, she shows, relied on periodicals and pamphlets as major media for making ideas more portable and durable across the empire. *Gandhi's Printing Press* thereby elaborates themes developed in *The Portable Bunyan*, subjecting them to new South–South contexts.

In *Gandhi's Printing Press* and beyond, Hofmeyr turns from the canon to the printing press, from literature to books, from concepts to covers, taking the core object of our work as scholars – books – and turning them upside down and inside out. Indeed, throughout Hofmeyr's scholarship, books appear in various places, states and mediums: on desks, in luggage, under water, frozen in ice, soaked, cut up, nibbled by insects, handled by customs inspectors, tasted and sniffed. Again, these interests operate across both work and life. Another of Hofmeyr's out-of-office activities – her own art practice – arose from the problem of having too many books. Tired of taking yet another load of books to the charity store, she began to use books as materials in an art class run by artist Bronwen Findlay. Long interested in the anatomy of the book, she was curious to see to what ends its materiality could be coaxed. First, she used books as paintbrushes, grasping the spine of the book, 'buttering' the foreedge with acrylic and then sweeping the book across the paper. The resulting painting was named after the book that had produced it: her earliest efforts included *The Autobiography of William Cobbett*, *Rebellion and Revolution* and *Sophie's World* (see figure 0.9). She then began making the book more malleable by saturating it in water. The sodden volume could then be 'spidered' into more interesting shapes when acrylic was again applied and the book impressed on the paper. This technique produces a pelagic, marine-like look, very far removed from the imagined solidity of the book (see figure 0.10).

Figure 0.9: One of the early artworks in Hofmeyr's book-art series, called *The Autobiography of William Cobbett*, produced by dipping the book of the same name in blue and gold paint

Figure 0.10: Hofmeyr in Bronwen Findlay's studio using a book as a paintbrush (2017). She dips the spine into black ink, producing marine-like images on a large canvas. (Photo by Bronwen Findlay)

Understanding books as printed matter, Hofmeyr uses them as stamps to make prints, as paintbrushes to apply paint to paper, and to make ephemeral frozen sculptures of pages in ice.

GETTING WET

Dockside Reading: Hydrocolonialism and the Custom House (Hofmeyr 2022) proceeds from similarly saturated books, particularly the observation that books, as they approached the ports of the imperial world, were regularly thrown overboard. What, Hofmeyr asks, happens to books under water or on the damp and salty dockside? Like the customs officials at the centre of the story, Hofmeyr is 'more interested in the book's material substrate than its textual interior and treats books as but one item among many', practising what she calls 'texternalisation' (Hofmeyr 2022, 14–15). In *Dockside Reading*, 'dry' institutions like copyright and censorship 'appear almost visceral, a quality seldom associated with intellectual property mechanisms generally imagined as noiseless and odourless' (2). This involves closely following the minutiae of archival traces which reveal the ontological methods of customs inspectors – determining what was sardine versus pilchard, incendiary versus benign novel – and the contestations among different port harbour institutions. These micropolitical matters ultimately construct and inform our understanding of macropolitical processes, such as the determination of which people are commodities and which are citizens. *Dockside Reading* therefore offers us a fascinating retake on the port city itself, the focus of much emerging historical work. As Hofmeyr puts it, the port and its infrastructure 'sought to overwrite the shipwreck' (12). As part of this infrastructure, the genres of the dockside, including the customs manual and the settler handbook, helped to create a 'textual landfill' (12) which enabled settlers to become landed and gain traction as settlers. This they ultimately did, at least in textual terms, via the farm novel, the most recognisable genre of southern African literature. Thus, Hofmeyr links farm and dockside, land and sea, and in so doing opens up a range of emerging potential trajectories for thinking about southern African literature today.

Antoinette Burton suggests in her chapter that it would be a mistake to see *Dockside Reading* as disconnected from Hofmeyr's earlier work, or as 'anything like a predictable, let alone a progressive, march to the sea'. Both books and oceans have always been 'immanent in her methodological approach', Burton argues, and '[b]ookish-ness and ocean-ness are, for her, key to grasping how worlds come into being, how history works, and what role motion plays in colonial place-making'. Meg Samuelson engages with this central connection between land and sea in Hofmeyr's oeuvre via Samuelson's own notion of 'amphibious form' (Samuelson 2017). She recommends that we find ways of reading the postcolonial novel that 'inhabit or accommodate more than one cultural biome' and which emanate from the South. Approaching these forms as '*ecotonal* might allow for other ways of thinking with them', she suggests. In a suggestive intertextual echo, Rimli Battacharya reflects on and extends Hofmeyr's work through sound, text and image, 'testing the tension between historical scholarship on print cultures and the myriad microtones of material cultures in movement'.

Dockside Reading had its beginnings in an earlier article Hofmeyr co-authored with Kerry Bystrom, 'Oceanic Routes: (Post-It) Notes on Hydro-colonialism', which imagined 'colored post-it notes floating on salty waves'. These 'sodden notes' provide a 'poetic image of writing on water' (Bystrom and Hofmeyr 2017, 1) and also point to the increasing attention to environmental realities in what is being called the age of the Anthropocene. In her most recent work, Hofmeyr turns even more fully to the sea itself, aware of the complicating pressures exerted on scholarship by the growing awareness of climate change. To better understand the physical character of and changes to the oceans that had long been her area of interest, Hofmeyr embarked on a series of online oceanography courses, with her colleagues Charne Lavery, Sharad Chari and Pamila Gupta. Turning to the ocean, it became clear, meant turning to a changing sea, with, for instance, the monsoon that underpins the

South–South connections of the Indian Ocean world faltering and shifting as global temperatures warm. Melting ice from the Antarctic continent is contributing to warming and freshening currents that flow into the southern reaches of the Atlantic and Indian oceans, affecting regional weather systems and inundating coastlines and islands. These concerns took Hofmeyr to Antarctica itself (see figure 0.11), as described in 'Reading in Antarctica' (Hofmeyr and Lavery 2021). Deeply interested, as always, in the lives of books and the phenomenology of reading, she assayed the archive that was the ship's library and reflects on the ways in which reading in Antarctica and the Southern Ocean is different from reading elsewhere. Necessarily affected by such environmental factors as the roll of the ship on the waves and the strange obliquity of the light, and with one's interests focused on ice, water and rare glimpses of earth, reading in Antarctica, she suggests, is a form of 'elemental reading'.

Figure 0.11: Wrapped up against the cold, Hofmeyr stands on a snowy rise on the Antarctic Peninsula in March 2019. The dark water of the bay and spines of peninsular mountains lie behind her. (Photo by Charne Lavery)

In 2018 Hofmeyr and Lavery established a research project and international network called Oceanic Humanities for the Global South, based at WiSER and the School of Language, Literature and Media (SLLM) at Wits, linking Indian Ocean studies to the environmental humanities. Again, Hofmeyr's research and institution-building work has provided a platform for a wide array of emerging research that is demonstrating new ways of reading for water, as well as from the South (see, e.g., Joseph 2022; Lavery 2021; Nuttall 2020; and Samuelson and Lavery 2019).

SUBMERGED, FLUID AND AQUEOUS WAYS OF READING

While each of the chapters that make up this book has been mentioned in the preceding pages, this section provides a more detailed overview of the ways of reading each essay offers, in conversation with Hofmeyr's work on three broad themes: African popular culture and orality ('High, Low and In-between'); fluid, diasporic and transnational methodologies ('Portable Methods'); and connecting, as well as ecological, oceans ('Oceanic Turns').

Khwezi Mkhize, in the opening chapter of Part 1, 'High, Low and In-between', focuses on genealogy as he positions Hofmeyr's 'emergence as a scholar at a crucial moment in progressive scholarship' in South Africa. He situates her within a generation of radical South African scholars in the 1970s and 1980s who were affiliated with a number of political and cultural movements and who believed South African scholarship was 'duty-bound to abscond from the archaic prison houses of Englishness and liberalism, and embrace the rich and multifarious expressive cultures indigenous to South Africa, especially those of its majority black populace'. Mkhize also points to Hofmeyr's insistence that theorising begin with the 'local', not the elsewhere, instantiating this in his own analysis.

James Ogude, writing from his then position as a colleague of Hofmeyr's in the Department of African Literature at Wits in the 1990s, discusses how African literature continued to be read at the time in relation to a Western canon. It was 'seen either as engaged in a project of reappropriating the Western canon or as simply writing back to it', he notes, adding that 'African literature's recourse to its own internal traditions remained submerged and silenced'. By foregrounding neglected African literatures and cultures, and specifically popular cultural forms, Ogude writes, Hofmeyr wrested African literature away from appendage-hood to Western literary studies.

Carolyn Hamilton draws on Hofmeyr's work on the impact on oral accounts of their publication as written sources – for example, in school texts. Publication 'conferred a rigid casing on forms that "previously lived by fluidity"', Hamilton writes, citing Hofmeyr. She shows that historians both then and now have frequently seen what Hofmeyr identified as fluidity as a weakness of oral accounts as historical sources. Yet Hofmeyr's formulation, pursued by Hamilton in her own work in this chapter, demands methodological as well as historical attention and can be put to use to remarkable effect. Fluidity, moreover, is an 'aqueous metaphor' that would travel a long way into the future, through Hofmeyr's subsequent work.

Karin Barber draws together Hofmeyr's scholarship on the encounter of oral genres and written forms with that on the movement of printed periodical texts through time and space. She does this by looking at how Yoruba-language newspapers in 1920s Lagos drew into print the oral genres they sought to preserve. If print was a way of 'fixing' valued oral genres and preventing their loss, Barber shows how the 'prevailing porosity, flexibility and heterogeneity' of Lagos print culture also enabled its transformation into a more oral-like form. Thus, she reads capaciously and fluidly across Hofmeyr's work in the Northern Transvaal and her own in colonial Lagos.

Ranka Primorac sets up Part 2's focus on 'Portable Methods' by describing in her chapter the range and impact of Hofmeyr's insistence on 'portability as malleability'. She starts with a reading of a popular Zambian novel, *Knitted in Silence* by Norah Mumba, in the context of a Zambian literary history that is in important ways distinct from the 'African novel' as it circulates in the global North. This, she argues, would not be legible without the conceptual apparatus provided by Hofmeyr's *The Portable Bunyan*, which links the operations of textual circulation with the temporality of conversion.

Christopher Ouma argues in his chapter that Hofmeyr's work provides a way to think 'at the intersection of oceans' and positions South Africa and specifically the Cape as a 'pivotal geography'. He shows how, following her 2007 article 'The Black Atlantic Meets the Indian Ocean', which sets out the contours of the emerging field, Hofmeyr reframed the Indian Ocean not only as a geographical space but as a method. Placing Hofmeyr's thinking alongside that of Brent Hayes Edwards (2001) in 'The Uses of Diaspora', Ouma argues that both scholars broaden the framework within which the word 'diaspora' operates as an analytical category, while complicating its cartographic logic in the process.

Madhumita Lahiri provides a model for using Hofmeyrian methodology in a new context, deploying the analysis of summary and slow reading from *Gandhi's Printing Press* in an illuminating close reading of the difficult novel *A Brief History of Seven Killings* by Marlon James. The 'brief' in the title is borne out in the novel's deployment and discussion of summary, even as the novel itself runs to hundreds of pages, and in the end constitutes what Lahiri calls a 'summary postcolony'. At the same time its complicated narrative, temporal structure and use of Jamaican English force the 'slow reading' that Gandhi advocated. This, Lahiri argues, provides a more locally grounded interpretative frame than 'the vernacular' through which the novel has been largely understood.

Lakshmi Subramanian describes Hofmeyr's cross-disciplinary contribution to Indian Ocean historiography: the focus on cultural studies, a more inclusive historical approach and particularly the inclusion of African participation in Indian Ocean worlds. Once an under-researched area in comparison to studies of the Mediterranean, Atlantic and Pacific oceans, and then requiring a shift from a Eurocentric approach to an analysis of indigenous networks, Indian Ocean studies were at the time India-centred in ways that were at once recuperative and exclusionary. Hofmeyr's sense of the Indian Ocean as a space of multiple universalisms shaped

Subramanian's extensive work on piracy and cosmopolitanism that, in the Indian Ocean, indexed different kinds of universalisms.

In Part 3, 'Oceanic Turns', Sunil Amrith's chapter provides an account of the growth of Indian Ocean studies as a response to area studies, globalisation and nationalism, and situates Hofmeyr's central place in its development. He demonstrates that Hofmeyr, through both institution-building work and scholarship – particularly *Gandhi's Printing Press*, as 'one of the most important books ever written about the Indian Ocean world' – first centred Africa in the Indian Ocean and then the sea itself. Both these moves are centred around the word 'complication' and the highly generative method implied by the 'complicating sea'.

Antoinette Burton sums up what Hofmeyr offers to scholarship as a 'characteristically dispersed approach' that undoes the metropole-colony binary. She provides an overview of Hofmeyr's intellectual oeuvre that connects the 'African print cultures' to the 'oceanic turns' that are marked in the subtitle of this volume. She argues that if the ocean can be considered a 'more-than-wet' phenomenon (following Peters and Steinberg 2019), then a similarly 'more-than-book' reading runs through Hofmeyr's work on print cultures, too.

Meg Samuelson follows Hofmeyr's turn to the sea and its 'shore-shaped literary formations' (Hofmeyr 2022, 15) in proposing 'amphibious' and 'ecotonal' as alternatives to the potentially exoticising descriptor 'magical realist'. Placing texts from Mozambique and Australia into conversation across the southern reaches of the Indian Ocean, she discerns an 'amphibious form' that is both 'fluctuant and fractal', even 'muddy', a literary mode both generated by southern littorals and capable of addressing the uncanny realities of climate change which are so clearly already affecting them.

Rimli Battacharya closes off this section in an extended meditation which proceeds from Hofmeyr's analysis of how the hermeneutical practices of the dockside are shaped by 'an intimate interaction with objects and their accompanying logistic grammars'. She draws out the multivalences of the word – 'sounded, transcribed, translated, recorded, chanted and sung' – of songs, dance, installation and cinema, as well as of satellite imaging and marine archaeology, placing them more centrally in a conceptualisation of the movements of plants, people and technologies, script and language.

The book closes with a pair of reflections that draw out the themes of methodological opening and creative criticism that are threaded through Hofmeyr's life and work as well as this book's chapters. Danai Mupotsa and Pumla Dineo Gqola's dialogue reflects on the value of circuits, circulations and 'pathways of ideas' in Hofmeyr's work; on her 'woven pursuits and intentions' as she navigates these; and on her 'productive irritability', which works to reveal the gaps in the always ongoing process of what they call 'field constitution'. Gabeba Baderoon's poem 'Proximate' – inspired by the fact that the name Isabel denotes 'oath', 'consecration', 'beauty' – draws together names, words, seas and making in a final 'consecration'.

THE LODESTAR

Along with her colleagues in the Department of African Literature, at the former CISA and at WiSER, the politics of location has been important to Isabel Hofmeyr. Being an Africa-based scholar producing excellent work on and from the global South has been at the heart of her intellectual project over several decades. As a scholar invested in building the African academy, Hofmeyr has devoted much of her time to graduate supervision, supervising twenty-eight PhD students and thirty-six MA students. Her graduates, drawn from the African continent at large, occupy positions in the academy, media and journalism, publishing, the NGO sector and the creative industries across Africa today. Hofmeyr has edited or co-edited twenty-nine special issues of journals, using them to bring visibility and excitement to emerging areas of scholarship and to offer methods and ideas for taking these new inquiries forward. In these ventures, she has worked with a range of scholars, including Liz Gunner, Sarah Nuttall, Preben Kaarsholm, Uma

Dhupelia-Mesthrie, Devarakshanam Goviden, Michelle Williams, Derek Peterson and Charne Lavery.

As Khwezi Mkhize affirms at the beginning of this book, Hofmeyr has produced a major work in every decade since the 1990s, each pushing our thinking across disciplines. Why and how her work has taken such transformative and 'mercurial turns', he argues, is ultimately traceable to her initial engagements with the 'problem space' of literary and cultural studies in South Africa. It is as fitting an end as it is a beginning. The choice to publish this book with Wits University Press, Africa's longest-running university press, and which celebrated its centenary in 2022, seems apposite to this project and this orientation. Countering Hofmeyr's long-standing critiques of imperial copyright, a predilection she shared with Gandhi himself, and embracing her African intellectual compass and location, so we too situate this book decidedly Southward in ongoing North–South publication circuits, knowing, of course, that, given the calibre of Hofmeyr's thought, it will find an audience wherever you are.

Isabel Hofmeyr is a lodestar: a person who serves as inspiration or guide, like the star used to guide the course of a ship. Or, as described in the final stanza of Baderoon's closing poem:

> On quests
> and their making, books
> and their making, seas
>
> your making leaves
> a lucent trail.

NOTES

1   Jay Pather, personal email communication, 17 July 2022.
2   Isabel Hofmeyr, personal email communication, 9 July 2022.
3   Cynthis Kros, interview with Isabel Hofmeyr as part of ongoing research on Jeppe High School for Girls, 2018.
4   *The Pilgrim's Progress* is a religious allegory, following the journey of one man, Christian, who faces many obstacles but eventually arrives in heaven.

5   The Kingdom of Kongo was a large kingdom in the western part of Central Africa, now part of the Democratic Republic of the Congo.

6   Vergès herself had written about the idea of 'writing on water'; Nuttall had researched and written about the islands of this African Indian Ocean as prisons, particularly in the work of Mauritian writer Lindsay Collen. The research project, Diasporic Economies and Cultural Corridors in the African South Indian Ocean, was an analysis of the 'coastal-island-inland' dynamics at work in configuring a set of cities geographically located in the 'African South Indian Ocean' region. It assessed the ways in which, through the process of globalisation, people and objects are clustered together and boundaries are drawn and redrawn around particular regional clusters. It led to a symposium held at WiSER on 'Indian Ocean Imaginaries' (September 2004), which explored some the earliest formulations of the African South Indian Ocean.

REFERENCES

Bystrom, Kerry and Isabel Hofmeyr. 2017. 'Oceanic Routes: (Post-It) Notes on Hydrocolonialism'. *Comparative Literature* 69 (1): 1–6.

Edwards, Brent Hayes. 2001. 'The Uses of Diaspora'. *Social Text 66*, no. 1 (Spring): 45–73.

Gupta, Pamila. 2018. *Portuguese Decolonization in the Indian Ocean World: History and Ethnography*. London: Bloomsbury Academic.

Gupta, Pamila, Isabel Hofmeyr and Michael Naylor Pearson. 2010. *Eyes Across the Water: Navigating the Indian Ocean*. Pretoria: UNISA Press.

Hofmeyr, Isabel. 1976. 'The State of South African Literary Criticism'. *English in Africa* 3 (1): 39–50.

———. 1993. *'We Spend Our Years as a Tale That is Told': Oral Historical Narrative in a South African Chiefdom*. Portsmouth: Heinemann; London: James Currey; Johannesburg: Wits University Press.

———. 2004. *The Portable Bunyan: A Transnational History of 'The Pilgrim's Progress'*. Princeton: Princeton University Press; Johannesburg: Wits University Press.

———. 2007. 'The Black Atlantic Meets the Indian Ocean: Forging New Paradigms of Transnationalism for the Global South – Literary and Cultural Perspectives'. *Social Dynamics* 33 (2): 3–32.

———. 2012. 'The Complicating Sea: The Indian Ocean as Method'. *Comparative Studies of South Asia, Africa and the Middle East* 32 (3): 584–590.

———. 2013. *Gandhi's Printing Press: Experiments in Slow Reading*. Cambridge, MA, and London: Harvard University Press.

———. 2015. 'Styling Multilateralism: Indian Ocean Cultural Futures'. *Journal of the Indian Ocean Region* 11 (1): 98–109.

———. 2022. *Dockside Reading: Hydrocolonialism and the Custom House*. Durham: Duke University Press; Johannesburg: Wits University Press.

Hofmeyr, Isabel and Charne Lavery. 2021. 'Reading in Antarctica'. *Wasafiri* 36 (2): 79–86.

Hofmeyr, Isabel and Michelle Williams, eds. 2011. *South Africa and India: Shaping the Global South*. Johannesburg: Wits University Press.

Joseph, Confidence. 2022. 'Multi-spirited Waters in Lynton Burger's *She Down There*'. In *The Palgrave Handbook of Blue Heritage*, edited by Rosabelle Boswell, David O'Kane and Jeremy Hills, 141–159. Cham: Palgrave Macmillan.

Lavery, Charne. 2021. *Writing Ocean Worlds: Indian Ocean Fiction in English*. Cham: Palgrave Macmillan.

Nuttall, Sarah. 2020. 'Pluvial Time/Wet Form'. *New Literary History* 51 (2): 455–472.

Nuttall, Sarah and Isabel Hofmeyr. 2001. Introduction to 'The Book in Africa'. Special issue, *Current Writing* 13 (2): 1–10.

Peters, Kimberley and Philip Steinberg. 2019. 'The Ocean in Excess: Towards a More-than-Wet Ontology'. *Dialogues in Human Geography* 9 (3): 293–307.

Samuelson, Meg. 2017. 'Coastal Form: Amphibian Positions, Wider Worlds, and Planetary Horizons on the African Indian Ocean Littoral'. *Comparative Literature* 69 (1): 16–24.

Samuelson, Meg and Charne Lavery. 2019. 'The Oceanic South'. *English Language Notes* 57 (1): 37–50.

Smith, David. 2009. 'The World's Most Loved Movies'. *The Guardian*, 4 June. Accessed 4 December 2022. https://www.theguardian.com/film/2009/jun/05/box-office-records-world-cinema.

Steiner, Tina. 2021. *Convivial Worlds: Writing Relation from Africa*. Oxon and New York: Routledge.

Vergès, Françoise, Sarah Nuttall and Abdoumaliq Simone. 2004. 'Diasporic Economies and Cultural Corridors in the African South Indian Ocean'. Research report.

PART 1

HIGH, LOW AND IN-BETWEEN

1

Transformations

Khwezi Mkhize

All original thought has foundations and a traceable genealogy. Isabel Hofmeyr has produced, in every decade since the 1990s, a major book that has transformed our thinking across disciplines. I have chosen to name my reflection on her work 'Transformations' precisely because of her always transformative relationship to various moments and turns in literary and cultural studies, particularly in South Africa. My argument here is that why and how her work has taken such mercurial turns is ultimately traceable to her initial engagements with the 'problem space' of literary and cultural studies in South Africa.[1]

I would like to tie the question of genealogy closely to South Africa because Hofmeyr's emergence as a scholar happened at a crucial moment in progressive scholarship in the country. It is important to remember that in the 1970s and 1980s she was among a generation of radical South African scholars – inspired by Marxism, feminism, oral history, oral narrative and cultural studies. Affiliated with various political and cultural movements, these scholars were armed with a sense that if South African scholarship was to ring true to the totality of its social and cultural references, then it was duty-bound to abscond from the archaic prison houses of Englishness and liberalism, and embrace the rich and multifarious expressive cultures indigenous to South Africa, especially those of its majority black populace.

Hofmeyr was also uniquely placed to address the problem of literary and cultural studies in South Africa by virtue of her long-standing location in the Department of African Literature at the University of the Witwatersrand (Wits). The only one of its kind, the department was founded by Es'kia Mphahlele in 1983, after his return from exile. Hofmeyr joined the department in 1984 and has spent her entire career there – in itself a unique and singular way to live out an intellectual life in the academy. Aside from Mphahlele with his substantial creative and critical work, a key figure in the department's early history, and certainly in the recuperation of major but neglected black writers of the early to mid-twentieth century, was Tim Couzens. His work on writers such as Sol Plaatje and the Dhlomo brothers (R.R.R. and H.I.E. Dhlomo) added significantly to the intellectual repatriation of black writers to the South African literary canon. Couzens was also a fine and path-breaking literary historian, whose biography of H.I.E. Dhlomo, *The New African: A Study of the Life and Work of H.I.E. Dhlomo* (1985), remains the only one of its kind. This scholarship took seriously the value of historical knowledge and thorough archival research, both of which are defining characteristics of Hofmeyr's work. The scholars who taught and produced important work while in the department – Bhekizizwe Peterson, James Ogude, Peter Thuynsma, Phaswane Mpe and Pumla Dineo Gqola are part of this illustrious list – undoubtedly provided an African-centred cosmopolitan milieu in which Hofmeyr could think about and inhabit the world while having the pleasure of taking for granted South Africa and Africa's centrality in it.

Hofmeyr, however, arrived at Wits and the Department of African Literature having already articulated a sharp sense of the task at hand for her generation of scholars. She had published one of her first articles, 'The State of South African Literary Criticism', in the journal *English in*

Africa in 1979. In a move strikingly resonant with contemporary calls to decolonise the discipline, she argued that the thing called 'South African literary criticism' was then not much more than the over-representation of white English sensibilities and their inheritance in the academy. 'On the most simple level,' she pointed out, 'this "tradition" is hopelessly selective. It excludes, for example, all the pre-nineteenth-century writing, the most notable exception being oral literature. It ignores all working class literature, both African and Afrikaans, and it shuns large chunks of white popular literature with vehemence. In total, then, this "tradition" which claims to represent South African Literature, quite staggeringly ignores the culture and literary endeavours of the majority of people in this country' (Hofmeyr 1979, 39–40).

For those of us who were formed at the height of the incursion of post-colonial theory into South Africa, it is not difficult to see, looking back, just how Hofmeyr's call for the 'provincialisation' of English literature, though rooted in specific debates about South African literary criticism, was always already part of a global movement that sought to disarticulate literary studies from its imperial habitus and to give serious attention to subalterns as literary and cultural producers.

A number of implications follow Hofmeyr's call to 'de-anglicise' literary studies in South Africa and to take popular culture seriously as a productive intellectual and political space. The first comes with appreciating that wresting the discipline away from the 'phantoms of our peculiar brand of prac. crit.' implies the apprehension and inscription of the field of social formation – and its varied and often vexed social relations – in which the literary artefact circulates in its various incarnations (Hofmeyr 1979, 39). Of course, these questions reflect the influence of British cultural studies in South Africa, particularly the work of E.P. Thompson and Raymond Williams, but, as we shall see, the implications of her thinking in relation to the local went far beyond the refraction of metropolitan influences. Her conceptualisation of the work to be done reads like both a manifesto and a summation of the field. She argued that the history of South African literature should include the modes and discourses of all South Africans, be that discourse oral, be it in newspapers, archives, magazines and pamphlets . . . Consequently, we need a theory of literature that includes the cultural products and practices of all classes. Such a critical position should take an anti-élitist stance which rejects the distinction between 'high' and 'low' culture, and begins instead to explain the complexities of a dynamic society and its culture. (Hofmeyr 1979, 44)

Indeed, the kind of work that Hofmeyr was involved in during the 1980s and 1990s reflected these deep commitments to social history and to the careful literary reading of things produced in the field of the social across the divides of race, class, gender and genre. An early work of literary criticism, 'The Mining Novel in South African Literature: 1870–1920' (Hofmeyr 1978), which came out of her first master's thesis, gives a materialist reading of the emergence of the mining novel in South Africa. The subgenre was, of course, racialist in bent, but Hofmeyr's survey uncovers a striking relationship between the bourgeoning mining industry of the 1870s to the 1920s and a mode of representation that sought to give it an ameliorating aesthetic form. Within the ambit of the emergent but sharp capitalist accumulation that accompanied the mining revolution, the image of 'the digger as "gentleman" and "pioneer"' that was opulent in the mining novel could, she argued, not only 'incorporate a wide range of suggestion and signification that implied Britishness, Imperialism, honour, manliness, courage, valour', but was also a rugged and more recent addendum to the colonialist literature of the frontier, which narrated the seizing of a providential white man's land (Hofmeyr 1978, 5). These literary and materialist concerns traced a pathway for understanding the continuities of the imaginaries of racial capitalism and white writing across a century.

Hofmeyr is also a major contributor to our understanding of the development of nationalism, language and literature in early twentieth-century South Africa. Another early major piece of hers, 'Building a Nation from

Words: Afrikaans Language, Literature and Ethnic Identity, 1902–1924'
(Hofmeyr 1987), appeared in Shula Marks and Stanley Trapido's edited
volume *The Politics of Class, Race and Nationalism in Twentieth-Century
South Africa*, in which Marks and Trapido pointed out the importance of
the early twentieth century in the reshaping of ethnic and national identities across the racial spectrum in South Africa. Far from being the stuff
of primordial origins unaffected by the vicissitudes of capital on either
side of the racial spectrum, the ethnic identities that emerged around
1910 were new ones, fashioned 'when the state was being constructed
as a single entity out of the British colonies, the conquered Afrikaner
republics and African kingdoms in the region' (Marks and Trapido
1987, 2). The social and cultural history that was being produced in
South Africa during this time did much to reorient our understanding
of nationalisms and national(ist) identities as 'historically contingent'.
As Hofmeyr put it, 'nationalist ideologies have their genesis in the social
relations precipitated by industrialisation' (Hofmeyr 1987, 96). Afrikaner
ethnicity was no different. 'Building a Nation from Words' demonstrated
one of the signature characteristics of Hofmeyr's scholarly identity: an
astute sense of the humanistic scholar as a historical detective carefully
dissecting the chaotic assemblage that is the archive and chiselling a
coherent pattern of meaning out of it. In the piece Hofmeyr convincingly
showed that Afrikanerhood proper, as an enveloping insignia of racial
and ethnic nationality – or what she called 'a monolithic *volk*' – emerged
during the first two decades of the twentieth century. Prior to that, 'the
language Dutch–Afrikaans was extremely diverse by region, dialect and
social class', and its creole origins were deeply marked by 'the language of
the slaves', the presence of the Khoisan, the inchoate strands of colonial
communities in the Cape, and the disorienting effects wrought by industrialisation and proletarianisation (Hofmeyr 1987, 96).

It was out of this context of social mixture that the Dutch intelligentsia
began 'groping toward' a definition of an Afrikaner volk, language and
literature, and it was through newspapers in particular that this intelligentsia assembled and addressed the strewn strands of 'Afrikanerdom'.

For Hofmeyr, a pivotal figure in the proselytisation of 'Afrikanerhood' was the journalist and historian Gustav Preller. As Hofmeyr observes, Preller saw the task of building the Afrikaner nation in terms of linguistics and of print. If Afrikaans was to be shared across the ethnicity's disassembled social structure, it had to be, first, made respectable by being stripped of its associations with 'colouredness' and, second, standardised, a task that 'entailed giving the language some substance by creating books and written material . . . [which,] in turn, requires markets, publishers, printers and distributors' (Hofmeyr 1987, 104). One of the major insights provided by 'Building a Nation from Words' is that (to borrow from Pierre Bourdieu) the field of cultural production in which the literary artefact gains its social prominence demands as much attention and care as aesthetic concerns. While achieving this balance may seem fairly straightforward, the force of Hofmeyr's historical detail and the cutting elegance of her prose make this work prone to rereading and reuse. Also instructive is the manner in which Hofmeyr works through the writing of identity without falling into the pitfall of conveniently positing the Afrikaner nation as an 'invention'.

'Building a Nation from Words' is also of interest for exhibiting another aspect that characterises Hofmeyr's work through the next two or so decades: the fact that her engagement with print culture and book history actually emerged out of the transformations of South African literary and cultural criticism outlined in her early conceptualisation of the function of the discipline, rather than as a simple 'importation' of these fields into South Africa. If the world has come to embrace Isabel Hofmeyr as a leading scholar in these disciplines, it is precisely because she brought her primary intellectual concerns and local contexts into the exploration of shared issues. It is not fortuitous, for instance, that 'Building a Nation from Words' and Benedict Anderson's *Imagined Communities* shared the same historical conjuncture (the 1980s): both were dealing with the need to explain the emergence and persistence of nationalism at a time – the nadir of the Cold War – when its stubborn persistence seemed to defy the rise and dominance of postmodernism.

An additional key point relates to Hofmeyr paying attention to how texts – oral and written – and meanings are produced. Given her intellectual foundations, it was perhaps inevitable that Hofmeyr would venture into oral history and oral literature. From the publication of Jan Vansina's seminal *Oral Tradition: A Study in Historical Methodology* in 1965 and Ruth Finnegan's *Oral Literature in Africa* in 1970, Africanists have taken oral tradition to be a vital living archive in the production of knowledge about the continent's varied societies and peoples, and an indication of how the disciplines involved were to encounter the study of Africa. For foundational African literary scholars such as F. Abiola Irele, oral literature's place in the study of African literature was an ontological necessity because it provided that body of texts 'which lies behind us as a complete and enduring literature, though constantly being renewed, and which most profoundly informs the world views of our people, and is thus at the same time the foundation and expressive channel of a fundamental African mental universe' (Irele 1990, 12). In South Africa the turn to this body of knowledge was equally necessary, if only for the added reason that the racially overdetermined social formation made subaltern experience retrievable in large measure through the pursuit of the inscription and analysis of the *embodied* knowledge of oral forms. And so Hofmeyr's first book-length study, *'We Spend Our Years as a Tale That is Told': Oral Historical Narrative in a South African Chiefdom* (1993), took to reconstructing 'an active storytelling tradition' among the Sotho and the Ndebele of Mokopane. Aside from the imperatives of knowledge production in South Africa, *'We Spend Our Years as a Tale That is Told'* was also driven by the need to bridge the distance between 'literary and historical concerns' in the study of oral performance (Hofmeyr 1993, 1). Given the social and political changes that had been imposed on African societies by colonial conquest during the nineteenth century, the dominance of the written word and its genres of authority would seem poised to similarly overdetermine the script of African modernity. But, as Bhekizizwe Peterson recently pointed out, at the level of genre and literary production, for African writers, narrators and interlocutors the colonial encounter, far from being unidirectional, 'allowed for exploring new synergies and possibilities between orature and literacy, indigenous narrative traditions and other European genres' (Peterson 2020, 134). Peterson was, of course, thinking about the discursive matrix in which modern African narrative forms spawned their multifaceted dealings with the question of representation. He was also working with a major theoretical insight from Hofmeyr's work on oral performance: that orality had its way of invoking an awkward coexistence with written forms and their claims to religious, literary and bureaucratic supremacy:

> In the initial confrontation of orality and literacy, it is, in fact, the former that transforms the latter, rather than the other way around (as common-sense wisdom would lead us to anticipate). In this process of transformation, a predominantly literate religion . . . becomes 'oralised' in its confrontation with African society, so that instead of being a religion of the printed word, it becomes a relation of the image and the spoken word. (Hofmeyr 1993, 14)

These insights refine our understanding of the colonial encounter in a number of ways. For example, Hofmeyr convincingly demonstrates that in order for the 'universally translatable' word of God to take root among African converts, missionaries were in reality often beholden to 'orality, performance, festival, spectacle and image, or, in other words, the central resources of African culture' (Hofmeyr 1993, 50). At the same time, Africans who interacted with colonial authority resorted to the visual representation of oral communication in order to cut through the cold distance of its paper bureaucracy. As Hofmeyr so eloquently puts it, 'By bathing documents in the stream of orality, they subordinated them to the prevailing practices and procedures of an oral world' (Hofmeyr 1993, 62).

Ever the detective who brings a fine literary eye to the archive and to matters historical, Hofmeyr, in 'We Spend Our Years as a Tale That is Told', takes oral performance into a terrain of theoretical possibilities.

The upending of the written word's and the oral word's seclusion from each other spills into the book's multiple meanings in the 'African mental universe'. Hofmeyr unhinges books from their primary semantic function and rubs them against African interpretive communities' varied apprehensions of their social and spiritual energies. Rather than focusing on reading as the singular locus of textual meaning, reading is subordinated to the multiple social lives of texts and to their charged object status. Her article 'Metaphorical Books' explores how, among a number of African communities, it is 'the material "objectness" of the book that predominates', and in which the 'fetishistic' power of books gave experiences such as gaining literacy magical inflections (Hofmeyr 2011, 104–105).

It is not difficult to see the continuities between 'We Spend Our Years as a Tale That is Told' and The Portable Bunyan: A Transnational History of 'The Pilgrim's Progress' (Hofmeyr 2004). Notwithstanding the latter's explicit framing in the field of book history, The Portable Bunyan extended Hofmeyr's fascination with the interaction of religious and spiritual texts with African belief systems. The fresh insight that she brought to these long-standing concerns is the crucial argument that the canonical texts that have come to signify English literature with a capital E, such as John Bunyan's The Pilgrim's Progress, were in fact popularised through their complex and promiscuous translation and publishing histories in the empire, and only retrospectively made English or national literature. The power of reading The Pilgrim's Progress from the margins of post-imperial history entails, first, a correction of 'the story of Bunyan's influence, [which] has been narrated back to front' and, second, being able to see that the process of canon formation obfuscates the profound role that the margins have played in the making of literary reputation (Hofmeyr 2004, 32).

If Hofmeyr's Gandhi's Printing Press (2013) argued for the colonial cosmopolitan port city of Durban as the testing ground for Gandhi's philosophy of satyagraha, then, read in the light of Hofmeyr's intellectual biography, this insight seems remarkably consistent with what she has done throughout her career, which is to stake in a fine-grained reading of the 'local' a starting point for new theoretical insights and transformations. From this perspective, it should not be surprising that Gandhi's philosophy of non-violence, which set the stage for much anti-racist resistance in the twentieth century, had deep colonial origins in South Africa. Perhaps Isabel Hofmeyr's greatest gift to us lies in thinking with and in relation to that which is closest to us as a necessary condition for engaging prevailing debates and reconfigurations of knowledge. Through her work we have seen the world come to South Africa, not the other way round. In a moment in which theory seems to portend some importation of metropolitan scholarship of one kind or another, her work reminds us that we have much to offer both to the world and, indeed, to the thing called theory.

NOTE

1   David Scott (2004: 4) defines a problem space as 'an ensemble of questions and answers around which a horizon of identifiable stakes (conceptual as well as ideological-political stakes) hangs'. In the case of my reading of Hofmeyr's work, the problem space can be identified through the need to think beyond the discipline of literary studies in the academy and its generalised neglect of the expressive cultures that constituted its social formation in the 1970s. This task, as Hofmeyr's work has repeatedly shown, has methodological implications that are constitutive of how we think, write, research and produce knowledge.

REFERENCES

Anderson, Benedict. 1983. *Imagined Communities: Reflections on the Origin and Spread of Nationalism*. London: Verso.
Couzens, Tim. 1985. *The New African: A Study of the Life and Work of H.I.E. Dhlomo*. Johannesburg: Ravan Press.
Finnegan, Ruth. 1970. *Oral Literature in Africa*. Oxford: Oxford University Press.
Hofmeyr, Isabel. 1978. 'The Mining Novel in South African Literature: 1870–1920'. *English in Africa* 5 (2): 1–16.
———. 1979. 'The State of South African Literary Criticism'. *English in Africa* 6 (2): 39–50.
———. 1987. 'Building a Nation from Words: Afrikaans Language, Literature and Ethnic Identity, 1902–1924'. In *The Politics of Race, Class and Nationalism in Twentieth-Century South Africa*, edited by Shula Marks and Stanley Trapido, 95–123. London: Longman Group.
———. 1993. 'We Spend Our Years as a Tale That is Told': Oral Historical Narrative in a South African Chiefdom*. Johannesburg: Wits University Press.

———. 2004. *The Portable Bunyan: A Transnational History of 'The Pilgrim's Progress'*. Princeton: Princeton University Press.

———. 2011. 'Metaphorical Books'. *Current Writing: Text and Reception in Southern Africa* 13 (2): 100–108.

———. 2013. *Gandhi's Printing Press: Experiments in Slow Reading*. Cambridge, MA: Harvard University Press.

Irele, F. Abiola. 1990. *The African Experience in Literature and Ideology*. Bloomington: Indiana University Press.

Marks, Shula and Stanley Trapido. 1987. 'The Politics of Race, Class and Nationalism'. In *The Politics of Race, Class and Nationalism in Twentieth-Century South Africa*, edited by Shula Marks and Stanley Trapido, 1–70. London: Longman Group.

Peterson, Bhekizizwe. 2020. 'Reasoning Creatively in *Mhudi*'. In *Sol Plaatje's 'Mhudi': History, Criticism, Celebration*, edited by Sabata-mpho Mokae and Brian Willan, 125–146. Johannesburg: Jacana Media.

Scott, David. 2004. *Conscripts of Modernity: The Tragedy of Colonial Enlightenment*. Durham: Duke University Press.

Vansina. Jan. 1965. *Oral Tradition: A Study in Historical Methodology*. Trans. H.M. Wright. London: Routledge and Kegan Paul.

2

African Popular Literatures Rising

James Ogude

I was fortunate to have joined the Department of African Literature at the University of the Witwatersrand (Wits) in February 1991. To my knowledge it was then the only department dedicated to the teaching of African literature, albeit literatures written in English. Started in 1983 as a division of the Department of Comparative and African Literature by one of Africa's foremost writers and critics, Es'kia Mphahlele, it soon grew into a fully established department. By the time I joined it, less than a decade later, it was offering a rich staple of African literature courses ranging from a focus on regional literatures from across the continent to the black diaspora, especially the Caribbean region. However, it also offered thematically driven courses covering related topics such as gender and women's writing in Africa, slavery and memory, orality and literacy, and a variety of other courses at postgraduate level. Yet, in spite of this rich and exciting syllabus, it was clear that the curriculum was in many respects dominated by canonical writers on the continent and its black diaspora. The Department of African Literature at Wits was not unique in this approach. A number of English departments on the continent – even the literature department at my alma mater, the University of Nairobi (UoN) – remained driven by the canon of African literature. In fact, I can hardly remember any course dedicated to women writers at UoN, in spite of its claims to be encouraging a decolonised curriculum. Instead, the most notice-able marker of a decolonised curriculum became a singularly focused return to oral literature. While a certain insistence on the study of oral literatures in Africa was desirable, if not long overdue, the impression created was that no other literatures deserved as much attention. So when I came to the department at Wits and encountered a compelling attention to women's literature and a sustained focus on gender and feminist theories, I was impressed by the novelty this small department with a limited number of faculty was showing in imagining its curriculum. Yet, even in this department, it was clear that a great deal still needed to be done to extend the boundaries of the curriculum.

By the year 2002, Isabel Hofmeyr, who had taken over as professor and chair of the department after Professor Njabulo Ndebele moved to the University of the Western Cape in 1993, had embarked on a radical reimagination of the curriculum within the department.[1] Building on her PhD work, published by Wits University Press under the title 'We Spend Our Years as a Tale That is Told': Oral Historical Narrative in a South African Chiefdom (Hofmeyr 1994), she started asking difficult questions about our curriculum, especially the postgraduate curriculum. Hofmeyr introduced the course Popular Literature and Cultures at postgraduate level, and followed this up with an application to South Africa's National Research Foundation (NRF) to raise funds that would allow the department to extend its research in the area of popular literature and its publics.[2] The grant was needed to encourage master's and PhD students to undertake research in this neglected area. In fleshing out the problem in the proposal, Hofmeyr, referencing Preben Kaarsholm and Deborah James (2000, 189), wrote:

Popular narratives are particularly sensitive artefacts, which encode the hopes and fears of social classes excluded from official histories. Such popular narrative forms embody complex intellectual analyses of what social and political life is and might be. Such texts provide privileged access into popular understandings of how social affinities, networks and subjectivities operate and bind people together . . . In situations of unstable transition and fragile democracy, such cultural forms are particularly important since many people lack meaningful access to political power.

Although the impact of the department's scholarship on popular literature and cultures is now widely acknowledged, what is not well known is the role Hofmeyr played in the development of a particular strand of research in this field, which started with her NRF proposal. Her novel intervention in the area of popular fiction and its publics unleashed a forceful intellectual energy in scholarship that ushered in a sense of newness that many had been waiting for and provided new ways of understanding the broad area of African cultural production beyond the canon. Hofmeyr was driven by what she saw as major gaps in scholarship, especially in relation to African literature. She felt that there was no comprehensive and compelling attention being paid, here in South Africa and on the rest of the continent, to research into African popular culture and literature. Hofmeyr rightly argued that the study of African literature continued to revolve around a limited number of internationally published canonical texts, largely by elite writers coming from the Heinemann African Writers series.[3] She would insist that as much as these canonical writers were important, grassroots intellectual traditions and lesser-known writers were seldom examined or studied in the academy. By implication, Hofmeyr was suggesting that although the aim of privileging African literature had been to supplant the English canon, scholars continued to follow that canon's bad example. They had replaced the English canon with the African canon instead of reaching out to the diverse cultural streams within the continent.

Moreover, African literature was seldom explored in relation to all its hinterlands and was often annexed by international trends. This was all the more significant because African literature continued to be read in relation to the Western canon. It was seen either as engaged in a project of reappropriating the Western canon or as simply writing back to it. A bastard child of the Western literary tradition, it had failed to create its own mythos, as Edward Said (1994) would have put it. Stated differently, African literature's recourse to its own internal traditions remained submerged and silenced. In a profound sense, Hofmeyr was foregrounding unknown and hidden patterns in the broad areas of African literatures and cultures that had been neglected. Her intervention came on the back of a resurgence of the need to foreground African studies within the academy, where they had hitherto been seen as an appendage to Western literary studies.

Indeed, in a gathering of eminent South African scholars of culture at the Centre for African Studies at the University of Cape Town in September 1993, Hofmeyr challenged her colleagues to rise above South African provincialism – or what has now come to be known as South African exceptionalism. She questioned the complacent assumption that South Africa is both the beginning and the horizon in African studies. In a response to the papers presented at the conference, she observed:

> The . . . issue relates to the often asymmetrical or idiosyncratic way in which African Studies has, or more properly has not, been appropriated in South Africa. The point has been made that in South Africa we do not do African Studies. We do South or at best Southern African Studies. There has been little systematic and sustained engagement with Africanist scholarship. This lack of engagement is particularly striking in these papers, particularly when one considers that one of the key and driving questions behind Africanist scholarship has been how to understand local knowledge. (Hofmeyr 1996, 115)

In essence, Hofmeyr was challenging her South African colleagues to rise above South African insularity, and asserting that if they wanted to enrich scholarship in African studies, they needed to tap into a body of knowledge that had been produced by their African counterparts beyond the Limpopo. On this point, she added: 'It seems to me that if interdisciplinary African Cultural Studies is to expand here, then work of the type we are discussing would need to baptise itself in, and enter a dialogue with, this type of scholarship' (Hofmeyr 1996, 115). The silent but salient point in Hofmeyr's sharp observations was that South African scholarship had perhaps spent more time engaging with Northern scholarship than with the rest of the continent, and that what masqueraded as African studies had long been annexed by Northern scholarship.

Hofmeyr would go on to challenge her colleagues to reflect more seriously on notions of the appropriation and reception of texts beyond normative ideas of reading. In fact, she was urging them to reflect more seriously on why and how texts are read, and on ways of reading that challenge elite modes of text reception. She was asking them to try to understand how texts travel and how their meanings mutate in the process, especially when they are passed on from one person to the next and the next, in a seamless yet complex mode of sharing. What is centred here is the story, which often keeps evolving and acquiring larger-than-life meanings. This type of reception and reading requires us to abandon our learned modes of reading. In the consumption of popular literature and cultures, we find a preponderance of these transgressive modes of reception and reading – hence the urgent need to position popular literature and culture at the heart of scholarship, especially here in Africa. Hofmeyr's point was that, unlike with popular cultural forms associated with huge Western production houses, which also determine ways of consuming their products, the situation in Africa is different. In Africa, local mass publishing does not exist. Instead, the bulk of book production is 'small-scale, regional and artisanal' (Newell 2002, 153). I am not suggesting here that multinational products of mass production do not circulate widely in Africa. They do, but the ways in which they are circulated and consumed are often tenaciously regional, class-driven and deeply uneven.

The foregoing analysis brings me to the final point I need to make with regard to Hofmeyr's intervention, which is that popular literature and culture also offer a challenge to postcolonial literary theory in its multiple variants. Hofmeyr argued that until recently the lens through which scholars both here in Africa and abroad had viewed the literature and intellectual history of the continent had been postcolonial theory. Like many others, she was concerned about the way postcolonial theory tended to homogenise the literature of the continent and other 'Third World' countries into easily accessible packages (Ahmad 1992; Barber 1995; Tomaselli 1998). Indeed, her concern was that certain variants of postcolonial theory continue to rely on the outdated models of opposition and resistance, which posit the 'centre' as the point towards which everyone 'writes back'. Perhaps her more important point in relation to reading, touched on above, is the way in which postcolonial theory further straitjackets African readers and writers by assuming that everyone is obsessed with Western imperialism – that 'the West continues to occupy everyone's imagination' (Larkin 1997, 408). In effect, what the postcolonial framework does is to 'create a ghetto for literature from once-colonised countries within English departments and degree schemes' (McLeod 2000, 249). Thus, Hofmeyr did not simply anticipate the fault lines associated with postcolonial theory: she was also suggesting that one needs only to turn to popular literature and cultures to fully grasp those complex and layered fears, desires and aspirations of African readers, which are embedded in their everyday lives. She was pointing out how attentive recourse to understanding African literature in relation to its hinterlands can challenge our complacent modes of literary reception while drawing attention to those issues of affect that drive our 'other' cultural and literary products – the hidden meanings and patterns. Her work on how John Bunyan's *Pilgrim's Progress* travelled, appropriated and translated into a number of African languages to serve a range of competing religious interests in Africa is a good illustration of her thinking in this regard.[4]

Linked to issues of the conditions of production and consumption of popular literature and cultures, Hofmeyr's intervention also drew attention to what these processes mean for the formation of publics and audiences. She was seeking to extend our understanding of how the so-called public spheres are constituted in African societies, but by turning to local practices rather than reading these through the lens of received theories. Hofmeyr started by engaging with broader traditions of debate relating to the formation of publics and audiences in Africa (Barber 1997), particularly the idea that the patrimonial nature of many African societies would effectively rule out the possibility of the emergence of a sizeable public sphere in which democratic debates could take place (Chabal and Daloz 1999). Debate, this strand of scholarship assumed, could only take place within elite institutionalised spaces. Hofmeyr had instead argued, very much as Atieno Odhiambo (2002) had done, that one needs to pay close attention to the 'paraliterate' zone of popular literary production and consumption, since it is here that much popular intellectual activity will take place. Odhiambo, making specific reference to the Kenyan context, had argued that the ordinary *wanainchi* (people) create their own 'mini republics' in sites such as the *matatu-taxi*, football stadiums and *nyama choma* (meat-roasting) venues – sites within which the unsayable could be spoken outside the reach of officialdom. According to Hofmeyr, these zones often operate on the borders of, and between, official institutions, be they chieftaincies, schools or churches. She was clearly drawing on South African examples, but these zones vary immensely depending on the particular regions and countries of the continent.

Hofmeyr's point nevertheless remains valid: these zones will inevitably produce a variegated set of literary and cultural practices, which in turn underpin a variety of social networks and imaginative forms of congregation that produce complexly layered public spheres. She was therefore disputing the notion of the constitution of the public sphere in many European countries, which is often understood as bringing reasonably homogeneous groupings of 'modern' subjects into being through a particular mode of address – for example, that which is enabled by the mass media (Anderson 1983; Calhoun 1992). Without denying the role that texts also play in Africa in hailing audiences or readers, Hofmeyr was careful to point out that other texts or cultural forms (such as music) speak to their audiences as part of patrimonial networks. In other words, in such texts audiences are addressed not simply as anonymous interchangeable subjects, but also in particular terms – terms that are shared by a community of people (see Ogude 2001). Her point is that in Africa there is no single overriding mode of address. Instead, there is an interplay of 'traditional' and 'modern' and, beyond that, also 'post-modern' modes that may seek to disrupt or even challenge the other two. An in-depth understanding of how texts address their audiences would therefore pursue a configuration of all these zones.

Through a series of seminars on theory, method and genre in the area of popular fiction and culture and their implied practices and audiences, a new intellectual formation in the making was born. These seminars not only attracted some very fine students but also tapped into the experiences of leading scholars in the area of the 'popular' in Africa, such as Karin Barber, Paulo de Moraes Farias, Stephanie Newell and Preben Kaarsholm, and our own internal group of faculty (among them Hofmeyr, Bhekizizwe Peterson, Sarah Nuttall and me). Of interest was a stream of intellectual clusters that would drive the seminars and research interest in the department. These clusters included Religion and Reading Formations; Writing, Global Cultures and Self-Styling in East and Southern Africa; Print Cultures: West, East and Southern Africa; Unruly Readers/Compliant Writers in West, East and Southern Africa; and Love in a Time of Plague: Reworkings of Romance.

The impact of this new trajectory in research is now widely acknowledged and perhaps most evident in the cohort of excellent scholars that the Wits Department of African Literature trained during this period. They include Joyce Nyairo, Cathy Muhoma, George Ogola, Michael Titlestad, George Outa, Okot Benge, Muff Andersson, Sope Maithufi, Dishon Kweya, Elsie Cloete, Maina Mutonya, Tom Odhiambo, Grace Musila, Dina Ligaga, and the late Monde Simelela and Phaswane

Mpe, among others. These scholars now occupy important spaces within the academy, both here in southern Africa and abroad, and they have distinguished themselves through quality scholarship and research production. The immediate impact of the work in the area is also evident in the range of books and special issues of journals that were produced under the rubrics of 'popular literature' and 'popular cultures' during that period, some of which have remained definitive in the field.[5] I have in mind, for example, my own book volume, edited with Joyce Nyairo and titled *Urban Legends, Colonial Myths: Popular Culture and Literature in East Africa* (2007), which was a product of this intellectual enterprise and has been very influential in the East African academy and useful to those scholars of culture working in the region.[6] In a sense, the tree that Isabel Hofmeyr planted back in 2002 has produced many more trees, and the forest they have formed has extended to many parts of Africa.

It is a remarkable and fitting tribute to Isabel Hofmeyr that, under her leadership, the Department of African Literature at Wits grew into a beacon of intellectual excellence, nurturing a group of students who were locally rooted in their research while remaining intellectually alert and acutely attentive to transnational currents in scholarship. The department became what many recognise as a home to a popular cultural and literary scholarship on the continent, and its scholars are seen as leaders of an intellectual tradition that has flowered in different directions. It comes as no surprise, then, that the recently released *Routledge Handbook of African Popular Culture* (2022) was edited by one of the finest products of the department, Grace Musila, who is now its head.

NOTES

1   When Professor Hofmeyr took over from Njabulo Ndebele in 1993, she was both the head and chair of the department. As head, she was dealing with the administrative affairs of the department, while as chair, she was the intellectual leader. Although Hofmeyr had relinquished the headship at the end of 1996, handing over to the late Bhekizizwe Peterson, she remained in a position of intellectual leadership, responsible for, among other things, the academic project in the department. With visible growth in our postgraduate programme, especially at master's and PhD level, it was clear by the year 2000 that we needed to revise our postgraduate courses, which

had hitherto remained relatively stable. By this time I had taken over from Bheki Peterson as department head, while Hofmeyr remained chair.

2 Isabel Hofmeyr, 'Popular Literature and Its Publics', a proposal submitted to the National Research Foundation (NRF), June 2002. Document in author's possession.

3 A collection of writings in English by African novelists, poets and politicians published by the London publisher Heinemann between 1962 and 2003.

4 See, for example, Isabel Hofmeyr (2001, 2004b, 2006, 2007).

5 See, for example, Hofmeyr (2004a, 2005); Hofmeyr and Kaarsholm (2006); Hofmeyr, Ogude and Nyairo (2003); Nyairo and Ogude (2005); Ogude (2001); Ogude and Nyairo (2003, 2005); and Ogude and Ojwang (2011).

6 Evan Mwangi of Northwestern University observed in his review of the book that 'the hallmark of the essays in this book is their theoretical sophistication and acute examination of East African politics and cultures. The writers conduct close readings of particular texts while remaining attentive to the historical and political developments in Africa. The result is a book that is comprehensive, entertaining, and intellectually engaging' (Mwangi 2008).

REFERENCES

Ahmad, Aijaz. 1992. *In Theory: Classes, Nations and Literature*. London: Verso.

Anderson, Benedict. 1983. *Imagined Communities: Reflections on the Origin and Spread of Nationalism*. London: Verso.

Barber, Karin. 1987. 'Popular Arts in Africa'. *African Studies Review* 30 (3): 1–78.

———. 1995. 'African Language Literature and Post-colonial Criticism'. *Research in African Literatures* 26 (4): 3–30.

———. 1997. 'Audiences in Africa'. *Africa: Journal of the International African Institute* 67 (3): 347–362.

Calhoun, Craig J., ed. 1992. *Harbermas and the Public Sphere*. Cambridge, MA: MIT Press.

Chabal, Patrick and Jean-Pascal Daloz. 1999. *Africa Works: Disorder as Political Instrument*. Oxford: James Currey.

Hofmeyr, Isabel. 1994. *'We Spend Our Years as a Tale That is Told': Oral Historical Narrative in a South African Chiefdom*. Portsmouth: Heinemann.

———. 1996. 'Response to Bunn and Taylor'. In *Transgressing Boundaries: New Directions in the Study of Culture in Africa*, edited by Brenda Cooper and Andrew Steyn, 114–115. Cape Town: University of Cape Town Press; Athens: Ohio University Press.

———. 2001. 'John Bunyan, His Chair and a Few Other Relics: Orality, Literacy and the Limits of Area Studies'. In *African Words, African Voices: Critical Practices in Oral History*, edited by Luise White, Stephan Miescher and David William Cohen, 78–90. Bloomington: Indiana University Press.

———, ed. 2004a. 'Popular Literature in Africa: Post-resistance Perspectives'. Special issue, *Social Dynamics* 30 (2): 131–143.

———. 2004b. 'Portable Landscapes: Thomas Mofolo and John Bunyan in the Broad and Narrow Way'. In *Disputed Territories: Land, Space and Identity in Settler Societies*, edited by Gareth Griffiths and David Trigger, 131–153. Hong Kong: Hong Kong University Press.

———, ed. 2005. 'Mass Media and Popular Narrative'. Special issue, *Social Identities* 11, no. 2.

———. 2006. 'The Pilgrim's Progress as World Literature: John Bunyan and George Simeon Mwase in Nyasaland'. *1650–1850: Ideas, Aesthetics, and Inquiries in the Early Modern Era* 13 (2006): 175–199.

———. 2007. 'Evangelical Realism: The Transnational Making of Genre in *The Pilgrim's Progress*'. In *Reception, Appropriation, Recollection: Bunyan's 'Pilgrim's Progress'*, edited by W.R.Owens and Stuart Sim, 119–145. Oxford: Peter Lang.

Hofmeyr, Isabel and Preben Kaarsholm, eds. 2006. 'Popular Cultural Materials and Public Spheres: Perspectives from Africa, India and Europe'. Special issue, *Current Writing* 18 (2): 1–13.

Hofmeyr, Isabel, James Ogude and Joyce Nyairo. 2003. '"Who Can Bwogo Me?" Popular Culture in Kenya'. *Social Identities* 9 (3): 373–382.

Kaarsholm, Preben and Deborah James. 2000. 'Popular Culture and Democracy in Some Southern Contexts: An Introduction'. *Journal of Southern African Studies* 26 (2): 189–208.

Larkin, Brian. 1997. 'Indian Films and Nigerian Lovers: Media and the Creation of Paralleled Modernities'. *Africa* 67 (3): 406–440.

McLeod, John. 2000. *Beginning Postcolonialism*. Manchester: Manchester University Press.

Musila, Grace, ed. 2022. *Routledge Handbook of African Popular Culture*. Abingdon-on-Thames: Routledge.

Mwangi, Evan. 2008. 'A Study in Popular Culture'. *Nairobi Sunday Times*, 12 February.

Newell, Stephanie, ed. 2002. *Readings in African Popular Fiction*. Oxford: James Currey.

Nyairo, Joyce and James Ogude. 2005. 'Popular Music, Popular Politics: "Unbwogable" and the Idioms of Freedom in Kenyan Popular Music'. *African Affairs* 104 (415): 225–249.

Odhiambo, Atieno. 2002. 'Hegemonic Enterprises and Instrumentalities of Survival: Ethnicity and Democracy in Kenya'. *African Studies* 62 (2): 224–249.

Ogude, James. 2001. 'The Vernacular Press and the Articulation of Luo Ethnic Citizenship: The Case of Achieng' Oneko's *Ramogi*'. *Current Writing* 13 (2): 42–55.

Ogude, James and Joyce Nyairo. 2003. 'Popular Music and the Negotiation of Contemporary Kenyan Identity: The Example of Nairobi City Ensemble'. *Social Identities* 9 (3): 383–400.

———, eds. 2005. 'East African Popular Culture and Literature'. Special issue, *Africa Insight* 35, no. 2 (June).

———, eds. 2007. *Urban Legends, Colonial Myths: Popular Culture and Literature in East Africa*. Trenton: Africa World Press.

Ogude, James and Dan Ojwang, eds. 2011. 'Eastern African Literatures and Culture'. Special issue, *Africa Today* 57, no. 3.

Said, Edward. 1994. *Culture and Imperialism*. London: Vintage.

Tomaselli, Kenyan G. 1998. 'Recovering Praxis: Cultural Studies in Africa: The Unnaming Continues (Reply to Wright, 1998 and McNeil, 1998)'. *European Journal of Cultural Studies* 1 (3): 387–402.

3

Fluidity and Its Methodological Openings: Mobility and Discourse on the Eve of Colonialism

Carolyn Hamilton

INTRODUCTION

In *'We Spend Our Years as a Tale That is Told'*: *Oral Historical Narrative in a South African Chiefdom*, which examines the relationship between orality and literacy, Isabel Hofmeyr (1993) drew attention to the impact on oral accounts of their publication in early South African school readers. She pointed to the way in which written texts separated speakers from their speeches, were static and unaccommodating of responses, and lacked the flexibility of oral storytelling. Using an aqueous metaphor that prefigured the circulations of the Indian Ocean and the hydrocolonialism of her later work (Hofmeyr 2022), she commented that publication conferred a rigid casing on forms that 'previously lived by fluidity' (Hofmeyr 1993, 54).

The fluidity that Hofmeyr pointed to in 1993 was, for most historians of the time, the core 'weakness' of oral accounts as historical sources. It was – and is still today for many researchers – a problem to be obviated by recording (usually by writing down) an oral text and 'fixing' it so that it stays the same. However, Hofmeyr's formulation suggested a different possibility: that of grappling with the significance and dynamics of fluidity both at the time of the text's encasement in written form, and in its iterations in social and political life in earlier eras, when the local world was one of oral communication and circulation.

This possibility has been realised in a critique of the concept of oral traditions, and of the ways in which oral accounts thus conceptualised have been used by historians. The critique points to a new way of approaching both oral historical accounts and early written accounts based on previously oral-only repertoires and discursive practices. This approach entails paying attention to fluidity as a characteristic feature – rather than a deleterious effect of oral communication and the passage of time – that demands methodological, and historical, attention in its own right. The approach brings past responses, debates, assessments and revisions into view (Cohen 1989, 1994; Hamilton 1987, 2002, 2021; Hofmeyr 1993; Landau 2010). The key arguments here are that engagements of the past were part of processes of the navigation of change; that oral accounts, as much as written ones, bear the traces of that navigational work; and that such navigations continue to this day. The approach thus offers historians two opportunities: that of exploring the ways in which history was engaged with in past political discourses, and that of delving into the nature of creative political thought and deliberation both in the eras before colonialism and subsequently, when newly colonised groupings sought to establish themselves in the emerging colonial order.

The use of oral accounts to throw light on eras before colonialism presents particular methodological challenges because historians have to rely on narrated materials that were often recorded or written down (encased) later in time. Here the adaptation of Hofmeyr's approach to circulation, more fully developed in *The Portable Bunyan: A Transnational History of 'The Pilgrim's Progress'* (2004), provides further assistance. For the use of oral accounts relating to the remote past, the work involves not only tracing circulatory pathways in and out of oral and written texts and across seemingly discrete geographies, but also tacking backwards and forwards across the apparently absolute divide between what are teleo-logically described as the 'pre-colonial era' and the 'colonial era'. The process entails examining, first, how ideas from and about the past, and often the movement of people with those ideas, shaped recorded and written texts; and, second, how latter-day formulations shaped understandings of that past, in what we might think of as an iterative spiral through time.

For historians, this process offers a remarkable opportunity to move away from the practices of mining oral accounts for facts about earlier political developments and of using ethnographic data recorded in the early twentieth century to elucidate such developments. The focus on flu-idity in the form of creative and deliberative responses to change thus signals a decisive break from long-congealed notions of societies prior to colonialism as being characterised by timeless, traditional practices framed as 'culture' rather than any number of alternatives – including political, intellectual or creative practices. In proposing that there are dis-tinct traces of strong intellectual carry-overs and carry-backs across the seemingly absolute pre-colonial/colonial divide, this essay leverages the work of Hofmeyr to prompt scholars to consider engaging the history of earlier eras and earlier ways of discoursing in their own right, recognising the possibilities offered by methods that find a way back into that past through texts from later times.

This approach to discursive fluidity brings into view past practices of political fluidity, flexibility and mobility, accompanied by the circu-lation of news, ideas, information and goods that were both signals of and responses to changing conditions. These developments add up to an understanding of fluidity as a characteristic feature of past social and political praxis.

This essay highlights the ubiquity of settled thinking to foreground the power – both disruptive and generative – of Hofmeyr's methodological engagement of fluidity, realised not only in her first book but elaborated across her accumulated body of work. It argues that fluidity in past political and historical discourses, as well as in past political practices, has long been obscured by three entrenched and interlocked forms of settled thinking: colonial recording practices seeking a fixed record of the past; the linked colonial ascription of timeless cultural practices to newly colonised subjects; and the colonial view of historically established 'tribes' settled in boundaried territories.

The essay does this by means of a discussion of recent work on the political formations of eastern southern Africa (present-day KwaZulu-Natal and neighbouring areas) in the century or so before colonialism, from roughly the early 1700s until around 1830 (Hamilton and Wright, forthcoming). What emerges from that work is an understanding of kinetic processes, of fluid and flexible polities forming and re-forming in new configurations and characterised by considerable political mobility, with people drawing on diverse networks of carefully curated connections. These processes were informed by active networks for the circulation of ideas and the movement of things, and were bolstered by equally dynamic discoursing about changing contexts. Fluidity is then seen both as a feature of oral accounts and of political formation-ing (the neologism is necessary to capture the idea of the fluid forming and re-forming of political entities) and as foundational to the methodological practice involved in using oral accounts as sources. That practice finds inspiration not only in Hofmeyr's 'We Spend Our Years as a Tale That is Told' but also in her larger oeuvre. It entails the giving of attention to the movement of people, ideas and texts in overlooked networks of circulation, which is in many respects the hallmark of Hofmeyr's work.

SETTLED THINKING

In the region with which this essay is concerned, the official recording in writing of what were regarded as 'tribal histories' commenced in the middle of the nineteenth century, when the newly installed British colonial authorities in Natal sought to rule through established chiefs and to confine Africans to specific pockets of 'tribal' lands (Guy 2013; Hamilton 1998; Hamilton and Leibhammer 2016; McClendon 2010). This type of recording, and linked practices of identifying and locating people, became increasingly systematic over time (Lekgoathi, Kros and Wright 2022). A variety of people outside government who identified, or were identified, as native experts – among them missionaries, Bantu Studies scholars, folklorists and anthropologists – also recorded or documented oral material of various kinds. Until the 1960s, however, academic historians paid little attention to oral accounts, which for the most part they regarded as unreliable historical evidence.

Following Jan Vansina's interventions (beginning in 1961) in developing specific methodologies for the use of oral traditions, historians began to mine bodies of recorded oral material for historical evidence and even to record oral accounts. To this day, southern African historians use methodologies stemming from Vansina's work. Few of them pay close attention to the thick discursive matrices – the circumstances of the telling of tales – or the histories and forms of the materials from which they extract their factual nuggets. Limited also is the number of scholars who investigate the processes involved in recording and rendering the spoken word into what are often multiple versions of text, produced over time and in a variety of locales. Only some attempt to reconstruct anything of the history of the accounts, or of the world of historical debate in which they were involved before, and at the time of, becoming fixed in their recorded form. And fewer still pay attention to choices of phrasing, or words and concepts, used in the local African languages or versions thereof (Hamilton 2011, 2021; Hofmeyr 1993).

In the 1960s the decolonisation of much of Africa saw a sharp upswing of historical studies into the African past before colonialism. In contrast to earlier works, which, insofar as they considered that past, portrayed the rise of the Zulu kingdom as attributable to the genius of its founder, King Shaka, scholars began to consider the role of factors such as demographic pressure, environmental change and external trade (Gluckman 1960; Guy 1979; Omer-Cooper 1966; Thompson 1969). In the 1970s and 1980s Marxist scholars conceptualised the Zulu kingdom, and what they saw as a number of precursor polities, as states (Bonner 1983; Guy 1979; Hedges 1978; Slater 1976). A key institutional development identified as enabling the processes of state formation was a new form of labour organisation – notably, *amabutho*, or 'age-regiments' – centralised under powerful rulers (Wright 1978). The upshot of two centuries of writing, from a variety of perspectives, about the history of the region before colonialism has been to conceive of these polities – whether described as chiefdoms, kingdoms, empires or states – as circumscribed entities settled in demarcated lands, with distinct historical identities under historically legitimated ruling houses characterised by forms of centralised power.

The corollary of the focus on the rise of big kingdoms was the conceptualisation of many of those who were not encompassed in these political formations as 'refugees'. Much has been written about King Shaka having depopulated vast swathes of territory, and about how such ideas were used by European settlers as an argument for the land being empty and available for settlement, and for a convenient formulation of the local inhabitants of Natal as rootless refugees in need of shelter. For all its internal variations across time, the accumulated knowledge of the centralised kingdoms and its corollary of rootless refugees amounts to well-established habits of settled thinking.

TRACKING CHANGE AND MOVEMENT

Over a century of settled thinking focused on the nineteenth-century Zulu kingdom, whether portrayed positively or negatively, as the most developed example of these established centralised polities. At the same time, the effects of European interpretive frameworks were concentrated on it as the first extensively documented political formation in the region. However, as a result of timing, the Zulu kingdom was also the local political formation that first felt the impact of an expanding colonial presence and the (at first distant) encroaching colonial frontier that increasingly constrained options for movement within southern Africa. It was thus a new case, rather than an example that illuminates, by extrapolation, less well-documented earlier political formations in the same region.[1]

In our latest work, John Wright and I focus our attention on political formations that pre-date the Zulu kingdom (Hamilton and Wright, forthcoming). We use an approach that is attentive to, among other things, the histories of accounts and their discursive contexts; the variations and contradictions within them; and the persistent presence of opaque and contradictory matter. Central to our approach is taking careful notice of how ideas travel across space as well as over time, moving across the oral and the written, with ideas and practices from early times influencing ideas and practices in colonial times, and colonial ideas and practices shaping understandings of earlier times.

As Hofmeyr's work affirms again and again, travelling changes the shape of texts (Hofmeyr 2004). In a manner resonant with her approach, we establish fluidity, and the travelling of ideas, as a foundation of our methodological practice. This requires the kind of multi-sited methodological approach that marks much of Hofmeyr's work. Thus we make a point of consulting accounts, both recorded oral materials and written texts, from a wide variety of descendants and other commentators with diverse later histories.

Many of these descendants and commentators came to be located in places other than the areas where the historical political formations with which we are concerned were based. This has meant exploring understandings of the early history of the KwaZulu-Natal region expressed at various times, often by speakers and writers based outside of the region, not only in isiZulu but also in siSwati, isiXhosa and Sesotho (and variations thereon), and in English. One advantage offered by the diversity of speaking/writing positions with which we engage is that it assists us in tracing how ideas about the past travelled and changed. It positions us to grapple with the ways in which varied subsequent experiences and locations – what Hofmeyr (1993, 175) terms 'the intervening period' – shape historical discussion of the earlier political formations. This in turn illuminates how actively and divergently people moved over time, developing and dissolving relationships in changing contexts. While some of the movement was the result of colonial and apartheid policies, most of the movement which emerges in these historical accounts pre-dates formal colonialism. Movements into, within and out of the region are abundantly attested to in the available historical materials, but previously attracted little attention because of the way in which the focus on aggregation, centralisation and settlement has been sustained over time.

Abundant attestation to movement is found in the main bodies of recorded materials for the region: notably, the James Stuart collection (assembled between c. 1890 and 1920), which contains the accounts of some two hundred commentators, interlocutors and expositors,[2] and the more synthesised compendium by Alfred T. Bryant (1929), a missionary turned Bantu Studies academic (Etherington 2016). The two corpuses are filled with details of politically contingent and ongoing regional shifts and movements over time of substantial groupings of people relocating to new areas and establishing new allegiances. They also record – in multiple ways – the discoursing on foundational movements in archaic and more recent times by the people with whom Stuart and Bryant consulted. Both Stuart and Bryant noted that these engagements typically involved discussions of opaque and ambiguous allusions. These allusions were open-ended and often engendered deliberative engagement from the interlocutors involved, as in this discussion about people identified as 'ntungwa' between Stuart and his assistants Socwatsha kaPhaphu and Maziyana kaMahlabeni, recorded in 1905:

> *They rolled down by means of a grain basket (ba gingika nge silulu)*, i.e. were all put into a basket which was rolled down, and when they got down it was opened and they came out and scattered over the country . . . The abeNguni are not said to have *come down by means of a grain basket*, but Socwatsha thinks they must have done so, like the amaNtungwa, on the ground that the Qwabes and Zulu, who are really amaNtungwa, speak of themselves nowadays as abeNguni. (Webb and Wright 1979, 281)[3]

Active interpretive engagement with movements in distant times also characterised the early historical writings of the intellectual Magema Fuze, where it is part of a bricolage of inherited ideas about local movements and ideas about pan-African migrations gleaned from other literature (Fuze 1922; Mokoena 2011).

Quotidian movements are thickly attested to in the Stuart and Bryant corpuses, being present in the accounts of new wives moving to marital contexts; appointees being sent to inhabit distant areas; foreign experts gaining local pre-eminence; sons and brothers setting up their own establishments; and so on.

Movement likewise characterises the first novel in isiZulu, *Insila ka Tshaka*, John Dube's imaginative evocation of the times of Shaka, which opens with the perspective of a traveller approaching the king's Dukuza residence (Dube 1931). The novel is filled with the details of the hospitalities that facilitated travel along the road, court arrivals and departures, and the achievement of positions in various places by the main protagonist, Jeqe (first at Dukuza, then later to the north-east among the followers of Shaka's enemy, Soshangane, and still later to the north of the Zulu kingdom, eSwatini).

James Scott (2017) prompts us to think about how the historical disciplines, reinforced by assumptions accumulated over time, read settlement as a sign of political order, and sedentism, demographic aggregation and large entities as desirable signals of success. Concomitantly, these disciplines habitually treat mobility as a sign of political disorder and a signal of failure. Scott lays out a compelling argument for looking afresh at the available sources and their assumptions, and developing an understanding of mobility in settings such as KwaZulu-Natal in this period not as anomalous but rather as commonplace, strategic, politically logical and successful. Alive to the attestation in the sources to movement, Wright and I have come to reconsider long-standing habits of thinking about the history of the KwaZulu-Natal region as demonstrating processes of state formation. The reconsideration involved does not challenge the evidence of the emergence of powerful polities in the hundred years or so before colonialism. If anything, it adds to that. But it gives close attention also to political fluidity, flexibility and mobility, arguing that those features were constitutive of the political fabric of the time.

In the period between around 1730 and around 1826, the region between the uPhongolo and uThukela rivers (an area of roughly only 160 square kilometres) saw the emergence and dissolution of a number of major formations, among them Ndwandwe, Hlubi, Mthethwa and Qwabe. The differences among these formations related to whether the aggregations concerned were primarily defensive or expansive, and whether the ruling powers were incomers or long-time inhabitants of a region. Supplicant incomers sought patronage and security in new places and offered adherence and labour in return. Incomers who bene-fited from the prior exploitation of resources elsewhere, a knowledge of other places and an ability to mobilise networks of distant connections were able to establish themselves in new places in assertive ways. Similar differences characterised vulnerable in situ people subject to conquest and powerful in situ people in command of strategic local affordances. The variety in the political formations of the time reflected the ways in which these combinations played out.

Focus of this kind on the dynamism of the regional political processes of the time, and on politically valued and much-used strategies of mobility, calls into question long-established ideas about what was politi-cally exceptional. Well-known nineteenth-century migrant kingdoms such as Ndebele under Mzilikazi and Ngwane under Matiwane are cases in point. The challenge here is to consider whether, or to what extent, the later mobility of formations like Ndebele and Ngwane – much discussed in relation to the notion of mfecane and presented as a crisis response, whether in relation to unusually severe drought, colonial pressures, slave trading or even an exceptionally aggressive new regional power – was dramatically different from what was typical in the region. The process of reconsideration described above suggests that, in the face of intensifying pressures, these were heightened but not unusual responses.[4] Moreover, it offers a critique of the all-too-ready characterisation of movements of people as the scattering of displaced refugees, and makes it worth noting that under certain circumstances people moved in order to seek the alleviation of onerous conditions and hardship, or refuge and protection from enemies. Some people were forced or pressured into moving, and some among them were forced into marginal existences. In addition, some people were captives taken to new places against their will. However, movement was as much a source of opportunity as it was a strategy of survival, and was often both.

In all instances relations between incomers and those in situ, and their layering into shared landscapes, required considered political conceptualisation expressed in the discourses of the time, often referencing the past in equally considered ways. Such conceptualisations involved what Hofmeyr (1993, 181) recognised as analysis embedded in narrative 'which encodes political ideas and historical thinking in particularly effective ways'. It entailed a form of iterative political work (more on this later).

The plethora of evidence about political movement is complemented by the abundant evidence related to the movement of goods. Many of the political developments described above involved strategically moving into position to control trade and transit routes, and mountain and river crossings. Ivory, brass, beads, finery, herbal remedies, potent substances, cattle, provisions and raided grain, among other things, were all in motion. So were porters, guides, envoys, spies, adventurers, ritual specialists and others with valued skills, relatives on their way to and from family visits, regiments on missions to relocate people, and even *buyisa*'d[5] ancestors. All this movement and mobility was underwritten by a variety of ritual and social practices designed to protect and support people who were moving, a case in point being the placing of stones on ubiquitous *izivivane* (travellers' cairns) with their associated invocations of ancestors' protection. Moreover, as is to be expected, the movement of goods and people was accompanied by the transmission of technologies, knowledge, expertise, new ideas, information and news. Movement and the circulation of goods and ideas were thus all at once agents and results of processes of change, and signals of dynamic political developments.

What emerges from a wide-ranging discussion of movement over time is the ability of people to take advantage of the affordances of carefully cultivated and constantly curated networks of cross-cutting connections, whether they were moving of their own volition or being forced to move, or were involved in moving things. These connections took multiple forms. One of them (the constraints of the essay form limit discussion to one type of connectivity) was the strategic management of carefully distributed exogamous marriage connections and of exchanges of information and political intelligence-gathering facilitated by the movement of women – notably, women who thus connected their natal and marriage homes. Women did not simply move away into new married contexts but maintained natal connections and actively visited, and were visited by, relatives. Similarly, women who were sent from their homes to live and work among the king's *izigodlo*[6] effectively connected their natal homes to the court, the workings of which they were closely and continuously exposed to. As *izigodlo* women who married men designated by the king, they also connected the court to their married contexts. Moreover, by sharing information among themselves, married *izigodlo* women facilitated the lateral movement of information across these married contexts.

The significance of the movement of women was, however, not confined to matters of information, communication and the multi-directional relay of political intelligence. Married women continually managed the political heft of their natal contexts in their married ones. They relied on their natal contexts to underpin their status in their married contexts, and in securing the successful accessions of sons or contesting the successions of others. They also used the affordances of their married contexts to direct benefits back to their natal contexts, and vice versa. Marriage strategies thus gave the families of both sons and daughters opportunities to secure multiple connections that were capable of supporting flexible immediate and future strategies.

The movement of women and the nature of their structurally relational political positioning was therefore centrally constitutive of the political fabric. At the same time, existing marriage connections were not the only factor facilitating flexible political activity. The *history* of marriages was also significant, as was the history of other kinds of connections.

PAST DISCOURSES AND DISCOURSING ACROSS TIME

The capacity to activate earlier connections and past and present networks – and to mobilise alternative possibilities at different points in time in response to new conditions – depended on ongoing communication and the work of historical memory, and sometimes on the refurbishment of such memory. The seeking of support, refuge or new opportunities was often bolstered by the mobilisation of historical arguments about past marriages, other connections, historical reciprocity, kinship or even past grievances. In short, the nature of political life meant that the production of history was a vital aspect of political discourse.

Discourse and discoursing are centrally concerned with words, communication and debate, often entailing extended expression of thought on a subject. It involves ways of constituting knowledge, together with the social practices, forms of subjectivity and power relations that inhere in such knowledge. Until a 2010 intervention by Paul Landau, Hofmeyr (1993) was a lone voice in pressing for engagement with intellectual discourses in southern Africa before colonialism, and in suggesting ways of doing this.

Recent research leveraging off Hofmeyr's insights now points to a long history of discourses and practices designed to manage and maximise the options that could be taken up in the face of changes; and capable of facilitating the mobility, flexibility and fluidity that were constitutive of the political fabric in eras immediately before, but also into, the reign of Shaka. The kinds of changes involved were diverse. They might range from the effects of drought and difficulties in cultivating marginal fields, through opportunities such as the introduction of new kinds of crops that supported larger populations and shifts in trade (from locally unvalued items to locally vital items), to the emergence of aggressively expanding neighbours. Taking up options required having multiple potential allies and access to a wide range of resources, including mountain and cave refuges, military support, loan cattle, alternative land to settle, multiple forms of capital, and specialist knowledge and expertise desired in other places. The matter of having viable options was no accident. It was the result of careful strategising. It involved maintaining relationships rooted in historical obligations and preserving memory of them. All of this required assiduous curation and ongoing work.[7]

As soon as we allow ourselves to entertain the idea that in former times people expended intellectual energy in thinking critically about political life and about the past, fluid features of their accounts that were long ignored or generalised as problems of broken relay, faulty memory or even invention emerge as signals of past debates and deliberative interventions, as political discourse in action and as involving iterative discursive activity. Indeed, the local term today translated as 'history' is *umlando*. The verb *ukulanda*, typically translated as 'narrate' or 'tell a story', carries within it notions of fetching, tracing or pursuing, placing the emphasis on the activity involved. This local term resonates conceptually with the title of Hofmeyr's 1993 study, and with fluidity in the multiple senses discussed in this essay.

Colonialism (and later apartheid) framed the immediately pre-colonial era of the region as a time of bounded 'tribes' with singular identities, located in particular areas and led by genealogically validated chiefs. It imposed this static conception on Africans even as the closing colonial frontier was reducing opportunities for mobile political responses. Over time, colonial procedures and processes, and – some time later – academic practices, came to authorise particular aspects of the past and to establish them as a fixed record, first in the form of colonial documents and then of recorded oral tradition, what Hofmeyr (1993, 175) termed 'literate impositions'. As a fixed record supporting singular tribal identities, allegiances and locations, the record itself curtailed the capacity of people to offer and withdraw support for chiefs, to foreground chosen aspects of identity or to move physically. In short, a set record and authorised history worked alongside laws, fences and boundaries to limit the political option of moving. However, the evidence suggests that even when faced with these colonial conditions and restrictions, Africans were adept at curating inherited historical knowledge in ways that served them in their new circumstances. At least at first – and perhaps for longer than we realise – the full repertoire on which they drew, with its capacity to store knowledge well beyond what was most immediately, colonially, relevant, continued to be assiduously curated and cultivated as an archive of political possibility. This is yet manifest in the forms of thick local historical knowledge about the distant past circulating in family networks, often in local languages, which are concerned with historical matters other than the rise of major kingdoms.

This resilient historical custodial praxis – involving the careful development and maintenance of diverse networks, options of connection, and histories of reciprocity and of negotiated successions – was honed over hundreds of years of iterative political activity. It did not attempt to store the past in the form of a definitive record, nor did it involve expediently attesting to whatever was newly most convenient. Rather it entailed – and continues to entail – a complex understanding of the past as full of resources for re-engagement in the face of change.

Hofmeyr (2004, 28) conceptualises *The Pilgrim's Progress* as becoming, through its circulations, a portmanteau text, 'an archive in which various intellectual positions could be billeted . . . provid[ing] a shared landscape and asset of reference points around and in which debates could be rehearsed'. A focus on fluidity allows us to bring into view similar processes of billeting and intellectual activity in a very different, much earlier setting, with remarkable effect.

NOTES

1   See Kopytoff (1987, 78) for a general claim about nineteenth-century polities being 'mature forms' that were then frozen as a result of colonialism.
2   Material in the collection, held at the Killie Campbell Africana Library in Durban, has been published as *The James Stuart Archive of Recorded Oral Evidence Relating to*

the History of the Zulu and Neighbouring Peoples in six volumes (published consecutively in 1976, 1979, 1982, 1986, 2001 and 2014).

3   The words in italics in the quotation signal that the original notes upon which they are based were in isiZulu, not English.

4   This is one of the matters at issue in what has become known as the 'mfecane debate'. See Cobbing (1988) and the collected essays in Hamilton (1995). See also Kopytoff (1987, 7) on the political culture of African societies as having a mobile 'frontier cast'.

5   The term *ukubuyisa* refers to the ceremonialised return home of the spirit of a person who died in distant parts.

6   This term is not readily translatable into English. The most recent volume of the *James Stuart Archive* glosses the term, as used here, as referring to 'women of the king's establishment; girls presented to the king as tribute or selected from the households of his subjects; and as his "daughters", disposable by him in marriage' (Webb and Wright 2014, xxi).

7   The discussion here chimes with new anthropological work on the social generation and experience of what is often termed 'potentiality' in times of significant change, notably the potentialities involved in movement – of people, ideas and goods. Such potentiality is understood to be a pervasive aspect of a prevailing sociality and ethical orientation, and as a process in action, captured in the idea of 'potentialising'. See, for example, Paolo Gaibazzi (2022). See also Giorgio Agamben (1999) on potentiality in relation to time, history and change.

REFERENCES

Agamben, Giorgio. 1999. *Potentialities: Collected Essays in Philosophy*. Stanford: Stanford University Press.

Bonner, Philip. 1983. *Kings, Commoners and Concessionaires: The Evolution and Dissolution of the Swazi State*. Cambridge: Cambridge University Press.

Bryant, Alfred T. 1929. *Olden Times in Zululand and Natal*. London: Longmans, Green and Company.

Cobbing, Julian. 1988. 'The Mfecane as Alibi: Thoughts on Dithakong and Mbolompo'. *Journal of African History* 29 (3): 487–519.

Cohen, David. 1989. 'Undefining of Oral Tradition'. *Ethnohistory* 36 (1): 9–18.

———. 1994. *The Combing of History*. Chicago: University of Chicago Press.

Dube, John. 1931. *Insila ka Tshaka*. (Place of publication and publisher unknown.)

Etherington, Norman. 2016. 'A.T. Bryant's Map of the "Native Clans in Pre-Shakan Times"'. In *Tribing and Untribing the Archive: Identity and the Material Record in Southern KwaZulu-Natal in the Late Independent and Colonial Periods*, edited by Carolyn Hamilton and Nessa Leibhammer, vol. 1, 239–261. Pietermaritzburg: University of KwaZulu-Natal Press.

Fuze, Magema. 1922. *Abantu Abamnyama, Lapa Bavela Ngakona*. Pietermaritzburg, privately printed.

Gaibazzi, Paolo. 2022. 'Potentiality in Crisis: Making and Living the Potential in Angola's Boom and Bust'. *History and Anthropology*. https://doi.org/10.1080/02757206.2022.2037584.

Gluckman, Max. 1960. 'The Rise of a Zulu Empire'. *Scientific American* 202 (4): 157–168.

Guy, Jeff. 1979. *The Destruction of the Zulu Kingdom: The Civil War in Zululand, 1879–1884*. Johannesburg: Ravan Press.

———. 2013. *Theophilus Shepstone and the Forging of Natal*. Pietermaritzburg: University of KwaZulu-Natal Press.

Hamilton, Carolyn. 1987. 'Ideology and Oral Traditions: Listening to the Voices "From Below"'. *History in Africa* 14: 67–83.

———, ed. 1995. *The Mfecane Aftermath*. Johannesburg: Wits University Press; Pietermaritzburg: University of Natal Press.

———. 1998. *Terrific Majesty: The Powers of Shaka Zulu and the Limits of Historical Invention*. Cambridge, MA: Harvard University Press.

———. 2002. 'Living by Fluidity: Oral Histories, Material Custodies and the Politics of Preservation'. In *Refiguring the Archive*, edited by Carolyn Hamilton, Verne Harris, Jane Taylor, Michele Pickover, Graeme Reid and Razia Saleh, 209–227. Claremont: David Philip; Dordrecht: Kluwer Academic Publishers.

———. 2011. 'Backstory, Biography and the Life of the James Stuart Archive'. *History in Africa* 38: 319–341.

———. 2021. 'Recalibrating the Deep History of Intellectual Thought in the KwaZulu-Natal Region'. In *Public Intellectuals in South Africa: Critical Voices from the Past*, edited by Christopher Broodryk, 21–43. Johannesburg: Wits University Press.

Hamilton, Carolyn and Nessa Leibhammer, eds. 2016. *Tribing and Untribing the Archive: Identity and the Material Record in Southern KwaZulu-Natal in the Late Independent and Colonial Periods*. 2 vols. Pietermaritzburg: University of KwaZulu-Natal Press.

Hamilton, Carolyn and John Wright. Forthcoming. *Politics and Identity Making in KwaZulu-Natal, 1700–1830* [provisional title]. Cambridge: Cambridge University Press.

Hedges, David. 1978. 'Trade and Politics in Southern Mozambique and Zululand in the Eighteenth and Early Nineteenth Centuries'. PhD dissertation, University of London.

Hofmeyr, Isabel. 1993. *'We Spend Our Years as a Tale That is Told': Oral Historical Narrative in a South African Chiefdom*. Portsmouth: Heinemann.

———. 2004. *The Portable Bunyan: A Transnational History of 'The Pilgrim's Progress'*. Princeton: Princeton University Press.

———. 2022. *Dockside Reading: Hydrocolonialism and the Custom House*. Johannesburg: Wits University Press.

Kopytoff, Igor. 1987. 'The Internal African Frontier: The Making of African Political Culture'. In *The African Frontier: The Reproduction of Traditional African Societies*, edited by Igor Kopytoff, 3–84. Bloomington: Indiana University Press.

Landau, Paul. 2010. *Popular Politics in the History of South Africa, 1400 to 1948*. Cape Town: Cambridge University Press.

Lekgoathi, Sekibakiba, Cynthia Kros and John Wright. 2022. 'Conversations with Sekibakiba Lekgoathi'. In *Archives of Times Past*, edited by Cynthia Kros, John Wright, Mbongiseni Buthelezi and Helen Ludlow, 104–126. Johannesburg: Wits University Press.

McClendon, Thomas. 2010. *White Chiefs, Black Lords: Shepstone and the Colonial State in Natal, South Africa, 1845–1878*. Rochester: University of Rochester Press.

Mokoena, Hlonipha. 2011. *Magema Magwaza Fuze: The Making of a Kholwa Intellectual*. Pietermaritzburg: University of KwaZulu-Natal Press.

Omer-Cooper, John. 1966. *The Zulu Aftermath: A Nineteenth-Century Revolution in Bantu Africa*. London: Longmans.

Scott, James. 2017. *Against the Grain: A Deep History of the Earliest States*. New Haven: Yale University Press.

Slater, Henry. 1976. 'Transitions in the Political Economy of South-east Africa before 1840'. PhD diss., University of Sussex.

Thompson, Leonard. 1969. 'Co-operation and Conflict: The Zulu Kingdom and Natal'. In *The Oxford History of South Africa*, vol. 1, edited by Monica Wilson and Leonard Thompson, 336–345. Oxford: Oxford University Press.

Vansina, Jan. 1961. *De la tradition orale: Essai de méthode historique*. Tervuren: Musée royal de l'Afrique centrale.

Webb, Colin de B. and John B.Wright, eds. 1979. *The James Stuart Archive of Recorded Oral Evidence Relating to the History of the Zulu and Neighbouring Peoples*, vol. 2. Pietermaritzburg: University of Natal Press.

———, eds. 2014. *The James Stuart Archive of Recorded Oral Evidence Relating to the History of the Zulu and Neighbouring Peoples*, vol. 6. Pietermaritzburg: University of KwaZulu-Natal Press.

Wright, John B. 1978. 'Pre-Shakan Age-Group Formation among the Northern Nguni'. *Natalia* 8 (December): 23–29.

4

Oral Genres and Home-Grown Print Culture

Karin Barber

sabel Hofmeyr's path-breaking work on orality, print and ways of reading demarcates a vast African textual history, and provides chart and compass with which to explore it. A key feature of her work is the way she combines a close focus on the materiality of texts with a capacious vision of their imperial and global interconnections. The letterheads, stamps and typewriters through which the imposition of bureaucracy on an oral world is grasped in 'We Spend Our Years as a Tale That is Told' (1993); the abridgments, excerpting, illustrations, translations, magic lantern shows and dramatic enactments by which The Pilgrim's Progress was disseminated, as described in The Portable Bunyan (2004); the format, layout and composition of the newspaper that Gandhi produced on his hand-operated printing press in Phoenix, Natal, in Gandhi's Printing Press (2013); books as cargo, sampled in customs sheds like other imported goods rather than being read from cover to cover, in Dockside Reading (2022) – attention to these material forms opens the way to a highly original and productive conceptualisation of multi-directional textual movements and interactions. This comprehensive and inclusive vision does not float detachedly above the material world but arises from it, from the material processes of production, circulation and consumption. This work shows how much we stand to gain from attending to the specifics of mode, genre and format, and how important it is to recognise that when texts travelled, they did so not abstractly but in steamships and trains, and were changed as they went, re-created in different ways by local readerships and intermediaries. A book, or a text, is both a product of global processes and the result of what people do with it on the ground, and what they think it is, is for and is about.

This conception of texts in motion, interconnected, shape-shifting, but produced and reproduced on the ground, has at its centre the idea of textual temporality. Hofmeyr's work is highly sensitive to the fact that texts, by their very textuality, are projected through time as well as space, and that these two dimensions are mutually constitutive. How do texts exist in time, in what sense can they be said to be multi-temporal, and to what extent do they partially escape time by virtue of the very process of entextualisation – the putting of passages of words 'out there' for interpretation, recuperation and future re-creation? These questions cannot receive generalised or universal answers. We need to look at the ways in which textuality is locally conceptualised and locally experienced. This in turn depends on the local historical contexts and structures of power that shape processes of textual production and practices of reading, including how texts are produced, by whom, for whom and in what circumstances. In this essay, I put together two of the key vectors of Hofmeyr's research – the encounter of oral genres with writing, and the movement of printed periodical texts through time and space – by looking at how local weekly newspapers in a particular West African colonial setting construed their own temporality and that of the oral genres they sought to preserve in print.

The Yoruba-language newspapers (with English sections) of the early 1920s in Lagos, Nigeria, invoked ideas of immediacy and permanence simultaneously. The editors and contributors to the papers had a double perspective. On the one hand, they mimicked oral presence, striving to make the print-medium project an oral-like speaking voice for their readers – and this effect was amplified by the prevailing porosity, flexibility and heterogeneity of Lagos print culture more widely. On the other hand, they saw print as immutably fixed, and affirmed that it was the only way to preserve valued oral genres that they feared would otherwise soon be lost forever.

The Yoruba newspapers which exploded into activity in the town in that period were owned, edited and to a great extent authored by entrepreneurial individuals in the outer circles of the small educated elite. They were less prestigious than the dominant English-language press run by people in the inner circles. Their main aim was to attract a new potential readership, made up of the large number of people who could read Yoruba but not English, in order to draw them into the civic debates and heated political campaigns of the period. They experimented incessantly and exuberantly with forms of address that would engage people whose lives were mostly lived orally. They appealed to readers, exhorted them, quoted hymns and songs and asked them to join in, said prayers and asked them to say 'Amen', and quoted proverbs that required recognition and completion by the reader. Almost everything could be addressed to a second person, whether singular or plural, and events were often not recounted in the third person but expressed as commiseration with or congratulation to the people concerned. Local news revolved around prominent figures – mostly men – and when their activities were reported on, they were hailed with fragments of *oríkì*, the intensely addressive oral genre of praise poetry through which status is not only recognised but also conferred and confirmed. The famous doctor Ògúntọ́lá Ṣapará was frequently saluted with 'Ẹbọra nínú iṣẹ́ gbígba ẹbí ọmọ' (Magician of midwifery); the successful lawyer and prominent political leader J. Egerton Shyngle with the admiring epithet 'Èṣùú ṣọmọkùnrin tó fi Shyngle ṣeré!' (You'd have to be mad to mess with Shyngle!). Dozens of other 'leading lights', as the newspaper *Akede Eko* called them, were unfailingly evoked and hailed by brief praise epithets such as these, as the newspaper writers reproduced the forms of salutation to be heard every day on the street and at public events.

The sociable immediacy of these papers drew on the informality of the prevailing 'printing culture' (Barber 2001, 16–17), where numerous print shops were ready to typeset and print in small runs any kind of document, from church programmes to invoices, quickly and relatively cheaply. Anyone who wanted to put a document into print could do so, whether in English or Yoruba. The weekly papers themselves were extremely porous, accessible to anyone who wished to contribute: the letter to the editor was the default format even for regular columnists. Editors solicited contributions and accepted reports on social events, personal notices, in memoriams, and readers' thanks to well-wishers. The line between paid insertions and social news items was often blurred.

This accessibility gave rise to a multi-vocal quality which was also multi-temporal. In her discussion of late nineteenth-century trans-national periodicals exchanges, Hofmeyr (2013) draws attention to the widespread practice of culling, reprinting, excerpting and summarising material from other periodicals imported from overseas. As these imports could arrive months after their original publication, most of the material the local papers chose to reprint was not tied to a specific date. Thus, 'reading such undated and unattributed sequences creates mul-tiple senses of time' (Hofmeyr 2013, 83) – a condition which Gandhi's philosophy of 'slow reading' made a virtue of in his own periodical, *Indian Opinion*. The Yoruba-language newspapers participated in this empire-wide practice. They culled English-language material from many other publications, frequently offering responses, translations or summaries in Yoruba. This practice dramatically increased these newspapers' internal heterogeneity by incorporating voices from Sierra Leone, the Gold Coast, Britain and elsewhere. The 'multiple senses of time' noted by Hofmeyr extended, in the Lagos Yoruba-language press, to locally produced material. There were temporal slippages and disjunctures even between items authored by the editor himself. When I.B. Thomas, the editor of *Akede Eko*, went on an editorial trip to eastern Nigeria, he sent back vivid weekly dispatches so that readers could follow his movements as he travelled by steamer and truck from town to town. However, these reports reached the editorial office so long after they had been written that on 16 May 1929, when the front page of the paper announced his return and welcomed him back to Lagos at the end of his trip, on page 6 Thomas was still on the train to Aba, only halfway through his journey, passing through the farm villages of the Dewo people – 'who look exceedingly wild and who all carry cutlasses and knives'! The report from the east carried its own aura of immediacy, which was apparently not dimmed by the fact that it was several weeks behind the times. Each item occupied its own temporal slot. This multi-temporality, and the general plurality, heterogeneity and adaptability of the newspapers' content, had affinities with oral modes. A corpus of Yoruba personal *oríkì*, for example, is inherently diverse, made up of name-like formulations that were composed at different times by different people in reponse to different actions or events, and accumulated over a lifetime. This heterogeneity is intensified by the addition of further, stylistic disjunctions through grammatical elision and the juxtaposition of contrasting elements.

But at the same time as Yoruba newspaper editors exploited the flexibility of the local printing culture, pulling out all the stops to make their printed discourse sound like a flow of oral speech, they also proclaimed the power of print to fix and preserve oral genres in perpetuity. While they observed that literacy spelled the death of oral traditions (because 'no one wants to be an oral poet any more, everyone wants to be a clerk'), they also maintained that it could be their saviour ('if we don't write it down, it will be lost forever'). For the educated elites in Lagos and in the Yoruba hinterland, as for their counterparts in South Africa (Attwell 1999), this was a central and well-established preoccupation. Some of the earliest Yoruba-language publications were collections of proverbs, riddles and Ifá divination verses, presented as the foundations on which a better future could be built. In the preface to his history of Ibadan in 1911, I.B. Akinyẹle wrote that history is encapsulated in a rich heritage of poetic forms such as *oríkì* and in the 'deep' registers of the Yoruba language, but that oral genres, and even the language itself, are in danger of disappearing unless they are written down so that they can be studied by students in school. In this view, history is culture – it is soaked into cultural forms still in circulation. At the same time, culture is on its way to becoming history as the bearers of praise poetry and of esoteric registers of the language pass away. The solution to this situation is to put these traditions into print before it is too late.

The Lagos elite of the 1920s were well aware of the great oral genres of praise poetry (*oríkì*), historical narrative (*ìtàn*), divination poetry (*ẹsẹ Ifá*) and proverbs (*òwe*), which in the inland towns were fundamental to how personhood was affirmed, social relations consolidated, power established and criticised, the interplay of human and spiritual forces diagnosed and ameliorated, and events marked, evaluated and remembered. But the elite usually concerned themselves with more recent and less hallowed urban popular genres. Lagos was a feverishly commercial port city, oriented to novelty, where literacy was the passport to white-collar occupations, and a command of flawless English rhetoric the source of prestige. On the outer fringes of this elite, the editors of the Yoruba papers – while they were brilliant Yoruba-language stylists – were to varying degrees distanced from the long-established oral genres that flourished in traditional great households. To them, it was above all popular topical songs composed by known local poets that constituted the textual treasures needing preservation. In May 1923, the editor of *Eleti Ọfẹ* put out a call for contributions from readers. He wanted them, he explained, to write down and send in examples of 'orin ilẹ wa' (the songs of our country). Not only would he publish them, he added, but 'a ò kọ̀ láti sanwó' (we're even willing to pay for them). By printing these contributions, he elaborated, he would save from extinction precious poems that provoke thought and preserve the memory of exemplary people. Two weeks after making this announcement, he showed the result: a song by the popular poet Bẹ́gbàájí, commemorating a wealthy man who had built a splendid house at Òbùn-Èkó in Lagos Island, but died suddenly in 1899 before he was able to spend a single night in it. It had the plangent refrain 'Kabiyawu

Buramọ! Ọkọ ṣan'gbo, ọkọ o r'ere jẹ!' (Kabiyawu Buramọ! The cutlass clears the bush, the cutlass does not enjoy the harvest!).[1] Most of the poetic texts that the Yoruba newspapers collected and printed were of this kind: by popular singers, on local topical themes and of fairly recent times – twenty or thirty years earlier or less (some were contemporaneous). They were presented as repositories of edification, moral example and wise reflections on life: perhaps Bẹ́gbàájí's song about Kabiyawu Buramọ conveyed the wisdom of accepting that 'no condition is permanent' and that wealth does not protect one from misfortune.

The stated aim of this effort to preserve oral texts was to make them available for the benefit of future generations. Even genres whose appeal rested on contingency and an openness to the present moment were presented as having value above all for people yet unborn. One of the most remarkable textual experiments of colonial Lagos was the narrative subsequently identified as 'the first Yoruba novel', *Itan Igbesi-Aiye Emi Segilọla* (The Life Story of Me, Ṣegilọla). It took the form of a series of letters to the editor of *Akede Eko*, I.B. Thomas, from July 1929 to March 1930, purporting to be from a repentant former good-time girl, Ṣegilọla, and narrating her past exploits and transgressions with a mixture of glee and regret. This narrative was plugged into real places – the familiar streets, harbours and churches of Lagos; into real popular culture – the songs, dances and anecdotes of Ṣegilọla's youth, which were still in circulation; and into real time – so that real and fictional dates matched at the time the letters were published. Not only this, but when readers wrote to the newspaper commenting on her story, she more than once suspended the narrative for a whole episode in order to respond. It is this sense of an emergent, contingent narrative entangled in a specific time and place that gives *Ṣegilọla* its compelling effect of reality and consequently its power as a moral warning. Readers were kept on tenterhooks, waiting to see if Ṣegilọla would manage to finish her story before she died – or before the precarious finances of the newspaper caused it to collapse. But after the end of the serial, when Thomas had collected the letters into a book, he wrote in his preface (Barber 2012: 82, 83):

Bo ba jẹ pe a le ri ẹnikẹni lati mu ọgbọn ṣ'ẹkọ ninu iwe itan 'Sẹgilọla' yi, nigbana ni inu wa yio dun pupọ lati ri pe wahala ati ayan olọṣi obinrin na ko jẹ asan nipa kiko itan aiye rẹ yi silẹ gẹgẹbi ẹkọ fun at'ọmọd'ọmọ awọn iran wa ti nwọn tun mbọ l'aiye lẹhin ọla; inu wa yio si tun dun pẹlu fun pe iwe irohin wa 'Akede Eko' ni o gba iyin on ọla na, nipa titẹ itan igbesi aiye 'Sẹgilọla' ka fun gbogbo agbaiye.

If anyone benefits from the wise lessons in this story of 'Sẹgilọla', we will be glad that the trouble and perseverance of this wretched woman in writing the story of her life down as a lesson for future generations was not in vain; and we will also be glad that our news-paper 'Akede Eko' has the distinction of being the publisher of the life-story of 'Sẹgilọla' for all the world to read.

Note the elaborate phrasing: 'at'ọmọd'ọmọ awọn iran wa ti nwọn tun mbọ l'aiye lẹhin ọla', which I have translated simply as 'future generations', could be rendered more fully as something like 'successive generations of our descendants who are still to come to the world in future times'. Thomas certainly gave full weight to the idea of generations yet unborn.

Print, then, was credited with the power to fix and preserve text far into the future. As elsewhere in the world, its capacity to do so was connected with its publicness and the recognition this brings. The quota-tion from Thomas's preface shows that the idea of the text being projected into the future is closely linked to the idea of its being made available 'for all the world to read'. Being in the open, being seen and acknowledged by many, reaching 'the four corners of the world', as the Yoruba pressmen often put it, was a form of durability. Extension in space was conceptu-ally inseparable from extension in time. And in colonial print cultures, the publicness of the press was tinged with an association with authority. The content of the Lagos papers was often critical or even subversive of the colonial government, but print as a medium enjoyed a faint halo of officialdom. The knowledge that one copy of every newspaper printed in Lagos was kept by the colonial government (for censorship but also for the record)[2] reinforced the notion that the whole enterprise of publishing involved creating a repository of material that would be preserved into the future.

If their projection of the printed text as fixed for all time was subverted by the Lagos newspapermen's own exploitation of print's potential for flexibility, it was also the case that the oral genres which they saw as always on the very brink of extinction were more resilient than they thought. The core oral traditions of *oríkì* and *ẹsẹ Ifá* had a footing in time different from the chronology the educated elites espoused. Oral poets affirmed the vitality of their formulations in terms of their unchanging relationship to a point of origin: in the case of Ifá divination verses, the point when the god Ọrúnmìlà brought the sacred corpus to the world and imparted it to his disciples; in the case of *oríkì*, to the foundation of towns, the establishment of dynasties and, even more fundamentally, to the differentiation of entities, the essential nature of each of which is condensed within its *oríkì* epithets. In these genres, time does not pass in such a way as to increase the distance between origin and present moment. In utterance, the Ifá verse opens upon an immanent truth. A precedent is narrated that forms a diagnosis of the present disposition of forces, and an action such as a sacrifice is prescribed to help a favourable outcome emerge. Neither history nor prediction, Ifá verses are a disclosure capable of endless reactivation and recapitulation. In the case of *oríkì*, a knowledgeable performer addressing a present subject will draw on the *oríkì* of that person's forebears, thereby activating their powers and potentials in order to enhance their living descendant's aura. And rather than being seen as a description, a narration or an accolade, *oríkì* are conceptualised as a summons, acting to call forth what a subject already has it within them to be: the verb *jẹ́*, 'to be', also means 'to answer'. In the oral traditionists' own view, then, these genres join past and present, and power flows through the channels that connect them. Because these genres were so crucial to people's being in the world, Ifá diviners and *oríkì* singers did not express the fear that they were about to be erased by the spread of literacy; nor did they think that writing them down was the only way to preserve them.

Even the topical urban songs that the Lagos literati collected and published were less ephemeral than they feared. After preparing a scholarly edition and translation of the Ṣẹgilọla narrative (Barber 2012), I was invited to give a talk on the subject at Lagos State University. As an example of the novel's use of popular topical songs, I cited one about an old man called Yesufa who had attacked passers-by with a gun from his rooftop – this, I had dicovered from newspaper reports of the time, was a real event that had taken place in 1907. I put the words up on a slide, explaining that 'in this novel some of the old topical songs of Lagos are preserved', upon which people in the audience began gently singing the refrain. The song was still in circulation.

Time, to the Lagos literati, pointed forward to a better, more enlightened and more progressive future. 'Yoruba culture', associated with the past – or soon to become so – was to be recuperated and preserved in order to send it forward to future generations who would benefit from the wisdom and moral lessons it embodied. The present became the pivot between that rich but vanishing past and that desired but distant future. The present itself – to which the local press actually owed its extraordinary vitality and inventiveness – shrank, in this view, to a precarious sliver, a vanishing point. The oral traditions' own orientation to time was almost the perfect inverse of this: the present absorbed both the past and the future. In *oríkì*, it was the present that recruited and activated the powers of the past; the past was always accessible and available for the enhancement of the living. In Ifá, the future was always immanent in the present, and the past took the form of models by which the present could be diagnosed.

Print is always a means of selecting and editing, and often also of authorising and standardising. It can never be a faithful reproduction and perpetuation of the original oral genre or discourse that it records. Isabel Hofmeyr's *'We Spend Our Years as a Tale That is Told'* describes what happened when missionaries in the Northern Transvaal began putting Sesotho tales and riddles into school reading books. The obvious loss of all the qualities associated with improvised oral performance was only part of it. When these genres entered the school curriculum, the classroom usurped the role of non-formal household-based education, and the authority of the oral storytellers as a source of knowledge was undermined. The formerly 'baggy and capacious' narrative form shrank, was purged of fantastical elements, came to be associated only with young children and became the bearer of explicit moral lessons (Hofmeyr 1993, 34). At the same time, printed books and schooling brought in new textual openings, 'a whole new range of stylistic possibilities and generic classifications' (Hofmeyr 1993, 57), including new kinds of characterisation and new plots drawn from bioscope and radio.

In colonial Lagos, as in the Northern Transvaal, putting oral genres into print involved not only a shift from one medium to another, but a shift in the location of control. It was the educated elite, not the oral artists, who decided which texts and genres should be 'preserved' for the benefit of future generations, and in what form. But their cultural authority was fragile. The literacy that gave them status also partly estranged them from the life of those very traditions. Privileged yet socially and culturally uneasy, they determined to use the tools of print to preserve what they felt they were already losing touch with. But the role they assigned to these texts in their future existence would have changed them significantly. They were envisaged as generic moral lessons, models of behaviour or unspecified wisdom, and treasured as evidence of the value of Yoruba culture. To the Lagos literati of the 1920s, then, these genres were heritage-to-be – something projected into the future so as to be valued as something coming from the past.

In the meantime, however, and in spite of the long shadow cast back by imagined future generations, there were textual innovators on the ground already experimenting with new ways of engaging, in print, with a profusion of everyday Yoruba verbal resources. The Yoruba newspaper editors themselves drew on proverbs, anecdotes, jokes, slang, and fragments of praise poetry and Ifá verses to produce new print genres. While warning of the imminent loss of Yoruba traditional knowledge, they were pioneering not only the 'first Yoruba novel', but the new forms of print poetry, parables, histories, dramatic dialogues and travel narratives that crowded the pages of the Yoruba weekly papers. The very fragility of the writers' social and cultural position may have played a part in stimulating this impressive, though often overlooked, creativity.

NOTES

1   *Eleti Ọfẹ*, 6 June 1923, p. 7.
2   This, indeed, is the origin of the only existing collection of Yoruba-language newspapers, now preserved in the Nigerian National Archive, though in a very fragile state.

REFERENCES

Akinyẹle, I.B. 1959 [1911]. *Iwe Itan Ibadan ati diẹ ninu awọn ilu agbegbe rẹ bi Iwo, Oshogbo, ati Ikirun*. 3rd ed. Exeter: James Townsend.

Attwell, David. 1999. 'Reprisals of Modernity in Black South African "Mission" Writing'. *Journal of Southern African Studies* 25 (2): 267–285.

Barber, Karin. 2001. 'Audiences and the Book'. *Current Writing* 13 (2): 9–19.

———. 2012. *Print Culture and the First Yoruba Novel: I.B. Thomas's 'Life Story of Me, Ṣẹgilọla' and Other Texts*. African Sources for African History series. Leiden: Brill.

Hofmeyr, Isabel. 1993. *'We Spend Our Years as a Tale That is Told': Oral Historical Narrative in a South African Chiefdom*. Portsmouth: Heinemann.

———. 2004. *The Portable Bunyan: A Transnational History of 'The Pilgrim's Progress'*. Princeton: Princeton University Press.

———. 2013. *Gandhi's Printing Press: Experiments in Slow Reading*. Cambridge, MA: Harvard University Press.

———. 2022. *Dockside Reading: Hydrocolonialism and the Custom House*. Durham: Duke University Press.

PART 2

PORTABLE METHODS

5

Overcomers: A Historical Sketch

Ranka Primorac

> Luweme was an overcomer.
> — Norah Mumba, *Knitted in Silence*

The Zambian author and public intellectual Norah Mumba uses the startling, memorable noun 'overcomer' to describe Luweme, the protagonist of her recent novel *Knitted in Silence*, in a late chapter titled 'New Beginnings'. At that stage in the plot, Luweme has come a long way. She has grown from a silent, traumatised child into an empowered and articulate young woman. Her very presence inspires resolve, resilience and hope in those who know her. But the notion of an 'overcomer' – one who moves past obstacles and triumphs in the face of difficulties and dangers – does more than provide an abbreviated reference to the novel's fast-moving, adventure-time plot. It is also an index to how Mumba imagines the emergence of a modern Zambian subjectivity, and of how this imagining fits in with her country's literary history – a history that would not be legible to us today without Isabel Hofmeyr's *The Portable Bunyan: A Transnational History of 'The Pilgrim's Progress'* (2004).

Published in Lusaka in 2022, *Knitted in Silence* is an elaborate coming-of-age story. It details Luweme's birth into a family of farm workers near the village of Laweni in contemporary Zambia; her family background; her separation from her parents; the political intrigue she survives as a child after her mother's death; and her eventual rise to confident adulthood as she assumes spiritual leadership of her community and develops extraordinary powers of healing. The novel's architecture segments this multi-strand narrative material into three parts. The first part initiates a cluster of unforeseen life-changing events for some of the characters in Laweni. The second outlines threatening developments in the heroine's maternal village of Kavuluvulu. The third returns Luweme, via Lusaka, to where her life began, and to the discovery that her old home environment has changed in unforeseen ways. The work of a Christian feminist author who is a well-established literary and activist figure in her home country, *Knitted in Silence* is interested in class difference and prejudice, in questions to do with the nature of evil, and in the spiritual properties of evangelical Christianity. The novel culminates in the sweeping away of all obstacles via a deep cosmic synthesis – and a wedding. Humorous and light-footed as well as serious and thought-provoking, *Knitted in Silence* is Bunyanesque in that it conceives of human life as a constant flow of new beginnings. Were the text not finite, the series could go on without end. Published in trying times – in early 2022, during the Covid-19 pandemic – the novel has already caught the imagination of Zambian readers. In a country sometimes perceived as lacking a viable literary culture, one reader congratulated the author with the words 'Keep the flame burning', while another begged for a spin-off based on a side plot.[1] These readers were clearly familiar with the narrative conventions on which the novel relies. On social media, several said that they 'could not put the book down'.

Isabel Hofmeyr's *The Portable Bunyan* had a similar effect on the author of this chapter. The 2004 monograph is, among other things, a corrective to a cluster of influential studies of world literature that began to supplant literary postcolonialism as a hegemonic transcontinental paradigm in anglophone literary scholarship in the early 2000s. *The Portable Bunyan* imagines the 'portability' of *The Pilgrim's Progress* (Bunyan [1678] 1978) not simply as a literary text's unimpeded travel via translation – even as it demonstrates that Bunyan's narrative is a textbook example of a work whose 'reach . . . [is] beyond its home base' (Damrosch 2003, 4). Instead, Hofmeyr outlines how *The Pilgrim's Progress*, as it circulated beyond its culture of origin, began to function as a 'compendium of generic possibilities' (Hofmeyr 2004, 18): a repository of formal elements capable of being detached, abridged, recombined, trans-mediated and otherwise appropriated, merging with local forms and adapting to local agendas. In this way, the imported narrative of an ordinary man who undergoes a long ordeal before reaching his final destination arguably became a key ingredient of African imaginaries related both to modernity and to freedom.

Hofmeyr's insistence on portability as malleability resonates with Franco Moretti's injunction to scholars to think about the circulation of 'units that are much smaller or much larger than the text: devices, themes, tropes – or genres and systems' (Moretti 2000, 57). Yet *The Portable Bunyan* avoids getting snagged in Moretti's binary contrast between 'close' and 'distant' reading. For Hofmeyr, literary circulation is the circulation of material objects and involves fluctuation in the very idea of literariness. *The Portable Bunyan* allows us to see, for example, how it is possible that, as late as the 1960s, print copies of *The Pilgrim's Progress* in Bemba translation were capable of functioning as symbols of black modernity and social prestige on the Zambian Copperbelt. In *Uwakwenshi Bushiku (A Friend in Need)* – the first part of the diptych *Pio na Vera (Pio and Vera)* by the much-loved Bemba writer Stephen Mpashi (1968) – the slick young city detective called Pio (for 'Pius') sends his servant, Chola, to the kiosk to buy, among other books and publications, '*Ulwendo lwa Mwina Christu [A Christian's Journey in a Dream]* written by John Bunyan.'[2] That he buys books and reads, together with *what* he buys and reads, signals to Mpashi's readers not only the extent of Pio's mastery of the urban crisis detailed in the novel, but also how worthy of him are the difficulties he is facing.

Mpashi's Pio, like Bunyan's Christian, overcomes an extended set of obstacles, not only to solve a murder mystery, but also to earn the hand of his beloved Vera in the second part of the diptych. The romance and detection genres share with *The Pilgrim's Progress* the embedding of ethical normativity within teleological narrative structures (as the romantic subplot of *Knitted in Silence* also demonstrates). As a result of a specific set of economic and political conditions (see Primorac 2014), Mpashi remained an influential literary figure in Zambian literature during the eras of formal decolonisation and the frontline struggle, in the 1960s and 1970s. In addition to 'the spine of the journey' (Hofmeyr 2004, 116), the formal element that afforded the usability of *Pilgrim's Progress* to Zambian nationalist discourses and fictions produced during the frontline struggle is the investment Bunyan's text makes in the notion of *conversion* as 'a form of magical transformation' (Hofmeyr 2004, 17).

Conversion's magic lies in its instantaneousness. As a temporal narrative device, it therefore works against the grain of the classical Euro-realist imagination of change in subjectivity as a gradual, cumulative, secular process. In Cold War Zambia, however, the temporality of conversion worked well as part of a Christian-nationalist discourse that allowed sovereign statehood to be forged via Kenneth Kaunda's foundational political slogan 'One Zambia – one nation'. The slogan included versions of local whiteness without stipulating a need to 'reconcile' – as long as certain cultural compromises could be achieved, as I detail shortly. Not for nothing did Benedict Anderson (in a related context) liken conversion to 'alchemic absorption' (Anderson 1983, 15). And yet, as the basis of an emergent local realist convention, the heavy reliance on the temporality of conversion placed Zambian texts outside of what Hofmeyr calls 'the "normal" rules' of [Euro-realist] plausibility' (Hofmeyr 2004, 104).

In the frontline era of the 1960s and 1970s, the Zambian literary scene in English was constituted largely (though not solely) by ephemeral forms: pamphleteering, theatre productions and, for about a decade, locally published literary journals. The most tenacious of those proved to be *New Writing from Zambia* (NWZ), edited in its final years by journalist and writer David Simpson. In *NWZ*'s editorials, Simpson occasionally expressed a yearning for the appearance of a Zambian author of genius, who might endow his country with international literary glory by becoming 'wreathed in the mists of [creativity], which crystallise into poems' (Simpson 1992, 2). Even as he voiced such literary fantasies (tinged, we now see, with more than a hint of Eurocentrism), *NWZ* was in the process of helping to establish the formal and discursive conventions that were to become the foundation of independent Zambia's literary repertoires.

For example, the stories published in the journal repeatedly imagined character change as an outcome of quasi-miraculous transformation (Primorac 2012). Together with other Zambian authors in English, Norah Mumba's work absorbs and transforms those early 'ways people imagine their social existence, how they fit together with others, how things go on between them and their fellows, the expectations that are normally met, and the deeper normative notions and images that underlie these expectations', as Charles Taylor (2004, 22) puts it. In *Knitted in Silence*, sudden subjectivity about-turns are an everyday temporal and ontological possibility. At the same time, miracles – in this and other Zambian texts – must be earned.

In the 1970s, a locally influential literary representation that built on the Bunyanesque trope of carrying a heavy load also foregrounded the local allegorical trope of the mute child who learns to speak. Dominic Mulaisho's novel *The Tongue of the Dumb* (1971) made Zambian literary history by being published in Heinemann's African Writers series. The novel imagines the political preconditions for Zambia's state independence as a set of circumstances that enable even the most disadvantaged community member – the mute child of a socially exiled mother – to acquire a speaking voice. Natombi, the mother of Mwape, is unjustly isolated from her village community by political intrigue. The narrative of Natombi and Mwape's protracted suffering merges Christian and national allegories in its representation of the difficulties that building a just society in the wake of colonialism might entail. Mwape acquires speech at the novel's end only as the result of the villagers and their neighbours, Jesuit missionaries, coming together to affirm their common humanity in a changed set of political circumstances. The missionaries recognise that they need to undergo a substantial change of religious practice. If they are to join the villagers in a political community that allows for the voices of all its members to be heard, the Jesuits must convert to genuine Christian faith and embrace Africans as their fellow humans.

Knitted in Silence extends, updates and re-genders the narrative strategies of Mumba's male literary forebears. In the central part of the novel, Luweme, too, loses the ability to speak. For Mumba, however, the speechless child who acquires a voice is not merely an emblem of an ostensibly just community led by men. In describing the progress of Bunyan's story in the 'echo chamber' of the Protestant Atlantic, Hofmeyr underlines the 'surprising forms of convergence' such circulation could promote (Hofmeyr 2004, 232). *Knitted in Silence* stages the formal inter-section between what may be called the Zambian narratives of Christian-nationalist conversion on the one hand, and the domestic concerns of the secular classics of anglophone African women's fiction (analysed by Susan Andrade [2011]) on the other. Mumba is interested in both Pentecostal cosmology and in the 'small' details of women's everyday lives in the Zambian countryside. Her novel recasts Zambia's mainstream literary history by representing a young woman as a leader and an over-coming warrior.

In this sense, the novel partly parallels – without being directly influenced by – recent works by internationally visible authors such as Kenya's Yvonne Adhiambo Owuor, Uganda's Jennifer Nansubuga Makumbi and Zambia's own Namwali Serpell, whose prize-winning *The Old Drift* echoed and augmented Mulaisho's publishing success by becoming 'the great Zambian novel' of its generation. There are no mute children in *The Old Drift*. But the narrative trajectory of a central black female character, the 'Afronaut' Matha Mwamba, resonates with those of Mulaisho's Natombi and Mumba's Luweme. Matha, too, goes from being misused, disempowered and excluded to becoming the vanguard of social change. In each of these two seminal Zambian novels authored by women, such change is the outcome of a sudden about-turn. In each novel, too, the change is in keeping with the Kaunda-era slogan 'One Zambia – one nation', which was itself from the outset underpinned by Christianity.

Africa's internationally canonical literary works in English have been overwhelmingly produced outside the continent. Unlike *The Old Drift*, however, *Knitted in Silence* was published in Zambia. Mumba's literary activity has always taken place in a national literary ecology (Beecroft 1992), in which the works of contemporary African authors published in the global North are only occasionally available for purchase in local bookshops. The disparity in visibility and prestige between intercontinentally and locally circulating African fiction has led Ashleigh Harris (2019) to conclude that the African novel as a genre is being 'de-realized' on the African continent. Despite emerging from a historical context of acute political crisis (in the frontline era) and ongoing economic and infrastructural difficulties (ever since), Zambian novels published in English since independence constitute a coherent and culturally generative literary tradition. The feasibility and legibility of this tradition are distinct from the aesthetic and political requirements placed on the novel as a genre by the publishing industry based in the global North.

Zambia's anglophone novelistic canon is the collective achievement of successive generations of literary overcomers: an inter-generational exercise in surmounting a wide range of economic and logistical difficulties of the type Norah Mumba is only too familiar with. In a private conversation, Mumba told me that she had read *The Pilgrim's Progress* (albeit a long time ago). The portable compendium of generic possibilities that Isabel Hofmeyr wrote about so memorably remains an active and generative literary and cultural force in south-eastern Africa. More than that: it helps to reproduce the novel as a genre in contexts where literariness cannot be measured solely by the numbers of print books bought and sold. Its literariness is one of crisis, and in drawing on deeply embedded notions of persevering and overcoming, it has proved itself capable of treating miracles such as local book publication as an everyday occurrence.

NOTES

1   Norah Mumba, private communication, 12 March 2022.
2   From an unpublished translation of Mpashi by Wycliffe Mushipi and Kalinga Lutato, 2016.

REFERENCES

Anderson, Benedict. 1983. *Imagined Communities: Reflections on the Origin and Spread of Nationalism*. London: Verso.

Andrade, Susan. 2011. *The Nation Writ Small: African Fictions and Feminisms, 1958–1988*. Durham: Duke University Press.

Beecroft, Alexander. 1992. 'World Literature Without a Hyphen'. *New Left Review* 54 (November–December): 87–100.

Bunyan, John. [1678] 1978. *The Pilgrim's Progress*. Virginia Beach: CBN University Press.

Damrosch, David. 2003. *What is World Literature?* Princeton: Princeton University Press.

Harris, Ashleigh. 2019. *Afropolitanism and the Novel: De-realizing Africa*. Oxford: Routledge.

Hofmeyr, Isabel. 2004. *The Portable Bunyan: A Transnational History of 'The Pilgrim's Progress'*. Princeton: Princeton University Press.

Makumbi, Jennifer Nansubuga. 2020. *A Girl is a Body of Water*. Portland: Tin House.

Moretti, Franco. 2000. 'Conjectures on World Literature'. *New Left Review* 1 (January–February): 54–68.

Mpashi, Stephen. 1968. *Pio na Vera*. Lusaka: Oxford University Press.

Mulaisho, Dominic. 1971. *The Tongue of the Dumb*. London: Heinemann.

Mumba, Norah. 2022. *Overcomers*. Lusaka: Dengwa.

Owuor, Yvonne. 2013. *Dust*. New York: Alfred A. Knopf.

Primorac, Ranka. 2012. 'Legends of Modern Zambia'. *Research in African Literatures* 40 (4): 50–70.

———. 2014. 'At Home in the World? Re-framing Zambia's Literature in English'. *Journal of Southern African Studies* 40 (3): 575–591.

Serpell, Namwali. 2020. *The Old Drift*. London: Vintage.

Simpson, David. 1972. Editorial. *New Writing from Zambia* 8 (3): 2.

Taylor, Charles. 2004. *Modern Social Imaginaries*. Durham: Duke University Press.

6

Hemispheric Limits: Rethinking the Uses of Diaspora from South Africa

Christopher E.W. Ouma

Isabel Hofmeyr's ground-clearing essay, 'The Black Atlantic Meets the Indian Ocean: Forging New Paradigms of Transnationalism for the Global South – Literary and Cultural Perspectives' (2007), poses an important question and (subsequently) a theoretical challenge for transnational and globalisation studies that try to conceptualise the movement of people, ideas and cultures around the world. Hofmeyr asks: 'What of non-Western sources of globalisation or processes of transnationalism that happen without reference to Europe?' (2007, 3). This question is at the heart of the analytical logic of Hofmeyr's much-cited article. In very interesting ways, the question is imploring us – as Dipesh Chakrabarty (2000) does – to 'provincialise Europe'. Ngũgĩ wa Thiong'o (1992) has used another expression elsewhere: to 'move the centre'. Hofmeyr deploys the taxonomy of 'South' to locate what she argues are 'universalisms' that have big historical footprints in Africa's encounter with the rest of the world through the Indian Ocean. The Indian Ocean, she argues, pivots 'transnationalism within the South itself' (2007, 3) and, from the perspective of South Africa, therefore provides a very specific enunciation of transnational studies that particularly challenges the dominance of Paul Gilroy's (1993) formulation of 'the Black Atlantic' in that field.

My essay seeks to place Isabel Hofmeyr's thinking alongside that of Brent Hayes Edwards (2001, 2003) to make an argument for the ways in which both scholars not only broaden the framework within which the word 'diaspora' operates as an analytic, but also complicate its cartographic logic in ways that speak to how we might, for example, read from a place such as Cape Town – a place at the very tip of the 'two oceans'. Hofmeyr herself 'suggests that we look quite literally at our location in Southern Africa – between two oceans – and see what analytical purchase that may provide . . . what can we derive from thinking about three intersecting frameworks: the black Atlantic, the Indian Ocean and Africa itself?' (2007, 4).

The point Hofmeyr makes here is critical, not only in expanding away from a singular oceanic frame of reference, but also in suggesting ways of *multi-directional reading* from the geography of the Cape and, more broadly, southern Africa. She offers us a strategy of reading, as it were, from the Cape. Hofmeyr, Sarah Nuttall and Charne Lavery (2022) expand this strategy in the special issue of *Interventions* titled 'Reading for Water', in which broader debates on the Anthropocene are informed by 'hydropoetics' – ways in which water formulates a narrative aesthetic in various kinds of cultural production – and are brought together with 'oceanic studies'. In other words, reading for water makes visible the critical purchase of a multi-directional logic of oceanic studies such as the one Hofmeyr proposes in 'The Black Atlantic Meets the Indian Ocean'. Hofmeyr, Nuttall and Lavery extend the tropology of a multi-directional reading by proposing how 'reading for water moves laterally, vertically and contrapuntally between different water-worlds and hydro-imaginaries' (2022, 304). These strategies of reading are inherent in the locations from which we embark on them, such as the place of 'two oceans'. South Africa, and particularly Cape Town, provide this strategic position and in crucial ways supply what Edwards calls a location for the 'hemispheric limits'

(2001, 62) from within which the concept of diaspora is inhabited by the 'hydro-imaginaries' that Hofmeyr and others are reading for.

In his own field-defining essay, 'The Uses of Diaspora', Edwards also argues for a ground-clearing 'intellectual history of the term' (2001, 64), locating it at a moment in which it is 'taken up . . . in black scholarly discourse to do a particular kind of epistemological work' (46). This assumption chimes with Hofmeyr's concern about the geographical framing of 'diaspora' as the 'Black Atlantic', in which a specific cartographical logic applies and overdetermines the concept in relation to Africa. Edwards's article gives us a wider lens through which to appreciate Hofmeyr's specific intervention, through its genealogical, even archaeological, approach to the concept of diaspora and the history of its political economy. By tracing the term diaspora in what he calls 'black scholarly discourse', Edwards makes connections between 'Pan-Africanism' as a form of identity and imagination, and the emergence of the category 'African diaspora' up to the moment when it acquires what he calls 'racial essentialism or American Vanguardism' (57). This essentialism and vanguardism are linked to the ethical import of Hofmeyr's own intervention, which offers to locate South Africa and the Cape precisely as operating beyond them. In his broader work, *The Practice of Diaspora* (2003), Edwards's conceptual genealogy of the formulation 'diaspora' creates a broader canvas on which to trace the ways in which the political work of 'Pan-African' imagination during the interwar period is deployed into a cultural currency that comes to embody the term 'diaspora' in black studies, and therefore begins to acquire not only a North Atlantic provenance but also an American vanguardism.

In doing this work of intellectual history, Edwards lays out a conceptual map from which we can plot the taxonomic spectrum – 'Pan-African', 'African Diaspora', 'North Atlantic', 'South Atlantic' and so on. These formulations provide theoretical points of enunciation and ways to differentiate various cartographical provenances. To think of the global South as Hofmeyr is doing in her essay is to reconfigure these cartographical provenances. But Edwards's argument prefigures Hofmeyr's own concerns by 'provincialising' Paul Gilroy's (1993) formulation 'the Black Atlantic' – locating it at a specific moment overdetermined by the cultural turn within transnational studies and, more importantly, warning of the risks of North Atlantic vanguardism. Beyond the critical work that Ntongela Masilela (1996) and Laura Chrisman (2005) have done in unpacking the concept's deficiencies in relation to Africa, Edwards brings us the important dimension of Gilroy's context: black British consciousness and its various influences, most of which Gilroy's concept glosses over and flattens. As Edwards puts it:

> The issue, of course, is the stakes of the 'Black Atlantic' as a term that (particularly in the adoption of Gilroy's work in the U.S. academy) often usurps the space that might otherwise be reserved for diaspora. The success of the Black Atlantic has cleared space for a wide range of intellectual work in the academy; still, this development makes it all the more crucial to ask about the risks of 'Black Atlantic' as a term of analysis that is not necessarily consonant with the sense of diaspora as intervention that I have described. (2001, 61)

Edwards is doing important ground-clearing work here – wading through what has become a conceptual fog. By making distinctions between the concept of diaspora and that of the 'Black Atlantic', he is cautioning against the deployment of the latter term as shorthand for the former – which indeed happened frequently in the aftermath of Gilroy's work. Moreover, like Hofmeyr, Edwards is hinting at what he calls the 'hemispheric limits' that attend to the formulation 'Black Atlantic' – especially the way it is meant to produce a very confined and specifically monodirectional idea of diaspora studies – under the assumption that Atlantic histories of the type that Gilroy's formulation seeks to account for and other oceanic studies are mutually exclusive. Edwards says:

> This continuing discourse of diaspora begs the question of the introduction of the notion of the 'Black Atlantic', which would

seem to impose an assumption of geographical specificity (what we might term a *hemispheric* limit) and a 'racial' context on a field that might be much more broad and more various. (2001, 62)

Hofmeyr's essay 'The Black Atlantic Meets the Indian Ocean' begins with the supposition that the field is broad and various and could extend in generative ways, beyond the Atlantic, based on specific cartographies of enunciation. Hofmeyr foregrounds the way in which the Atlantic seaboard has calcified the intellectual discourse on capitalist modernity in relation to Africa, forging a dominant paradigm of the analysis through various categories that emerge from its exchange system: 'slaves', 'slavery', 'settler', 'native', 'migrant' and – the 'concept-metaphor' at stake – 'diaspora'. In her essay, she performs the intellectual labour that Edwards (2001) is asking for: she provides a genealogy of scholarly discourse on the Indian Ocean, outlining the various directions in which movement happened in this particular oceanic space while foregrounding the nuanced political economy that underwrote enslaved and indentured, free, migrant and settler identities. Hofmeyr's analysis throws up the kinds of modernity that not only intersect, but also remain surplus – she uses the word 'alternative' – to the Atlantic one. As a result, one is able to appreciate Hofmeyr's argument about the peculiarity of South Africa and the Cape in relation to the multiple modernities she touches on. The location entailed calls for a reconfiguration of received categories of Atlantic modernity, such as that of diaspora, and of how they shape South African literary and cultural imagination. In tracing the much longer history of Indian Ocean contact with eastern and southern Africa, Hofmeyr maps a broader historical terrain to propose an idea of the South that seriously heeds the interlacing and intersectional histories literally converging at the southern tip of the continent and the world. In this location, Hofmeyr broadly proposes ways to read reconfigured space by reading water. In the case of the Southern water where the Cape is located, this approach provides innovative perspectives.

To read from the Cape is therefore to consider, for instance, a wider and deeper historical perspective in which enslavement and indentured labour come together to result in race and sexuality forming categories of belonging at the crucible of Atlantic and Indian Ocean encounters, as Gabeba Baderoon (2014) argues. Baderoon develops an interventive art of reading the Cape by foregrounding how Muslims and their presence in South Africa expand the historical boundaries from within which to theorise South African identity – a longer durée – in which we can plot a temporal palimpsest that begins with Indian Ocean enslavement and becomes more deeply layered with the inauguration of apartheid. In other words, Muslims and their specific location in the Cape provide a tropology of critical historical memory across these periods. Such an injunction about time, history and the imagination of South African identity seeks not only to displace the competitive memory of apartheid and its Atlantic-dominated frameworks of understanding, but also to reconfigure South Africa's place in Southern history by reading from the Cape.

Reading from the Cape prolongs the historical view of South Africa as a Southern location, demonstrating a temporal palimpsest in which enslavement, colonialism and apartheid build onto each other. Yet, in light of Hofmeyr's essay, the temporal intersections bringing together the two oceans often complicate the mono-directionality of a palimpsestic reading. Baderoon employs both a palimpsestic and an intersectional reading of time and the formation of identity by centring Muslims. Such a reading takes into account the representational economy built over centuries, in which Muslims, Islam and Islam's cultural footprints form the cartographical palimpsest in which tourist consumption happens, but at the same time the counterpoint of indentured labour and enslavement lies at the very foundations of this enterprise. And so, to ask the question Pumla Gqola (2010) asks – 'What is slavery to me?' – is to confront the limits of competitive imperial memory drawn only from Atlantic frameworks of southern African history. It is to give conceptual substance to the category 'South' and to its Cape-inflected dimensions – 'two oceans', 'South Atlantic' and 'Southern Ocean', among other formulations.

For example, in looking at Yewande Omotoso's novel *The Woman Next Door* (2016), we are able to note ways in which suburban Cape Town is a geography acted upon and curated by imperial projects that began during the period of enslavement and calcified with apartheid. Omotoso creates a narrative in which the upper-middle-class suburb of Constantia is a chronotope, with space the basis of a specific sense of belonging that is being curated by imperial time. Constantia in the novel is an 'architext' for the competing and intersecting memories of enslavement, colonialism and apartheid. Here the afterlives of enslavement are etched onto the landscape, in this case centuries-old trees that line a driveway, marking slave burial grounds and indicating the contested histories of land dispossession that mark the 'post-apartheid' as a period of competitive memory. Omotoso stages an encounter between two octogenarians, one black and from the Caribbean and the other a white South African. Their relationship is mediated by the intersections of class and race, but with the specific racial histories of the South Atlantic intervening as contextual inflection. In this way, the South Atlantic becomes a platform that convenes an encounter between postcolonial and post-apartheid frameworks of belonging. Omotoso's narratives, by being positioned in the Cape, harness these triangulated anglophone African, Caribbean and South African identities, helping us to reconfigure those 'hemispheric limits' of the Atlantic and therefore our 'uses' of diaspora in the global South.

Reflecting on the Omotoso example helps us partially draw in Hofmeyr's injunction regarding South African literature's positioning within Southern logics, in the way it projects from its location as part of Southern universalisms. Baderoon takes the relationship between David Lurie and Soraya in J.M. Coetzee's *Disgrace* (1999) as an example of the intersections between race, gender and sexuality at the crucible of historical encounters between the two oceans, which over time developed a cultural grammar that brings together surplus capital, leisure, and the exoticisation of Muslim bodies and cultures. Baderoon draws on various forms of cultural production, prominent among them the work of the artist Berni Searle, which presents racialised and sexualised bodies as symptomatic sites of cultural consumption, but speaks broadly to structural histories of enslavement and colonialism and how they have marked the landscape of the Cape.

The irony of the formulation 'Mother City' in referring to Cape Town lies not only in the problematic gendered 'pedestal' but also in the way that Dutch colonial and settler history is often seen as the originary moment of southern African urbanism and civilisation. While this formulation belies the structural violence occasioned at the intersection of race and gender (the originary 'sin'), it also articulates itself as the dominant form of imperialism over the past couple of centuries. Indeed, the competing imperialisms that occasioned the 'trek' and led to the South African War, the formation of the Union and the emergence of apartheid provide the context for South Africa's sub-imperialism within the global South. They therefore necessitate the kind of reading Hofmeyr is asking us to deploy, expanding our perspective away from the Atlantic seaboard so as to be able to map the historical currents from the Indian Ocean that nuance our taken-for-granted categories, including those of 'settler', 'native', 'slave' and 'indentured labourer'.

Hofmeyr's essay remains a crucial scholarly intervention, creating a conceptual pathway for reading from the location of South Africa towards the rest of the world. To think about the intellectual category 'South' is to think, like Hofmeyr, at the intersection of oceans, to think of the Cape and South Africa as a pivotal geography but with multiple counterpoints. This type of reckoning means rethinking received categories such as 'Black Atlantic' and 'diaspora', categories that need to be relocated to inhabit the context of two oceans. It is apposite, therefore, that from this important essay, Hofmeyr's major contributions to Indian Ocean studies and oceanic humanities in particular have morphed into another important conceptual metaphor, encapsulated in the formulation that is the subject of her co-edited special issue 'Reading for Water' and her recent monograph, *Dockside Reading: Hydrocolonialism and the Custom House* (2021). Her work not only offers rich genealogical frameworks and creates conditions for building new concepts, but also provides interventionist ways of *reading* – a key analytic and intellectual pastime for Isabel Hofmeyr.

REFERENCES

Baderoon, Gabeba. 2014. *Regarding Muslims: From Slavery to Post-apartheid*. Johannesburg: Wits University Press.

Chakrabarty, Dipesh. 2000. *Provincializing Europe: Postcolonial Thought and Historical Difference*. Princeton: Princeton University Press.

Chrisman, Laura. 2005. 'Beyond Black Atlantic and Postcolonial Studies: The South African Differences of Sol Plaatje and Peter Abrahams'. In *Postcolonial Studies and Beyond*, edited by Ania Loomba, Suvir Kaul, Matti Bunzl, Antoinette Burton and Jed Esty, 252–271. New Delhi: Permanent Black.

Coetzee, J.M. 1999. *Disgrace*. London: Secker & Warburg.

Edwards, Brent Hayes. 2001. 'The Uses of Diaspora'. *Social Text* 66, no. 1 (Spring): 45–73.

———. 2003. *The Practice of Diaspora: Literature, Translation and the Rise of Black Internationalism*. Cambridge, MA: Harvard University Press.

Gilroy, Paul. 1993. *The Black Atlantic: Modernity and Double Consciousness*. Cambridge, MA: Harvard University Press.

Gqola, Pumla. 2010. *What is Slavery to Me? Postcolonial/Slave Memory in Post-apartheid South Africa*. Johannesburg: Wits University Press.

Hofmeyr, Isabel. 2007. 'The Black Atlantic Meets the Indian Ocean: Forging New Paradigms of Transnationalism for the Global South – Literary and Cultural Perspectives'. *Social Dynamics* 33 (2): 3–32.

———. 2021. *Dockside Reading: Hydrocolonialism and the Custom House*. Durham: Duke University Pres; Johannesburg: Wits University Press.

Hofmeyr, Isabel, Sarah Nuttall and Charne Lavery, eds. 2022. 'Reading for Water'. Special issue, *Interventions* 24 (3): 303–322.

Masilela, Ntongela. 1996. 'The "Black Atlantic" and African Modernity in South Africa'. *Research in African Literatures* 27 (4): 88–96.

Ngũgĩ wa Thiong'o. 1992. *Moving the Centre: The Struggle for Cultural Freedoms*. London: James Currey Publishers.

Omotoso, Yewande. 2016. *The Woman Next Door*. London: Chatto and Windus.

What's the Rush? Slow Reading, Summary and *A Brief History of Seven Killings*

Madhumita Lahiri

What mode of textual attention is best suited to dismantling structures of oppression? This question is as big as it is urgent: it is the fundamental methodological question for literary scholars working in the fields of postcolonial and decolonial studies. This essay addresses the question by asking a different one, posed by Isabel Hofmeyr in her monograph *Gandhi's Printing Press: Experiments in Slow Reading*: 'How do [Gandhi's] insights about summary and speed as a central feature of modernity and industrialised orders of information speak to conditions today?' (2013, 24–25).

Read against the fluid leaps of *Dockside Reading* (Hofmeyr 2021), the illuminating detours of *The Portable Bunyan* (Hofmeyr 2004) or the fluent locality of *'We Spend Our Years as a Tale That is Told'* (Hofmeyr 1993), *Gandhi's Printing Press* is a quiet book. In contrast to ongoing debates about Gandhi's political positions, Hofmeyr's book effectively puts aside the question of Gandhi as an ethical icon, situating him instead as a person of print culture.[1] In the process, Hofmeyr offers a compelling alternative to the Eurocentrism of most postcolonial literary methods, for she derives from Gandhi an analytic that can be easily applied elsewhere.

In Hofmeyr's account, reading is a key Gandhian activity. Because the Gandhian approach to *swaraj* (literally, 'self-rule') territorialises sovereignty in the individual rather than in a territory, proper reading practices can demonstrate how *swaraj* should operate. As Hofmeyr shows, 'The process of understanding true *swaraj*, or self-rule, is equally the process of learning to read in a patient, concrete, nonteleological way' (2013, 150). Reading, she argues, enables Gandhi to oppose the accelerating impulses of modernity, because 'serious reading can only be done at the pace of the human body and . . . each reader must read on his or her own behalf' (4). As a consequence, reading 'created small moments of intellectual independence' by 'pausing industrial speed' (4). This emphasis on slowness that she finds in Gandhi's approach to reading enables her to conclude that 'the style of reading we call literary is somewhat Gandhian: slow, scrupulous, patient, repetitive, cumulative' (162).

This essay applies the Hofmeyrian analytic as it surfaces in *Gandhi's Printing Press* to a text whose pages Gandhi himself would have undoubtedly abjured: Marlon James's 2014 novel *A Brief History of Seven Killings*. James's novel intersects with Gandhi's corpus in its thematic preoccupation with violence, yet whereas Gandhi's work sought to excavate the ordinariness of non-violence (what he termed *ahimsa*) as a historical force, James's novel explores the complex violence of Cold War Jamaica and the Jamaican diaspora. Repeatedly gruesome, and frequently sexually explicit, the novel's depictions of violence have prompted both criticism and praise (Jaffe 2019; Walonen 2018). They intervene, as Michael K. Walonen has shown, in long-standing debates, both popular and scholarly, about entrenched patterns of gang warfare. Gandhi's strategy of non-violent resistance worked, in part, by refusing the humiliations of violence; James's novel similarly demonstrates how violence deploys 'humiliation, which accompanies so many killings in the narrative, [and] serves as a form of social and political control' (Walonen 2018, 6). In the Gandhian corpus, European civilisation rationalises violence as a historical force; in James's novel, US popular culture serves that purpose, enabling his characters to narrate their experiences of violence in cinematic terms. Finally, much as Gandhi extracts *ahimsa* from the wider historical record and launches it as an agent of global historical change, James's novel foregrounds how Bob Marley's music and its accompanying message of peace move along the same transnational routes that perpetuate violence as well (Walonen 2018, 12).

In a 2011 article on Gandhi's *Hind Swaraj* (1909), Hofmeyr found in both Gandhi's work and the work of the colonial state 'a concern with the vulnerable reader at the mercy of the violent text' (2011, 286). She writes:

> *Hind Swaraj* takes shape at the point where the vulnerable reader encounters the violent text, the exact same point where the colonial state's censorship mechanisms spring into action. Censorship replicates the brute force of the colonial state in the realm of text and letters. The standard response of revolutionaries had been to bombard the state with even more incendiary publications. *Hind Swaraj* seeks to bow out of this textual arms race . . . while still taking account of the 'problem' of the vulnerable reader. (Hofmeyr 2011, 287)

Written a century later, James's violent text does not assume a vulnerable reader in the colonies, or even one in the postcolonies, but rather an indifferent reader in the former colonial powers: the reader's vulnerability to the text is produced by the novel rather than assumed by it. Yet this novel, too, castigates 'incendiary publications', in this case those of Cold War US imperialism. One of the novel's prominent characters is Barry Diflorio, the Central Intelligence Agency (CIA) station chief in Jamaica, and Barry's CIA work involves precisely the kinds of interactions that Hofmeyr highlights in her reading of Gandhi. When, for instance,

Barry's machinations in Ecuador are derided by another agent as a 'silly little letter-writing campaign', he complains to the reader:

> By letter writing he means the letters that I fed the press warning people about the communist threat . . . By letter writing he means the flyers I created for . . . a communist organization I created . . . By letter writing he means the Anti-Communist Front that I created . . . By letter writing he's talking about what it took to get [Otto] Arosemana elected [president of Ecuador] as well as thrown out . . . All the while keeping this shit out of the *New York Times*. (James 2014, 209)

Through such depictions of 'incendiary publications', *A Brief History of Seven Killings* shows the devastating failures of violent politics and their gruesome human toll. Perhaps the survivors of James's novel testify, in their own way, to Gandhi's argument about the powerful but usually overlooked force of non-violence; certainly the novel as such does not offer a hopeful interpretation of the forces of history. Instead, it spews an atmosphere of guilt, both through our guilty reading of other people's imagined suffering and our capitalist complicity (and, for US readers, imperial complicity) in the historical suffering thinly fictionalised in the novel.

Deploying letters, flyers and other paper propaganda to devastating political effect, James's imagined CIA agent fully resides in the world of print ephemera. As Hofmeyr has demonstrated, both in *Gandhi's Printing Press* and in *Dockside Reading*, such ephemera were central to the emergence of the colonial and postcolonial literary spheres. Barry's 'last big project', we read, will be 'anti-communist coloring books' (James 2014, 211). We see this colouring book two hundred pages later: it is presented to the gangster Josey Wales by a CIA field agent. Josey has been playing dumb, and the agent responds by infantilising him further:

> – Do you know what we mean by Cold War?
> – War don't have no temperature.
> – What? Oh no, son . . .

The white man take out a coloring book. When you keep playing fool with Americans you learn to expect anything, but this one throw even me off.

– A wha this?

I had it upside down because who need to flip around a cover to read the *Democracy Is for US!* title. The American look at me holding the book wrong and I know exactly what he was thinking . . .

– It's a breakdown, that's what it is . . . See on page six? This is the world in a democracy. See? People in a park . . . And watch that chick, hot, right? . . . Oh yeah, look at the tall buildings . . . That's the free market, son. And if anybody in this picture doesn't like what's going on they can say so.

– You want me to color this picture, boss?

– What? No, no. (James 2014, 412–413)

The comedy of this scene is enabled by the pre-existing rules of print culture: while Josey violates an implicit rule by holding the book upside down, the CIA agent violates an explicit rule by telling him not to colour a colouring book. James's imagined colouring book as an agent of Cold War imperialism intersects beautifully with Hofmeyr's elaboration of the pamphlet as a colonial genre. Arguing that pamphlets 'were a major medium for making ideas more portable and durable across the empire', she further notes that they were 'rarely straightforward secular commodities: seldom intended to render profit, they often related religious plots of eternal life rather than secular narratives of national time like the novel' (Hofmeyr 2013, 13, 15). James's CIA colouring book depicts the dream life of capitalism: the free market transfigured into a heavenly metropolis of parks, 'hot chicks' and tall buildings rather than the lived misery of the Kingston slums.

James's lauded literary novel, for which he was awarded the 2015 Booker Prize, explicitly thrashes about in what Hofmeyr terms 'the lower empire of periodicals': a 'world of recycled text, impersonal writing, and reader-as-redactor [that] has typified the experience of most "ordinary" print culture users' (2013, 159). The novel both emerges from this 'lower empire' and dramatises it: it draws on journalistic works such as Laurie Gunst's (1995) *Born Fi' Dead: A Journey through the Jamaican Posse Underworld* for its historical material (Walonen 2018, 4), while inside the novel one primary character, Alex Pierce, is a white US journalist. Alex understands his narrative journalism for print periodicals such as *Rolling Stone* and *The New Yorker* to be in explicit opposition to the rapidity and compression of conventional news. As he explains to another character late in the novel:

> Well, at some point you gotta expand on a story. You can't just give it focus, you gotta give it scope. Shit doesn't just happen in a void, there're ripples and consequences and even with all that there's still a whole fucking world going on, whether you're doing something or not. Or else it's just a report of some shit that happened somewhere and you can get that from the nightly news. (James 2014, 671)

Periodical culture is positioned here precisely as Hofmeyr has elaborated. With 'weekly, monthly, or quarterly tempos [that] are slower than the daily rhythms of the newspaper' and 'driven by the temporalities of circulation', these periodicals' 'modes of consumption are punctuated and sequential', for they 'have longer shelf lives' and are 'less date-driven' than the more widely studied genre of the newspaper (Hofmeyr 2013, 14).

Nearly seven hundred pages long, *A Brief History of Seven Killings* unfolds across three decades and features over a dozen distinctive narrators. It is divided into five sections, each with a title and date; inside each section are several chapters, each of which proceeds with a different narrator. The table of contents shows the section names and page numbers, but it provides no information about the chapters. This makes it impossible, for instance, to simply glance at the table of contents and perceive how multiple narrative voices are juxtaposed. In the first four sections, each chapter is titled with the speaker's name: one knows, upon starting a chapter, exactly whose perspective one is reading. In the fifth and final section, however, the text abruptly changes: instead of chapters titled with a character's name, we encounter chapters that are simply numbered, leaving us unclear, in our initial moments of reading, whose words we are absorbing. Until the final section, then, our reading experience of the novel arguably resembles that of reading a print periodical: we encounter several different voices, labelled as one would bylines, nestled together in a single print object.

The difficulty of enumerating the total number of different narrators in *A Brief History of Seven Killings* relates to James's strategic depiction of one narrator as several for most of the novel. The impossibility of accurately counting these voices reminds one of the polyphonic strategies of Gandhian print culture, where, as Hofmeyr showed, 'forms of authorship, such as fictitious correspondents and pseudonymous and semi-pseudonymous writing, proliferated' (2013, 79). In addition, the events related in this enormous novel occur on only five specific days: one each in 1979, 1985 and 1991 and the remaining two in 1976. These five days are so long that they dwarf the years between them, and as Sheri-Marie Harrison (2017) has argued, these days are also haunted by days and decades that came long before. The impress of a longer history is made through this slowing of narrative movement: rather than accelerating us through this 'brief history' of three decades, James's novel retards our progress, insisting that we slow down our reading and absorb the importance of just five days.

Hofmeyr has argued that Gandhi's 'slow reading' practice 'created small moments of intellectual independence' by 'pausing industrial speed' (2013, 4). *A Brief History of Seven Killings* makes fast reading impossible, for the reader is repeatedly interrupted by the text, not only through its use of multiple narrators and its shocking descriptions of violence, but also through its usage of different dialects of English. What has been described as 'the relentless orality of James's novel' (Watson 2022, 203) manifests in the use of several different patois: English here is not one language but several, each indelibly marked not only by its speakers' race, ethnicity, class and nationality, but also by their political and religious affiliations. The Hofmeyrian analytic of 'slow reading' is particularly useful for apprehending language usage in *A Brief History of Seven Killings*, for it allows us to sidestep the questions of locality and authenticity that are otherwise foregrounded in discussions of non-standard English.

The linguistic patterns of *A Brief History of Seven Killings* have generally been analysed through the category of the vernacular (for instance, in Watson 2022). They were also mentioned in Kalyan Nadiminti's important argument about 'vernacular anglophone realism', which he describes as a new trend in the global novel that 'subsume[s] the vernacular as an atmospheric effect for English writing' (2018, 377–378). Nadiminti's article focuses on South Asian writing in English, yet he argues briefly that

> one could apply the conceptual apparatus of vernacular anglophone realism to Caribbean and West African writers, like Marlon James alongside Chigozie Obioma . . . Both writers exhibit a strong tendency to voice the local for the consumption of both American and non-Western readers. They present members of a marginalized underclass as subjects of literary fiction, relying heavily on the diction and rhythm of Jamaica and Nigeria to depict their characters' inner lives. (Nadiminti 2018, 378)

Nadiminti's claim here relies on equivalence of 'the vernacular', on the one hand, and 'the diction and rhythm' of a place, on the other. While common, such a continuum of definition risks collapsing all non-standard American English into a single category and then naming it 'the vernacular': the vernacular ceases to indicate a different language and now names difference as such. Critics of the homogenising powers of global English who use 'the vernacular' in this fashion inadvertently purify the very concept that they aim to critique: the anglophone becomes a homogeneous and homogenising thing precisely because all that is non-standard is no longer considered English.

This issue is an urgent one in *A Brief History of Seven Killings* because Nadiminti's 'vernacular anglophone realism' works by 'gestur[ing] toward the tonal presence of a mother tongue that simultaneously reckons with the imposition of a second, often colonial, language' (Nadiminti 2018, 384). Yet James's novel unfolds in a national context where there is no 'mother tongue': rather, Jamaica has been shaped by a complete loss of pre-colonial languages in keeping with the genocide of pre-colonial populations. To transmute this absence, which scholars have often theorised as a traumatic loss, into a 'tonal presence' because of the non-standard nature of James's English is to collapse connected yet divergent experiences of coloniality into a dangerously undifferentiated whole. More than that, to describe James's use of Jamaican English as 'vernacular anglophone' is to ignore the ways in which dialectical and idiomatic difference emerges *within* a language, and particularly within English: Jamaican English indicates, I would argue, not a 'tonal presence' within 'the imposition of a second, often colonial, language', but the ways in which language never belongs only to its most powerful users. The English of this novel, moreover, is not simply Jamaican: the idiom and its speakers migrate and circulate, and to that extent the novel's English is as much global English as any other. *A Brief History of Seven Killings* is not, consequently, 'renegotiat[ing] the non-Western anglophone novel's tussle with translation – the translation of multiple languages and realities into the singular discourse of anglophone modernity' (Nadiminti 2018, 392). Instead of such manoeuvring, where presence predicates the encounter between the local and the global, *A Brief History of Seven Killings* negotiates absences: lost languages, buried bodies, and unsolved and even unconfirmed killings.

While recent theorisations of the vernacular have separated the concept from an easy equivalence with local authenticity (for instance, Kullberg and Watson 2022), this reorientation is particularly difficult in the analysis of works by black US writers such as James. In that context, the analytic deployment of the vernacular necessarily invokes the long tradition of the vernacular paradigm for African American literature, in which 'writers may speak for distinctively black communities insofar as they can inflect their texts with the accents and idioms of black oral culture' (Dubey 2003, 6). In this paradigm, the vernacular is binarised first and foremost with the literary rather than with the global. The terminology of the vernacular is thus used to indicate a black authenticity grounded in orality, physical presence and lived community (Dubey 2003). The vernacular in the Americas may or may not be local, but it is already marked in racial terms.

How, then, to describe the literary use of an English that is deeply inflected with a likely unfamiliar idiom? This is where Hofmeyr's focus on slow reading can be useful. Arguing that Gandhi's print periodical, *Indian Opinion*, 'specialised in "uneven" reading surfaces across which one could not hurtle', she suggests that the interruptions of such a text were designed to disrupt 'the tempos of industrialised information' (2013, 91, 158). The resulting practice of slow reading, in her account, mobilises 'bodily rhythm as a way of interrupting industrial tempos', placing the emphasis on 'how, rather than on what, one reads' (4, 160). A focus on 'how' allows us to see the linguistic interruptions of the text on a continuum with the text's other practices of interruption, such as the use of multiple narrators and detailed depictions of violence, encouraging us to focus on the reader's experience of the text rather than, as in the 'what' framework, approaching the text's utilisation of non-standard English separately from its other formal choices.

James's text intersects again with Hofmeyr's analysis in its use of summary. Writing of Gandhi's world as one whose 'imperial modernity relied on summary, telegram, telegraph, clipping, and extract for its operations', Hofmeyr argues that Gandhi 'came to appreciate these flows of summary as tied to the industrialisation of information itself' (2013, 17, 18). Gandhian print practice transforms the operations of summary, converting an accelerant of industrial modernity into an elicitor of careful reading. In Gandhian print practice,

> [t]he characteristics of journalism – telegraphic brevity, rapid summary, hurried reading, instantaneous obsolescence – become

their opposite: summary acquires a gravity that pulls the reader's attention down into the text where reading has to be deliberate rather than thoughtless and hasty. Condensation becomes an art form that produces a thoughtful or an 'ideaful' text that in turn requires a reader who is thoughtful in both senses of the word: exercising careful deliberation and extending sympathetic regard to the text. (Hofmeyr 2013, 70)

Summary, now turned into the 'art' of condensation, works 'to pull readers in and slow them down'. Instead of producing 'ever faster and more epitomised bits of information [bombarding] consumers', the Gandhian summary demands a reading practice of 'effort and friction' (Hofmeyr 2013, 89, 18, 91).

James's text includes multiple non-literary summaries, such as when we are given two brief accounts of how to use an M16 gun (James 2014, 110, 342). The novel also summarises a key text – V.S. Naipaul's 1962 travelogue, *The Middle Passage* – not once but thrice, to powerful effect. In the first instance, the text is not named: instead, we start reading a section narrated by Alex Pierce which begins with his first draft of an essay about Kingston:

> *There's a reason why the story of the ghetto should never come with a photo. The Third World slum is a nightmare that defies beliefs or facts, even the ones staring right at you . . . It cannot be photographed because . . . the inherent beauty of the photographic process will lie to you about just how ugly it is.* (James 2014, 81; italics in original)

In this instance, there is no mention of Naipaul; instead, Alex's voice interrupts our reading to exclaim: 'Shit sounds like I'm writing for ladies who lunch on Fifth Avenue . . . Who the fuck am I writing for?' (James 2014, 82). James's use of summary, I argue, operates in the fashion that Hofmeyr has described for Gandhi: on encountering a summary, whether of *The Middle Passage* or of machine gun usage, the reader stumbles. The text slows; the reader is absorbed.

Alex's drafted summary will surface again much later in the novel, now summarised through a different character. In a late passage, the imprisoned gangster Tristan Phillips tells Alex:

> Me go to plenty library in Jamaica and not one have book like the number of books me see in Rikers. One of them is this book *Middle Passage*. Some coolie write it, V.S. Naipaul. Brethren, the man say West Kingston is a place so fucking bad that you can't even take a picture of it, because the beauty of the photographic process lies to you as to just how ugly it really is. Oh you read it? Trust me, even him have it wrong. The beauty of how him write that sentence still lie to you as to how ugly it is. It so ugly it shouldn't produce no pretty sentence, ever. (James 2014, 452)

In both of these instances we are reading a summary of Naipaul's declaration, towards the end of his travelogue, that 'the slums of Kingston are beyond description. Even the camera glamorizes them, except in shots taken from the air' (Naipaul 1962, 216). Yet Tristan's summary hews closer to Alex's summary than to Naipaul's original. Hofmeyr has argued that the Gandhian reshaping of summary 'requires consideration . . . from us, a contemporary audience accustomed to seeing summary, abridgement, or précis as trivial intellectual procedures rather than as a form demanding particular orders of skill and craft' (2013, 70). James's text here seems to explicitly make this point: by delivering a summary of Naipaul's text that is more accurately a summary of Alex's early draft, the novel demonstrates what Hofmeyr terms 'the art of condensation' (70). Between these two instances, we are given a highly sympathetic summary of the same volume from Barry Diflorio. As he explains to the reader:

> You have to get to the point where you know how the country works better than the people who live here. Then you leave. The

Company suggested I read a book from V.S. Naipaul before coming here, *The Middle Passage*. It amazed me how he could land in some country, be there for mere days and nail exactly what was wrong with it. I went to that beach he wrote about, Frenchman's Cove, expecting lazy white women and men in sunglasses and Bermuda shorts, attended to by cabana boys. But even the cove got hit by a wave of democratic socialism. (James 2014, 139)

Landing on a passage shortly after the one that Alex and Tristan summarise, Barry accurately sums up Naipaul's description of the resort area known as Frenchman's Cove. In this instance, summary has collapsed into endorsement, and as he describes his own experience of the Cove he has to pull Naipaul back into the ranks of those who 'know how the country works better than the people who live here'. Barry is now also one of those 'people who live here', and when he finds that the Cove is nothing like what Naipaul describes, he concludes not that Naipaul was wrong but that the place itself has changed. The three summaries thus reveal just as much about the person summarising as about the text under summary: the 'art of condensation' has thus been mobilised to testify to each reader's character and opinions.

The novel's most decisive moment of summary occurs at the very end, when we start reading an essay with the same title as the novel in our hands. The ninth chapter of the final section – titled simply 'Nine' – begins:

A Brief History of Seven Killings
– *A Crack House, A Massacre, and the Making of a Crime Dynasty*
Part 3.
By Alexander Pierce (James 2014, 654; italics in original)

Although this title is that of the novel we are reading, the subtitle and the author's name are not. We read, in effect, a summary of our own current reading, presented in the genre of the print periodical. In this diegetic

A Brief History of Seven Killings, too, we have a thinly fictionalised character, fenced in by multiple other named characters, and specific dates, giving us a span of time for the few paragraphs that we read. And yet, only four paragraphs into this *Brief History of Seven Killings*, our nested reading is rudely interrupted. Unattributed speakers declare: 'You did feel really cute when you write that, don't?' (James 2014, 655). We are, it turns out, in the middle of a dangerous situation: the drug lord Eubie and his henchmen are violently detaining Alex Pierce.

Alex's *Brief History* centres on Monifah Thibodeaux, whom his own writing describes as 'a cliché's idea of a ghetto cliché had she not complicated her own narrative so much' (James 2014, 655). His listeners object to his story much as we might object to the *Brief History* we ourselves are reading: they ask, for instance, 'Why you have to describe her so ghetto?' (657). By situating us in sympathy with these fellow readers of the summary *Brief History*, James's novel produces a form of identification and commonality through reading rather than writing. This is somewhat different from the commonplace notion of writing as a humanising process, one ventriloquised within James's novel, for instance, when Eubie speaks, in the penultimate chapter of the novel, of 'enjoying the nice little crackhead profile, I mean, somebody have to recognise even scum is people too, you know, them heartwarming sinting that turn them back into "people" so that white woman can talk 'bout how they were so touched and shit' (671). Rather than drawing our attention to the possibly real people behind the characters we are reading, the deployment of summary here makes us keenly aware of other readers of the text, and of these characters. The kinship here is, as it were, across the surface of the text rather than through its depths. The text is thus 'marked by the residue of prior readers as well as the hypothetical knowledge of those to come': a phrase Hofmeyr (2013, 19) uses to describe the operations of British imperial print culture and which applies to the Cold War print culture narrativised in James's text.

Despite Eubie's objections to Alex's writing style – his sensationalism, his cultural insensitivity, his reliance on racist stereotyping – his decisive objection is to the content, and specifically to his assignations of blame: what he calls Alex's decision to 'take it 'pon yourself to play detective' (James 2014, 671). The dynamics of this summary thus also anticipate what the anthropologist Rivke Jaffe writes of her own experience of reading the novel:

> Readers with some knowledge of Jamaican history will have no trouble in identifying the real-life counterparts of the superficially fictionalized characters, some of whom are still alive and continue to have varying levels of influence in Jamaica's political and criminal scene. I realized that it made me nervous to see a writer pointing fingers so clearly at specific individuals and organizations, implicating them not only in the Marley attack but also in various other acts of torture and murder, and in sexual exploits that many in Jamaica consider taboo. Could one write like this and get away with it? (Jaffe 2019, 380)

Jaffe's response here is eloquent and personal, yet the novel itself has already staged her reaction. The use of summary within the novel thus allows the author to answer his imagined attackers: we as readers have no original insights to offer, having been already interpellated within the text. Alex's *New Yorker* story operates as a summary of the novel we are reading that nonetheless surfaces within that very novel, an operation made comprehensible to us through the Hofmeyrian analytic.

What Hofmeyr describes as 'imperial reading' requires not only 'reading within the time–space continuum of empire' but also 'becoming accustomed to lateral linkages among colonies and non-metropolitan centers' (2013, 86). James's text, too, makes these lateral linkages visible, explicitly foregrounding the dynamics of Cold War Jamaica while repeatedly insisting throughout the novel that what the CIA and capitalism are unfolding in Jamaica is both exemplary and enmeshed: only one part of what is unfolding elsewhere. This is a move reminiscent of Gandhi's politics of place. Hofmeyr's account of Gandhi constructing a 'summary India' through print indicates how we might understand James's novel, with its vast array of voices, as constructing a kind of 'summary Jamaica'. Crucially, James's summary Jamaica exists across the Western Hemisphere, for the novel as a whole stages US interventions in South America and the Caribbean as a key mover of both plot and character. We frequently encounter passages that summarise all the US machinations across the developing world, particularly in Africa, South America and the Caribbean. In this sense, we could even think of James's novel as a 'summary postcolony', for it represents in novelistic form the compromised sovereignty and nominal independence that has frequently defined the postcolonial experience. Moreover, by reframing *A Brief History of Seven Killings* as a summary postcolony, the much-noted discrepancy between the novel's length and its title's promised brevity becomes more than just a joke: the book is long for a novel, but for a summary of postcoloniality it is decidedly brief.

In reading Marlon James's novel through Isabel Hofmeyr's scholarship, I have excavated textual patterns that manifest the ongoing impress of imperialism and colonialism across the global South, whether in the early twentieth century or in the early twenty-first. Hofmeyr's careful study of Gandhi has made these practices visible, gifting us the concepts of summary and slow reading as they operate in imperial and anti-colonial print cultures. Slow reading, as I have demonstrated, provides a useful analytic for texts that use non-standard English, recognising it primarily as a formal and ethical choice rather than a representation of other languages or a ventriloquisation of racialised difference. Much as slow reading shifts our critical focus to the reader's experience, the use of summary within a text forces the reader's self-recognition. Once recognised, as Hofmeyr suggests, as 'the art of condensation', any summary can alert its reader to the simultaneous presence of other readers, and to reading itself as a test of focus and character.

NOTE

1   For an important recent example of such critiques, see Desai and Vahed (2016). For a rebuttal, see Burton et al. (2018).

REFERENCES

Burton, Antoinette, Faisal Devji, Mrinalini Sinha, Jon Soske, Ashwin Desai and Goolam Vahed. 2018. 'The South African Gandhi: Stretcher-Bearer of Empire'. *Journal of Natal and Zulu History* 32 (1): 100–118.

Desai, Ashwin and Goolam Vahed. 2016. *The South African Gandhi: Stretcher-Bearer of Empire*. Stanford: Stanford University Press.

Dubey, Madhu. 2003. *Signs and Cities: Black Literary Postmodernism*. Chicago: University of Chicago Press.

Gandhi, M.K. [1909] 1997. Hind Swaraj. In *'Hind Swaraj' and Other Writings*, edited by Anthony Parel. Cambridge: Cambridge University Press.

Gunst, Laurie. 1995. *Born Fi' Dead: A Journey through the Jamaican Posse Underworld*. New York: Henry Holt.

Harrison, Sheri-Marie. 2017. 'Global Sisyphus: Rereading the Jamaican 1960s through *A Brief History of Seven Killings*'. *Small Axe* 21 (3): 85–97.

Hofmeyr, Isabel. 1993. *'We Spend Our Years as a Tale That is Told': Oral Historical Narrative in a South African Chiefdom*. Portsmouth: Heinemann.

———. 2004. *The Portable Bunyan: A Transnational History of 'The Pilgrim's Progress'*. Princeton: Princeton University Press.

———. 2011. 'Violent Texts, Vulnerable Readers: *Hind Swaraj* and its South African Audiences'. *Public Culture* 23 (2): 285–297.

———. 2013. *Gandhi's Printing Press: Experiments in Slow Reading*. Cambridge, MA: Harvard University Press.

———. 2021. *Dockside Reading: Hydrocolonialism and the Custom House*. Durham: Duke University Press; Johannesburg: Wits University Press.

Jaffe, Rivke. 2019. 'Writing around Violence: Representing Organized Crime in Kingston, Jamaica'. *Ethnography* 20 (3): 379–396.

James, Marlon. 2014. *A Brief History of Seven Killings*. London: OneWorld Publications.

Kullberg, Christina and David Watson, eds. 2022. *Vernaculars in an Age of World Literatures*. London and New York: Bloomsbury Academic.

Nadiminti, Kalyan. 2018. 'The Global Program Era: Contemporary International Fiction in the American Creative Economy'. *Novel* 51 (3): 375–398.

Naipaul, V.S. 1962. *The Middle Passage*. London: Andre Deutsch.

Walonen, Michael K. 2018. 'Violence, Diasporic Transnationalism, and Neo-Imperialism in *A Brief History of Seven Killings*'. *Small Axe* 22 (3): 1–12.

Watson, David. 2022. 'Specters of the Vernacular: Neoliberalism, World Literature, and Marlon James's *A Brief History of Seven Killings*'. In *Vernaculars in an Age of World Literatures*, edited by Christina Kullberg and David Watson, 203–222. London and New York: Bloomsbury Academic.

8

Seeing Waters Afresh: Working with Isabel Hofmeyr

Lakshmi Subramanian

For a considerable time, until the 1960s, the Indian Ocean was markedly absent from the larger academy of maritime studies. There was a curious lack of interest in, and an academic neglect of, the Indian Ocean. Oceanic history was about the Pacific, the Atlantic and the Mediterranean Sea. Studies on the Indian Ocean, as far as they existed, were infected with the bias of a Eurocentrism that, subsequent to the colonial domination of the Indian subcontinent, saw that ocean as a British lake. The influence of imperialist historiography cast its long shadow right through the first half of the twentieth century, notwithstanding amateur nationalist attempts to recover and restore Indian maritime greatness, especially in antiquity. Subsequently, thanks to the intervention of professional historians who used the European archive to tell an Asian story, the field of Indian Ocean history came into its own. The uncovering of a dense web of social and commercial connections, the movement of peoples and ideas, the workings of complex mechanisms of credit and custom: all these things provided the validation and rationale for studying the Indian Ocean on its own terms, and for detaching it not only from the specific societies and polities that dominated its rim, but also from the hegemonic control of European capital that had subjugated oceanic spaces in the first place (Subramanian 2018).

The collective work of a new generation of historians came to deepen understanding of the Indian Ocean's history. This work both generated significant shifts in method and developed a clearer sense of the nature of the available archives. In South Asia, historians made use of the European East India Company's archives to question the Eurocentric bias that informed analyses of trade structures and communities in and of the Indian Ocean, establishing in the process the centrality of the Indian subcontinent in the trading economy of the ocean. But, by default, this process of rehabilitation involved a decentring of other important societies on the Indian Ocean rim, especially in Africa, whose participation in the dense network of exchanges remained obscure. Throughout the 1980s and the 1990s, while there was a meaningful expansion of scholarship on the Indian Ocean – and on its commodities, communities, social and political processes, empires and networks – the tendency to look at the ocean as an extension of land-based empires that oversaw massive networks of connections and transactions remained pronounced, especially in historical work. At that stage, confidence in the archive being drawn upon and in the historical method for studying waters and the societies and communities that peopled them remained resolute, with the result that Indian Ocean history was about the land mass that we know as India and the connections that India maintained with the other societies that peopled the rim of the ocean. Typically, these histories were built on the foundations of official archival holdings; of the official documentation of European trading companies that came to India from the sixteenth century onwards for trade and trade privileges; of the private papers of European traders; and of records of customs revenues and diplomatic negotiations kept by the Mughal state. Not surprisingly, then, histories of the Indian Ocean tended to focus on the operations of the Europeans and on their transactions with the indigenous commercial populations, whose own experience of the sea was not uniform. Seafaring merchants had a very different relationship with the sea from that of their land-based counterparts, whose operations in the hinterland markets made for a very different appreciation of oceanic trade. Both groups valued trade as the basis of their livelihoods and expected protection and support from the ruling dispensation, but with varying degrees of emphasis. These differences were foregrounded especially by those scholars whose imaginative use of the archive gave us evocative stories about the Indian Ocean that were a rich palimpsest of living memories, traces, connections and artefacts. M.N. Pearson (1976), Ashin Dasgupta and M.N. Pearson (1987), Om Prakash (1998) and Sanjay Subrahmanyam (1990), among others, helped to give coherence to the field by undertaking detailed and micro regional studies in order to address macro issues such as state and markets, circulation and price movements, communities and networks. Within the discipline of history, therefore, there was productive engagement with the notions of littoral society (Pearson) and connected histories (Subrahmanyam) to ascertain both the actuality of historical experience and the salience of theoretical frameworks.

A CULTURAL TURN?

Yet, by the end of the 1990s, there was a growing dissatisfaction with the impasse that Indian Ocean studies faced, and a realisation that disciplinary constraints stood in the way of writing about water spaces that were both unbounded and fluid. There was also a tension between the imperative to seek facts and the dynamics of a literary imagination that questioned the archive. These challenges eventually turned out to be productive, for they initiated a series of conversations among historians and social theorists, and literature specialists and cultural studies scholars, that led those involved to revisit the subject from a new perspective. In the field of cultural studies, a number of scholars got together with some of their colleagues to revisit the study of the Indian Ocean, and of its waters and its littoral; to share each other's research findings; and, in the process, to think more generally 'with water' and more inclusively about the ocean. This was a very different conversation from those we had in the past, when we had occasion to bemoan the failure of the land-centric bias of premodern states on the Indian Ocean rim to generate a useful archive, or even a vocabulary of conceptual terms, that might have enabled us to understand the economies of production and circulation around water resources – including their control.

Isabel Hofmeyr played a key role in making this change possible, and in setting up a formal platform to develop ideas that far exceeded our expectations. From the initial, informal parleys that happened under the aegis of the research concentration at the University of the Witwatersrand entitled South Africa/India: Connections and Comparisons, to the academic conferences that followed in 2009 and 2010, we were able to participate in the articulation of key themes and ideas that gave a new set of directions to Indian Ocean studies. As Amitav Ghosh, speaking of the Witwatersrand conference in 2010 put it: 'It was a rich feast: there we were, historians, anthropologists, literary critics, novelists and others, each stirring handfuls of our own spices into the pot of our common interest' (Gupta, Hofmeyr and Pearson 2010, ix).

To what extent was this initiative an offshoot of the cultural turn that, by 2000, had already shifted its attention to the study of oceanic spaces? What did the newly founded Centre for Indian Studies in Africa (CISA), directed by Dilip Menon, propose to do? Was it hoping for a more stimulating dialogue between history and literature, or between anthropology and cultural studies, in order to bring a fresh, non-national perspective to the field, especially in relation to the overemphasis on South Asia as the principal driver of the Indian Ocean world and to the resultant marginalisation of Africa within it? The answers to this would lie in the dynamic agenda that marked the work of CISA, especially in the ways it framed annual conferences and academic meetings to foster a South–South dialogue that would take cognisance of the need to recentre Africa and to look at histories *in* the ocean rather than *of* the ocean. The historical perspective was never abandoned; rather it was augmented and calibrated to ask a range of questions that had not been attempted before. In fact, the new initiative served to strengthen the early attempts of scholars at the University of Technology (UTS), Sydney, in 2000 to provide a cultural studies perspective to the Indian Ocean, during which a number of challenges had been identified: the location of Indian Ocean elements; the materiality of the seagoing experience; and the issue of archives to reconstruct traces and residual elements of unity and disruption in the ocean (Ghosh and Muecke 2000).

A number of us were more than happy to participate in the project and to think afresh about issues that had remained obscure in historical work. Mike Pearson used the occasion to write innovatively about religion in the Indian Ocean, and to reconstruct the lives of travelling teachers and Islamic itinerants, based in Java and East Africa respectively, who had been working across centuries under the aegis of very different empires. These preachers mediated religious disputes, taught the faith and in the process added to a sense of unity and community across the waters. Trade and religion worked in tandem for merchants who were exemplars of Islam, specifically of a maritime Islam whose features invited censure and surprise from many quarters (Pearson 2000). Admittedly, the diffusion of Islam in frontier areas – or what Richard Eaton (1978) referred to as 'shatter zones' – is well known, but what marked off Pearson's intervention was that he asked a range of new questions in the context of the Indian Ocean; tried to study developments within its space; and did not turn the ocean into an object of study subordinated to the magisterial gaze of the historian. This exercise generated rich empirical understandings and analyses, as well as conceptual frames that are now seen as commonplace in studies of the Indian Ocean. One such concept was that of littoral society, which Pearson later developed and amplified, while another was that of cosmopolitanism, which soon assumed more substantive dimensions. This was so especially with the writing of Anne Bang, whose work I got to know during the CISA workshops, and that of Hofmeyr, whose reading of Gandhi (Hofmeyr 2013) in particular lent an altogether new perspective on shared practices and sensibilities growing out of long periods of complex, and not always complementary, interactions in the oceanic space of empire.

For me personally, the initiative floated by the UTS was an encouragement to think more creatively about, firstly, the salty subaltern, whose presence was almost never acknowledged barring the token reference to the (famous or infamous) peddler of Van Leurian vintage, whose operations characterised the premodern trading world of the Indian Ocean; and, secondly, networks and how these actually worked in a rapidly changing context. Having worked on the ramifications of indigenous capital in the making of imperial projects in the eighteenth and early nineteenth centuries, I was hoping to make more of the materiality of the maritime world of the Indian Ocean, both of the actual seafarer who travelled as floating labour and subsequently as bonded/indentured labour and of those who resisted authority and flouted conventions to become outlaws and perfidious pirates. In both cases, the collaborative enterprise was invaluable. For the story of piracy, the insights I reached on space and spatial relations and on the politics of maritime radicalism came in the wake of rich conversations with Hofmeyr and critical geographer David Featherstone. I was especially attentive to suggestions regarding fault lines and how these were to be understood. Hofmeyr's brief intervention on Africa as a fault line (2010) proved to be immensely provocative in that it invited a deconstruction of uneasy silent histories of Indo-African conflict and cooperation and suggested how, in the end, modes of representation tended to be exercises in occlusion. Thus, when attempting to write and deconstruct imperialist and nationalist histories of predation in the Indian Ocean on the basis of a fractured and fragmented archive, I was all too aware of the occlusion that Hofmeyr referenced, especially in relation to spaces that did not conform to the neat divisions of trade fraternity, political uniformity and capital flows and thus remained marginalised as small nodes of illicit activity.

My subsequent work on predation and piracy in the Indian Ocean in the last decades of the eighteenth and at the turn of the nineteenth centuries was, in part, a response to this conversation, as it negotiated a fractured archive to recuperate the voices of the marginalised and to disrupt categories of resistance and agency that in the case of South Asia always remained anchored within landed spaces (Subramanian 2016). In the work I repositioned pirates and predation within a political economy of migration, grey markets and loose community affiliations that reacted strongly to the emerging colonial dispensation. I was able to do so by analysing the eruption of piratical attacks off the western littoral of India and exploring the networks the actors maintained across watery spaces that defied political borders; studying the use they made of community connections forged around religious lines; and looking at the ways they negotiated with grey markets for the resale of secured goods. Thinking with water helped to capture the materiality of experience in littoral societies and on sea journeys that generated new idioms of political communication. Pirates participated in an amphibious world in which they negotiated with local bosses who were land-based while extracting revenues from trade and protection, and left their wives with religious elders. At sea or on littoral waters they could and did break out on their own, articulating their distinct agenda based on custom that brooked no interference from law. Piracy was part of a local resistance to global pressure (Subramanian 2016). Piracy's manifestation in the Indian Ocean thus seemed to offer a useful lens to index a different kind of universalism, something that Hofmeyr referred to in her essay 'Universalizing the Indian Ocean' (2010). Interrogating the tendency to look at the Atlantic Ocean to frame our work on slavery and, may I add, piracy, she makes the valuable assertion that the discipline of Indian Ocean studies has the potential to complicate binaries, 'moving us away from the simplicities of the resistant local and dominating global and towards a historically deep archive of competing universalism' (Hofmeyr 2010, 722).

PRINT, NETWORKS AND CIRCULATION

Nowhere is the deep archive of competing universalism more evident than in Hofmeyr's work on Gandhi and print networks in the Indian

Ocean. While focusing on Gandhi's experiments to articulate practices of citizenship by slow reading and writing, she draws attention to the ways in which alternative conceptions of cosmopolitanism were being framed within an expanding print sphere in the Indian Ocean (Hofmeyr 2013). These grew out of a longer and deeper set of connections that helped to form identities that were distinct and transnational in their aspirations and expression, occasionally embodied in ambiguous terminology such as 'overseas Indians' or 'Indians outside India'. Hofmeyr parses the term 'colonial born' to index productive ambiguity as a necessary precondition to subjectivity, and in the process gives us a tool both to think with the actual experiences of subject-citizens in the empire and to decode the dense journalistic output that presses churned out in Indian Ocean cities from the late nineteenth century. For Hofmeyr, the materiality of printing, reading and writing is central to the formation of an Indian Ocean subject constituted by connections that criss-crossed an arc of colonial cities, where journalism actively configured and complicated identities. Access to English and participation in a common liberal project and its infrastructure saw Africans working in Indian-owned presses, and Indian printers assisting the articulation of African nationalist ideas suggested the workings of a transnational Indian Ocean public (Hofmeyr, Kaarsholm and Frederiksen 2011).

Some of these insights helped me to conceptualise the work on trade and social networks in the nineteenth and twentieth centuries, where the focus was on looking at subjectivity and imaginaries of diaspora groups and how these were articulated through print and universalist aspirations of religion and cultural practice. Working with diaspora groups related to labour and capital in South East Asia, I was aware of the contrasting historical experiences of merchant and labouring communities, and of how print and cultural practice intersected to give coherence to the experience of travel and settlement within spaces mediated by empire and its regulatory apparatus. What did 'being cosmopolitan' mean in the spaces outside the nation state? How did their individuals and communities negotiate their quotidian realities? My preliminary reflections were drawn from the case study of an individual, Munshi Abdulla, who acted as an exemplar for the research. He was an embodiment both of cross-cultural conversations and of the Chetty community, which was known for its apparent insularity but was reputed to produce exceptional traders and businessmen whose fortunes were made outside India.

My study of Chulia networks and of nineteenth-century figures such as Munshi Abdulla (the right-hand man of Sir Stamford Raffles) in Singapore helped to track two different moments in the history of the Indian Ocean and in the process of layering the notion of 'cosmopolitanism'. With his affiliations to a larger Hadrami diaspora and to localised Chulia Tamil networks that had in the past effectively deployed language and marriage to carve a niche space in coastal and littoral society, the munshi worked with missionaries, Europeans and Asian traders to emerge as the archetypal Indian Ocean subject – one who was multilingual, familiar with commercial protocols old and new, and therefore able to make the transition to a new system with relative ease. The munshi's cosmopolitanism was apparently not shared by other groups. For instance, the Chettis, who followed the British Empire into Burma and South East Asia, remained strongly connected to their natal base and responded largely to sub-nationalist aspirations around language. But located as they were in the growing networks of print and journalistic literacy, Chetti ideas of reform and self-cultivation indexed yet another notion of universalism, one that was shaped both by a traditional world view mediated by caste, religion and community reform, and by notions of responsible self-care that would help the community transition to modernity. It is not clear whether the community responded to the idea of either the colonial born or the greater Indian, but it would appear that, like Gandhi's efforts to cultivate the moral self and enable greater participation in citizenship practices, the community articulated a clear programme of self-improvement and larger social welfare (Subramanian 2010).

I would like to conclude this brief contribution by referring to an important essay that Hofmeyr wrote, 'The Complicating Sea: Ocean as

Method' (2012), and how this invokes the salience of universalism; of transnational interactions in resisting the reproduction of old categories of race and nation; and of looking at diasporas afresh. This, I think, marks Hofmeyr's most important and sustained contribution to methodology. Drawing on her work on the Indian Ocean and print culture, on Gandhi and the printing press, and on her current interests in looking even more closely at oceans and hydrocolonialism, the essay opens up the potential for comparative literary studies looking at the idea of the Indian Ocean. She draws attention to the importance of practicing awareness about historical realities as they happened and as they were represented, an exercise which holds the key to bridging the gap between the humanities and the social sciences, and between history and literature, and also asks new questions of the ocean and the histories within it (in relation both to their making and to their retrospective recall). This would include memories of sailing, of marine life, of climate change that will then truly integrate environmental history with social history. This, I think, is the way forward – something that Hofmeyr has already and presciently thought of in her current initiative on oceanic humanities for the global South.

REFERENCES

Bang, Anne. 2014. *Islamic Sufi Networks in the Western Indian Ocean (c.1880–1940): Ripples of Reform*. Leiden: Brill.

Dasgupta, Ashin and M.N. Pearson, eds. 1987. *India and the Indian Ocean 1500–1800*. Delhi: Oxford University Press.

Eaton, Richard Maxwell. 1978. *The Sufis of Bijapur, 1300–1700: Social Roles of Sufis in Medieval India*. Princeton: Princeton University Press.

Ghosh, Devleena and Stephen Muecke, eds. 2000. 'Editors' Introduction'. *UTS Review* 6 (2): 1–5.

Gupta, Pamila, Isabel Hofmeyr and Michael Pearson, eds. 2010. *Eyes Across the Water: Navigating the Indian Ocean*. Pretoria: UNISA Press.

Hofmeyr, Isabel. 2010. 'Universalizing the Indian Ocean'. *PMLA* 125 (3): 721–729.

———. 2012. 'The Complicating Sea: Indian Ocean as Method'. *Comparative Studies of South Asia, Africa and the Middle East* 32 (3): 584–590.

———. 2013. *Gandhi's Printing Press: Experiments in Slow Reading*. Cambridge, MA: Harvard University Press.

Hofmeyr, Isabel, Preben Kaarsholm and Bodil Frederiksen. 2011. 'Introduction: Print Cultures, Nationalisms and Publics of the Indian Ocean'. *Africa: Journal of the International African Institute* 81 (1): 1–22.

Pearson, M.N. 1976. *Merchants and Rulers in Gujarat: The Response to the Portuguese in the Sixteenth Century*. Berkeley and Los Angeles: University of California Press.

———. 2000. 'Consolidating the Faith: Muslim Travellers in the Indian Ocean'. *UTS Review* 6 (2): 6–13.

Prakash, Om. 1998. *European Commercial Enterprise in Pre-colonial India*. Cambridge: Cambridge University Press.

Subrahmanyam, Sanjay. 1990. *The Political Economy of Commerce: Southern India 1500–1650*. Delhi: Oxford University Press.

Subramanian, Lakshmi. 2010. 'Commerce, Circulation and Consumption: Indian Ocean Communities in Historical Perspective'. In *Indian Ocean Studies: Cultural, Social and Political Perspectives*, edited by Shanti Moorthy and Ashraf Jamal, 136–158. Abingdon-on-Thames: Routledge.

———. 2016. *The Sovereign and the Pirate: Ordering Maritime Subjects in India's Western Littoral*. New Delhi: Oxford University Press.

———. 2018. 'Introduction: The Ocean and the Historian'. *Journal of Indian Ocean Studies* 2 (1): 2–11.

PART 3

OCEANIC TURNS

9

A Turn to the Indian Ocean

Sunil Amrith

PRINT CULTURE IN THE INDIAN OCEAN

I first met Isabel Hofmeyr in London, in 2008. Both of us had quite recently begun to write about the Indian Ocean world, and with that in mind a mutual friend, the brilliant South African historian Hilary Sapire, introduced us. Hofmeyr was in the UK to give the McKenzie Lecture in the field of book history at Oxford. Her lecture was an early iteration of the ideas that would become *Gandhi's Printing Press* (Hofmeyr 2013), and I had just started working on the project that turned into my *Crossing the Bay of Bengal* (Amrith 2013). Over tea at the British Library, we discussed at length a piece that we both admired: Mark Frost's essay on the cosmopolitan intellectual culture of colonial Colombo (Frost 2002).

Frost sketched the contours of an intellectual and social world that had received little scholarly attention. Overshadowed by the study of anticolonial nationalism and obscured by the boundaries of area studies, this world had found no place in the metropole-periphery mould of imperial history. He wrote:

> During the latter part of the nineteenth century and until after the
> First World War the imperial cities of the Indian Ocean became
> thriving centres for cultural exchange and intellectual debate.
> Entrepots like Bombay, Madras, Calcutta, Rangoon and Singapore
> witnessed the emergence of a non-European, western-educated
> professional class that serviced the requirements of expanding
> international commercial interests and the simultaneous growth
> of the imperial state. (Frost 2002, 937)

Frost pointed to the 'informational explosion' (940) that linked the
Indian Ocean's port cities, sometimes re-energising much older Buddhist
and Islamic networks, and in other cases connecting previously discrete
social worlds anew. Through the mass diffusion of printed material,
hastened by the telegraph and the imperial post, the circulation of ideas
was unleashed. In this world the 'proximity of alternative mores, practices
and beliefs' (941) stimulated movements of social and political reform
that were not all nationalist, nor even anti-colonial.

Frost's intervention emerged from three distinct but converging
concerns. First, within the academy, a 'crisis' of area studies led to
a search for alternative spatial orientations. By the late 1990s, the
project of area studies struck many as outdated and compromised:
too bounded in its frameworks to comprehend a world of global
migration; too tied in its origins to the US government's Cold War
counter-insurgencies. As Hofmeyr (2007) pointed out in her earliest
published intervention on the Indian Ocean, the North–South orientation of area studies, oblivious to lateral connections, was ill-suited
to understanding the growth in South–South economic, political and
cultural connections.

Not all who questioned area studies were ready to throw in their
lot with the study of globalisation. For those who sought looser spatial
boundaries while retaining the texture of specific cultural and historical
experiences, oceans emerged as a promising framework for the organisation of academic knowledge, and the oceanic turn was embraced with an

enthusiasm that some, with hindsight, now dismiss as boosterism (Lewis and Wigen 1999).

A second stream of thought that fed Indian Ocean studies as they emerged in the 2000s was more specific to the region. It marked the encounter of an older tradition of Indian Ocean history (Chaudhuri 1985) – primarily empirical, focused on the history of trade and merchant diasporas – with postcolonial studies and intellectual history. A new set of questions concerned how, and how far, the Indian Ocean was a space of political imagination.

In response to Benedict Anderson's *Imagined Communities*, Partha Chatterjee (1991) had asked: 'if nationalisms in the rest of the world have to choose their imagined community from certain "modular" forms already made available to them by Europe and the Americas, what do they have left to imagine?' He reconceived nationalism as an 'inner' project of cultural renovation as much as it was an 'outer' project of political struggle (Chatterjee 1993). The new histories of the Indian Ocean world reframed the question of what they had 'left to imagine' by moving beyond the nation. The Indian Ocean, Frost and others showed, was a space of multiple, simultaneous and interacting political imaginaries – many of them religiously inflected, almost all of them with universalist aspirations (Bose 2006). Pan-Islamic, Buddhist, Confucian and Hindu movements each viewed the Indian Ocean as a continuous space.

The third impetus for a turn to the Indian Ocean came from its literary reimagining as a cosmopolitan, even utopian, space. Amitav Ghosh's remarkable hybrid of history, memoir and ethnography, *In an Antique Land*, evoked an Indian Ocean of peaceful mercantile exchange prior to the arrival of European gunboats. The tragedy of postcolonial nationalism, in this view, was that it borrowed too much from its colonial opponents and not enough from a polyglot, pre-colonial world (Ghosh 1994). Novelist Abdulrazak Gurnah, too, breathed life into the imagination of a lost idyll of Indian Ocean connections, in his case from the perspective of the East African coast (Gurnah 2001). There was more than an edge of romanticism in these literary imaginings, and they proved irresistible at a moment when the violence of the postcolonial state was everywhere in view.

THE VIEW FROM JOHANNESBURG

The Indian Ocean looked different from a South Africa barely a decade past the fall of apartheid, where the contradictions of political transition were confronted on a daily basis. Now that South Africa was no longer a citadel of white supremacy on a postcolonial continent, the path was open to thinking of it as part of the global South. For as long as racial segregation had been the fundamental question in South African history, the obvious frame of comparison and connection had been transatlantic. After 1994, South African artists and writers found another set of histories and imaginaries, many of them forgotten or marginalised, by turning to the Indian Ocean.

When Isabel Hofmeyr invited me to the University of the Witwatersrand in 2009 to visit the newly opened Centre for Indian Studies in Africa (CISA), I caught a glimpse of the energies feeding South African scholars' engagement with the Indian Ocean. Hofmeyr had already forged close relationships with Indian institutions and was immersed in joint work with Lakshmi Subramanian. These were models of South–South collaboration. I was struck by the diverse intellectual ecosystem in which CISA thrived. In its infancy, CISA's offices were – tellingly, I thought – located within the Department of African Literature. In the short period of my visit, I had numerous enriching conversations about the Indian Ocean world. I also attended seminars at the Wits Institute for Social and Economic Research (WiSER) on archiving South African liberation narratives, and formed a lasting friendship with Susan Pennybacker and the late Jim Miller, who were there to pursue their respective projects on South African political and musical exiles in London and beyond. It was clear from the start how well placed Hofmeyr and her South African colleagues were to blow open two perennial limitations of Indian Ocean studies – an India-centred parochialism, and a tendency towards reverent nostalgia.

Hofmeyr set a new agenda for the field: a manifesto for what she called 'post-area studies' scholarship (Hofmeyr 2007, 2012). The crucial significance of the Indian Ocean, she argued, was 'as a site par excellence of "alternative modernities"', by which she meant 'those formations of modernity that have taken shape in an archive of deep and layered existing social and intellectual traditions' (2007, 13). Bringing insights from the Indian Ocean into dialogue with the 'black Atlantic' might end up destabilising assumptions on both sides.

One assumption, belied by the Indian Ocean's multiple and historically long-lived circuits of coerced labour, which bore little resemblance to plantation slavery, was that 'slavery and freedom are neatly separable states' (Hofmeyr 2007, 14). A second was related to the notion of 'counterintuitive textual circulation', overturning models that had clearly been shaped expressly within an Atlantic paradigm (21). And a third was challenged when Hofmeyr pointed out that the term 'diaspora', honed into a core concept in Atlantic history, 'sits uneasily' in an Indian Ocean context where 'failed diasporas', to use her provocative term, were at least as common (18).

Conversely, reading across from the scholarship on the 'black Atlantic' highlighted blinkers in Indian Ocean studies, foremost among them a blindness to the importance of race. Many of the Indian Ocean's cosmopolitan projects reached a hard stop when it came to Africa: blackness was beyond their bounds. The risk, Hofmeyr rightly pointed out, is that we write 'romantic accounts' of the Indian Ocean 'with too much African-Indian solidarity' – which is not, however, to endorse 'colonial' accounts that conceded such alliances 'too little' solidarity (Hofmeyr 2012, 589).

GANDHI'S PRINTING PRESS

Gandhi's Printing Press: Experiments in Slow Reading (2013) is Hofmeyr's lasting contribution to the field. It is, to my mind, one of the most important books ever written about the Indian Ocean world. It is playful beneath its conceptual rigour, expansive beneath its admirable concision. Extending Frost's argument about the kinds of intellectual exchange that the Indian Ocean's port cities made possible, Hofmeyr argues that a city like Durban constituted 'an environment that obliged its inhabitants to experiment with who they were or could become' (2013, 7).

Hofmeyr delves into the 'doubleness' of the Indian presence in South Africa, and the intellectual and textual forms that emerged from this liminal state. She situates Gandhi's periodical, *Indian Opinion*, the focus of her book, at the 'point where Greater Britain and Greater India intersected in southern Africa' (Hofmeyr 2013, 11). That intersection allowed Gandhi – who still harboured ambivalence about the British Empire and had not given up on the prospect of imperial citizenship – to define India and Indianness capaciously, but always with a firm limit that excluded Africans: 'he installed Africa as a boundary of India', she writes (10). Like Thomas Metcalf (2008), Hofmeyr talks about how Indian elites in South Africa sought solidarity with other colonised peoples even as they benefited from 'India's sub-imperial relations with its indentured peripheries' (2013, 11).

Hofmeyr's immersion in the field of book history inspired her to push the argument further. It was not only the content of *Indian Opinion* that was distinctively of the Indian Ocean; its very form would not have been possible anywhere else. Published in multiple scripts, sometimes on the very same page, *Indian Opinion* was 'an entirely novel experiment' (Hofmeyr 2013, 5), unlike anything else being published in either India or Britain. This insight of Hofmeyr's was enormously valuable in my own attempt to make sense of print culture on the other edge of the Indian Ocean, in the port cities of South East Asia, where a similar polyglot dynamic was at work. Some of the earliest Tamil-language newspapers, for example, were published not in South India but in Singapore, Penang and Colombo. The very first Malay-language newspaper in the Straits Settlements, *Jawi Peranakan*, was started by the same publishing house as its first Tamil newspaper (the press was owned by a family of mixed Malay–Tamil ethnicity; Amrith 2013).

In Hofmeyr's analysis, *Indian Opinion* was the apotheosis of this new, oceanic form of textual circulation. It adapted the widespread form of the periodical, which 'on every page convened a miniature empire' (Hofmeyr 2013, 13) through juxtaposition, repetition and extracting, but it did so in a way that resisted the logic of print capitalism. Hofmeyr describes it as an 'anti-commodity, copyright-free, slow-motion newspaper' (4), each hyphenated adjective confounding our assumptions. *Indian Opinion* addressed itself to an expansive world of readers, more likely sequentially than simultaneously. Through its circulation, reading would become 'an experience of witnessing a provisional thickening of text pulled from across the world cohering briefly, before dispersing again into a range of other periodicals' (19).

Hofmeyr shows that before it was deployed for more narrowly nationalist aims, as a more narrowly 'Indian' text, Gandhi's *Hind Swaraj* (*Indian Home Rule*) (1997) began as an epistolary exchange with the dispersed, diasporic readers of *Indian Opinion*. In the very act of reading it, slowly and like so many scattered points of illumination, its readers would become 'miniature . . . zones of sovereignty' (Hofmeyr 2013, 152).

If there is a sense of loss in the closing pages of *Gandhi's Printing Press*, it is for something more modest than a lost cosmopolitanism or the embers of Asian–African solidarity. It is, rather, regret at the loss of the notional 'Gujarati reader' of *Indian Opinion*, from whom Gandhi turned away in his final years in South Africa. Gandhi's 'Gujarati reader' was the ideal reader: patient, self-reflexive, receptive, allowing each word to lodge in the consciousness and reverberate. As Gandhi returned to India and 'to a more nationalist future', Hofmeyr argues, 'the figure he had invented to elude a narrow idea of nation remained behind' (2013, 152). But the liberatory possibility of Gandhian readings remains, she concludes – 'pausing the addictive tempos of market-driven life, and creating small zones of independence outside the realm of the nation-state' (163). Therein lies the answer to the blunt Indian Ocean question Hofmeyr had posed a few years earlier: 'So what?' (Hofmeyr 2007, 13). Only from the specific conjuncture of an Indian Ocean's 'archive of deep and layered existing social and intellectual traditions' (13), she shows, could such an ethical and political vision have emerged.

TOWARDS HYDROCOLONIALISM

The 2000s and 2010s saw an outpouring of fine scholarship on the Indian Ocean's print cultures, much of it in dialogue with Hofmeyr. At some point I began to wonder whether the Indian Ocean was but a sea of printing presses. Inevitably, it turned out that Hofmeyr had already been thinking about this, as I found out when we both attended a conference in 2016 on the state of the field of Indian Ocean history. In her brilliant concluding remarks, Hofmeyr said there had been something missing from all but a few of the talks – the 'oceanness of the ocean', 'the seaness of the sea'.

Enter 'hydrocolonialism': the latest iteration of Hofmeyr's recursive excavation of the Indian Ocean's multiple meanings (Bystrom and Hofmeyr 2017; Hofmeyr 2019). Both solo and in a series of collaborations, notably with Charne Lavery through their oceanic humanities initiative, Hofmeyr grapples more fully with the materiality of the ocean in her recent work.

Hofmeyr and Lavery (2020) point out that most Indian Ocean histories, for all their sophistication, have 'little to say about the sea itself'. The ocean is but a space of transit, crossed by traders and merchants, empire builders and labourers. It is perhaps unsurprising that historians have paid little attention to the ocean's depths, given how late even oceanographers were to the study of the Indian Ocean. When the first International Indian Ocean Expedition was launched in 1959, ocean scientists called it 'the largest unknown area on earth'. Paul Tchernia, who worked in the physical oceanography laboratory of the National Museum of Natural History in Paris, described it as the 'forlorn ocean' (Amrith 2018, 233). The study of this ocean has advanced considerably since then, of course, but the Indian Ocean nevertheless remains an under-researched space.

Studying a 'world indelibly shaped by imperial uses of water' (Hofmeyr 2019, 13), Hofmeyr and her colleagues connect, intimately, two defining facets of the Indian Ocean: its cultural diversity and its endangerment by climate change. I have grappled with that intersection in my own work, and it has taken me in the direction of the history of climate science in the Indian Ocean and towards the study of how the messy borders of decolonisation shape the ways in which South and South East Asia now grapple with the climate crisis (Amrith 2018, 2020). Reading Hofmeyr and Lavery, however, opened my imagination to a different archive – one that is both rich and deep.

Hofmeyr and Lavery point out that, despite the silence of historians and oceanographers, the Indian Ocean was 'not unpopulated in people's imaginations'. The ocean, they write, 'bustles with water deities, djinns, mermaids and ancestral spirits – a mythical submarine world that reflects the cosmopolitanism of its land populations' (Hofmeyr and Lavery 2020). Hofmeyr's turn to the deepest archives of memory and storytelling to understand the Indian Ocean's depths should come as no surprise: she began her career, after all, as a path-breaking scholar of orality and oral tradition.

Thinking about hydrocolonialism brings to my mind South African artist Penny Siopis's remarkable series *Warm Waters*, which I first saw as part of the Indian Ocean Currents exhibition at Boston College in Massachusetts. Using glue, ink and oil on paper, Siopis depicts twisted, shadowy forms that rise from the warming waters. Hers is a view not from above but from underneath. She forces us to imagine possible futures, inviting us to envision different forms of society, different forms of economy, different forms of solidarity. 'What do we imagine?' she asks. 'Burning? Drowning? Absolute alterity?' I cannot think of a more appropriate visual accompaniment to Hofmeyr's oeuvre.

I find myself writing, in my head, a Hofmeyrian lexicon of the Indian Ocean. What terms would it contain? 'Slow reading' and 'hydrocolonialism', certainly. To my mind, its keyword would be 'complication'. The Indian Ocean is a 'complicating sea' in the hands of a scholar who rejects easy binaries and embraces contradiction. I can think of nobody else who would think to point out that we should pay as much attention to 'south-south slapstick' (Hofmeyr 2010, 726) as to declarations of South–South solidarity in trying to understand our messy, hydrocolonial present.

The opportunity to think through the Indian Ocean with Isabel Hofmeyr has been a highlight of my career as a historian. I look forward to many opportunities to continue the conversation.

REFERENCES

Amrith, Sunil. 2013. *Crossing the Bay of Bengal: The Furies of Nature and the Fortunes of Migrants*. Cambridge, MA: Harvard University Press.
———. 2018. *Unruly Waters: How Monsoons and Mountain Rivers Have Shaped South Asia's History*. London: Allen Lane.
———. 2020. 'Climate Change and the Future of the Indian Ocean'. In *Indian Ocean Current: Six Artistic Narratives*, edited by Prasannan Parthasarathi, 177–186. Boston: McMullen Museum of Art.
Bose, Sugata. 2006. *A Hundred Horizons: The Indian Ocean in an Age of Global Empire*. Cambridge, MA: Harvard University Press.
Bystrom, Kelly and Isabel Hofmeyr. 2017. 'Oceanic Routes: (Post-It) Notes on Hydrocolonialism'. *Comparative Literature* 69 (1): 1–6.
Chatterjee, Partha. 1991. 'Whose Imagined Community?' *Millennium: Journal of International Studies* 20 (3): 521–525.
———. 1993. *The Nation and its Fragments: Colonial and Postcolonial Histories*. Princeton: Princeton University Press.
Chaudhuri, Kirti N. 1985. *Trade and Civilisation in the Indian Ocean: An Economic History from the Rise of Islam to 1750*. Cambridge: Cambridge University Press.
Frost, Mark Ravinder. 2002. '"Wider Opportunities": Religious Revival, Nationalist Awakening, and the Global Dimension in Colombo, 1870–1920'. *Modern Asian Studies* 36 (4): 937–967.
Gandhi, Mohandas. 1997. '*Hind Swaraj*' *and Other Writings*, ed. Anthony J. Parel. Cambridge: Cambridge University Press.
Ghosh, Amitav. 1994. *In an Antique Land*. New York: Vintage Books.
Gurnah, Abdulrazak. 2001. *By the Sea*. London: Bloomsbury.
Hofmeyr, Isabel. 2007. 'The Black Atlantic Meets the Indian Ocean: Forging New Paradigms of Transnationalism for the Global South – Literary and Cultural Perspectives'. *Social Dynamics* 33 (2): 3–32.
———. 2010. 'Universalizing the Indian Ocean'. *Publications of the Modern Language Association of America* 125 (3): 721–729.
———. 2012. 'The Complicating Sea: The Indian Ocean as Method'. *Comparative Studies of South Asia, Africa and the Middle East* 32 (3): 584–590.
———. 2013. *Gandhi's Printing Press: Experiments in Slow Reading*. Cambridge, MA: Harvard University Press.

————. 2019. 'Provisional Notes on Hydrocolonialism'. *English Language Notes* 7 (1): 11–20.

Hofmeyr, Isabel and Charne Lavery. 2020. 'Exploring the Indian Ocean as a Rich Archive of History – Above and Below the Water Line'. *The Conversation*, 7 June. Accessed 1 April 2022. https://theconversation.com/exploring-the-indian-ocean-as-a-rich-archive-of-history-above-and-below-the-water-line-133817.

Lewis, Martin and Karin Wigen. 1999. 'A Maritime Response to the Crisis in Area Studies'. *Geographical Review* 89 (2): 161–168.

Metcalf, Thomas R. 2008. *Imperial Connections: India in the Indian Ocean Arena, 1860–1920.* Berkeley: University of California Press.

10

'The Sea's Watery Volume': More-than-Book Ontologies and the Making of Empire History

Antoinette Burton

> Like the box in Goethe's tale, a book is not only a
> fragment of the world, but itself a little world.
> — Susan Sontag, *Under the Sign of Saturn*

> We thus present a way of thinking of the ocean
> and its presence beyond the sea's watery volume, as
> a 'more-than-wet' phenomenon.
> — Kimberley Peters and Philip Steinberg,
> 'The Ocean in Excess'

> At the bottom there is blackness.
> — Alexis Pauline Gumbs, 'Being Ocean as Praxis'

At first glance, Isabel Hofmeyr's estimable career reads like the story of a book lover who ended up falling in love with the ocean. Two major studies that have shaped her reputation as one of the most important, and historically minded, scholars of the book and print cultures are *The Portable Bunyan: A Transnational History of The Pilgrim's*

Progress (2004) and *Gandhi's Printing Press: Experiments in Slow Reading* (2013). Both of these monographs are deeply engaged with how print, whether between covers or in more ephemeral forms, moves across time and space, carrying and producing geopolitical transformation all at once.

As an Indian Ocean phenomenon, Gandhi's printing press arguably pulled Hofmeyr into the world of ocean studies just as it was gaining currency. To this field she has loaned her considerable acumen and has contributed a raft of edited collections and articles that have illuminated, among other things, how central chronicles of ocean life have been to the political economy and the imaginaries of the global South. Most recent among them is Hofmeyr's 2022 *Dockside Reading: Hydrocolonialism and the Custom House*, which tracks books and other printed materials from ship to shore, developing an argument about the power of imperial institutions to colonise not only land but water as well.

Here I hope to be forgiven for glossing Hofmeyr's vast body of work through a somewhat telescopic lens. While the book and reading are salient aspects of her career-long projects of research and writing, they may be in danger of eclipsing the vast array of related and unrelated interests and subjects she has brought to our attention – including women and gender in storytelling, the relationship between orality and literacy, popular culture and popular literature, and the field of African literature and studies as objects of inquiry. These have all been central to her thinking over several decades and some are implicated, if not directly addressed, in the story I want to tell of book-to-ocean in her work.

The hyphens in the term 'book-to-ocean' appear to tell a tale of linear, progressive movement – dare I say, a kind of pilgrim's progress – that a mere list of Hofmeyr's publications might well support. If we operated under that apprehension, we might see 2008–2010 as a turning point, a moment when her publications start to signal the oceanic directions that *Gandhi's Printing Press* would fully manifest. Worth noting is the way in which her pursuit of links between India and South Africa, and also her expansive sense of the public sphere, propelled her towards 'Indian Ocean lives and letters' and towards the critically important stake in the ground that was 'The Complicating Sea: The Indian Ocean as Method' (Hofmeyr 2012). Although this essay appeared in 2012, 'the Indian Ocean as method' is a useful optic through which to read the work she did leading up to the Gandhi book and much of what she has done after. A prism for many of us seeking not just new subjects but new analytical and conceptual frames, as well as new ways of narrating, 'The Complicating Sea' is a pivotal moment in her auto-bibliography, indicating a practically full-blown oceanic turn.

Yet this Whiggish reading doesn't hold if we know Hofmeyr's work and appreciate what it has always been about. Her ocean interests grow up and out of many influences, not least her own autobiographical experience of South African history as it has unfolded in the past six decades. I would say, too, that her intellectual eclecticism – her intense curiosity, her ability to move between and across fields, and above all her highly distributed interdisciplinarity – all these militate against understanding *Dockside Reading* as anything like a predictable, let alone a progressive, march to the sea. Any account of Hofmeyr's body of work, and certainly one that seeks to understand how books and oceans meet in and map onto the larger canvas of her thinking, has to begin by understanding both subjects as immanent in her methodological approach. Bookish-ness and ocean-ness are, for her, key to grasping how worlds come into being, how history works and what role motion plays in colonial placemaking.

I am emboldened in this conviction by the work of Philip Steinberg and Kimberley Peters, professors of geography whose concept 'wet ontologies' is a means, as they put it, of 'giving depth to volume through oceanic thinking' (Steinberg and Peters 2015, 247). Their research helps us to unpick the hyphens in book-to-ocean logics. Steinberg and Peters's 2015 essay, 'Wet Ontologies, Fluid Spaces', makes a persuasive case for redirecting land-based geographic theory, where the sea has been considered immaterial, towards the ocean, which in their view is 'indisputably voluminous, stubbornly material, and unmistakably undergoing continual re-formation' (247). Drawing on a host of interlocutors who address the materiality of volume (and even the fluid properties of earth), they argue that water's materiality – its liquidity, its wetness – is taken for granted rather than being understood as a condition of its being. If water has form, it follows that 'the character of the sea – its vertical depth, together and coalescing with its movement, its horizontal surface, its angled waves – is a space not moved on, but *through* . . . and also *under*' (253). Wet ontology, in other words, allows us to see the sea as a space of volume, as well as to acknowledge how terrestrial our epistemologies are when it comes to talking about time, history, conflict, governance and the Anthropocene, no less. This reasoning leads Steinberg and Peters to embrace an assemblage approach: one that sees the ocean as a force that 'configures a world that is open, porous, mobile, and changing', a territorial 'whole' that emerges in response to the relations that compose and recompose it (255). Meanwhile, they are keen to emphasise the materiality of this oceanic volume in part because of their conviction that 'we must continually rethink the borders that we apply to various materialities and their physical states' (259).

Readers may be thinking that yes, this comports so well with how Hofmeyr has always thought of the book, as well as the variety of forms that the texts and print culture she has studied have taken. What is *The Portable Bunyan* if not an instance of (a) volume with depth, crosshatched by the social relations and political forces that marked its transnational life and continually remade it as it passed through English and African hands, from London to the Congo to the Caribbean and beyond? Hofmeyr's point was that the materiality of that volume must be countenanced, and that translation alone, while certainly an important means of helping to promote its message about a passport to heaven, is not sufficient for historicising the eventfulness of *Pilgrim's Progress* as a story or as a story form. The dynamism, its evangelical power, derives from that combination of stubborn materiality and continual re-formation that its circulation and the social life of its intertextuality guaranteed. Here we might say that Hofmeyr anticipated, or intuited, the coming waves of the new materialism, with its emphasis on the work of vibrant matter ('vital materiality') in configuring the shape of human and non-human worlds (Bennett 2009). And *Gandhi's Printing Press* drives that dynamic materiality home, tracking as it does this famous but little understood apparatus to and through the littorals of Indian Ocean world print culture. Hofmeyr calls that ocean ecosystem a 'cosmopolis' that both nurtured and circulated remarkable flows of textual knowledge and, in an imperial context, of contest and struggle (Hofmeyr 2013, 37). In light of Steinberg and Peters's work, it is interesting to think of *Gandhi's Printing Press* as an argument for a kind of wet cosmopolis, challenging land-based histories of print, rooting that challenge nonetheless in the machinery of the press, and situating global histories of print culture in the boundless liquidity of Indian Ocean worlds. In that sense, wet and more-than-wet reading is an analogue for the 'slow reading' of *Gandhi's Printing Press*.

Having laid out their case for wet ontologies, Peters and Steinberg came back, in 2019, with a corrective. Acknowledging that there was much to be gained by 'taking the ocean's liquidity to heart', they proposed that the ocean is not only liquid but also ice and mist and other forms that could 'emote the oceanic miles inland'. They therefore now sought to explore how the ocean 'exceeds material liquidity'. Hence their provocation of 'a more-than-wet ontology, wherein its fluid nature is continually produced and dissipated' (Peters and Steinberg 2019, 293).

Lest this seem like a minor recalibration, we might consider how it speaks to the challenges of undoing that binary of land and sea which undergirds so much of Western, and Western colonial, thinking and practice (Mawani 2018). We should also note how conceptually and narratively persistent are vocabularies that evoke the integrity or sovereignty of land, even among those determined to break out of terrestrial frames. As Peters and Steinberg (2019, 295) contend:

> [T]he ocean does spill and leak – and often in ways that are less obvious than the creeping or cascading of water across the land in the intertidal zone . . . The ocean is not an entity then; it is an extension. We argue . . . that it is extensive geographically, as a materiality that exists beyond the liquid, blue spaces on the map that are marked as 'water'. But we argue as well that it is extensive

metaphysically, in the way that philosophers . . . refer to extension as the property of a substance that allows it to be sensed and known – a substance's outward property – and that connects it with other substances with which it is in constant, mutual relation . . . We thus present a way of thinking of the ocean and its presence beyond the sea's watery volume, as a 'more-than-wet' phenomenon.

In an echo of this 'more-than' itself-ness, it is no mere metaphor to say that books and other textual formations are, in Hofmeyr's hands, read not as bounded sovereign entities but as porous, relational assemblages marked perhaps as 'property' but with substantial relationships that exceed their physical embodiment.

Indeed, seeing and believing the watery volume-ness of the book is a methodology, a practice of reading (of more-than-book reading) that runs through much of Hofmeyr's writing on print culture. For those who have bought the fiction of the self-contained volume, it may be surprising to learn that the work of the book, material and symbolic, has exceeded the verticality of the spine and the imprint of the site of production throughout the long life of the form. In other words, like the ocean-ness of the ocean, the book-ishness of the book goes well beyond the canonical terrains to which each has been assigned. As much of Hofmeyr's work has shown, in admirable detail and with equally careful attention to the particularities of space and time, the book – that epitome of the imperial modern – is voluminous. And, in her mode of reading, its volume is ontological, a condition of its being in the world.

There are some limits to my own reading, of course. Hofmeyr's oceans are not watery in the way that Peters and Steinberg's are. And they, in turn, are not keyed into either the Indian Ocean or the global South per se. Mine is not an argument for concordance, but rather an evocation of where vocabularies overlap and conceptual frameworks mesh.[1] There is a shared historicity to their interventions and Hofmeyr's – a parallel immersion, if you will, that makes them interesting to think about together. Ultimately, these 'more-than' geographic theories help us to situate Hofmeyr's work in the broadest currents possible when it comes to connections between oceans and books.

I have referenced how two of Hofmeyr's monographs modelled this line of thinking, well before Steinberg and Peters gave them a name. I want to turn now to one of the best examples of how Hofmeyr's more-than-book ontology approach has worked in practice, by offering an account of our collaboration on an edited collection, *Ten Books That Shaped the British Empire: Creating an Imperial Commons* (Burton and Hofmeyr 2014). Having met Hofmeyr for the first time on a visit to Johannesburg in 2009 and energised by that encounter, I was eager to find a way to collaborate. We landed on the idea for a 'ten books' volume, which started out with an intention that was more cause-and-effect (ten books that made the empire) than the influence/impact argument (ten books that *shaped* the empire) that eventuated. That shift emerged from our conversations about what processes of historical change look like through the lens of travelling texts, which in turn reflected Hofmeyr's characteristically dispersed approach to undoing the metropole-colony binary at the heart of much imperial history.

We went into the project with a few books in mind – Gandhi's *Hind Swaraj*, for example, and Baden-Powell's *Scouting for Boys* (the latter in part because we knew of Elleke Boehmer's [2005] work on it) – but we were also open to what scholars whose research we admired were interested in pitching. Geographical reach was also a factor – all inside the numerical frame of ten. We sketched a very basic collection proposal to draw people in, but the 'Imperial Commons' subtitle emerged from our collective experience of discussing drafts of chapters and the broader aims of the book. Hofmeyr's rare combination of scholarly firepower, intellectual generosity and quiet charisma made all the difference here. She organised and funded a retreat workshop in the Magaliesberg mountain range outside of Johannesburg, where most of us convened to discuss our chapter drafts and work out the full remit of the collection. Those who couldn't attend were beamed in virtually (impressively, I have to say, as this was well before the days of Zoom). We spent our days workshopping drafts, moving from the particulars of the text at hand to the view from ten thousand feet and back again. In between we ate and talked, and walked, and talked some more. My distinct memory of the experience is of Hofmeyr's ability to guide the conversations so that the dynamics of each book among the ten became a central component of the imperial commons discussion. And whereas we had already indicated to the contributors that the production, circulation, reception, re-formation and recomposition of the books at hand were to be a subject of their essays, the Magaliesberg experience made it happen.

What emerged throughout Hofmeyr's spirited engagements was her constant reminder of the fluidity – internal and external – that each book's trajectory revealed. I recall an excited discussion of the vocabulary it was most apt to use to describe these trajectories. We landed on 'recycle' and 'upcycle' – notably environmentalist nomenclature – to capture both the social relations that propelled each title outward and the ways in which the books themselves exceeded their original intentions as they travelled. Those were exhilarating moments of the kind most of us can count on one hand over the course of our careers. They are all the rarer in such convivial, collaborative company, an atmosphere that Hofmeyr designed, supported and fostered. And though we didn't have 'wet' or 'more-than-wet' ontologies at our disposal, these orientations were in the air, thanks again to Hofmeyr's long-standing commitment to thinking about how books cross boundaries set up by geopolitical systems such as empires, sometimes challenging them and also, it must be said, often mirroring them as well.

A word on how we worked through the introduction to our book, which we wrote jointly. We wanted that essay to be both a gloss on the whole book and an argument about what the ten books added up to. The imperial commons idea came out of the workshop conversations, but we were eager to keep the concept baggy, suggestive of a formation in process, as Steinberg and Peters posit. We do use the word 'assemblage' to describe this print culture commons, in contradistinction to the manly authority of the English-language book. We set the commons up as an antagonist to more vertical notions of imperial power, and we offer the circulation of books across different geographies and temporalities as a way of imagining alternative routes to colonial ideas and subjects. Looking back, I can see that we were swimming around the wet and more-than-wet ontology question, in part because the conceptual vocabulary that Peters and Steinberg use draws in turn on Gilles Deleuze, Félix Guattari and other contemporary theorists, all of whom float in and out of debates about the new materialism and its navigation of the borders of the human and the non-human worlds.

'Non-human' can certainly conjure up life forms, but it evokes vibrant matter too. Thus, the ten books of our collection are boundary objects *and* floating signifiers, full of energetic agency but unmoored and resistant to a developmentalist model of history, let alone a teleological one. Reading *Ten Books* alongside Peters and Steinberg now, it's clear that we share their investment in a de-territorialised account of world-making (they in oceans, we in books). Thanks to Hofmeyr's interest in the limits of copyright – which found its way into *Dockside Reading* – we were also focused on the transactional mobility of the book, whether across imperial land and sea or in terms of what kinds of re-formations its material circulation involved. All of which is to say that I feel the influence of Hofmeyr's wet and more-than-wet ontologies in our work together, insofar as our collection treated books as fluid, voluminous, relational and in constant motion.

It's tempting to end this reflection with a paean to Hofmeyr's most recent book, whose subtitle – *Hydrocolonialism and the Custom House* – offers 'a larger framework for theorizing . . . shore-shaped literary formations' (Hofmeyr 2022, 4). But in keeping with my refusal of a 'destination: seaside' reading of her career-long work, I will end with a perhaps lesser-known essay she wrote for a special issue of a journal tracing the longitudinal impact of a very big twentieth-century book: E.P. Thompson's 1963 *The Making of the English Working Class*. In her 2015 article, Hofmeyr asked how this classic tome travelled, in its material form, in and through the Black Consciousness movement in apartheid

South Africa. Juxtaposing it with Steve Biko's 1978 *I Write What I Like*, she compared the notes, scratchings and other marginalia in library copies of each text in order to weigh evidence of reader and community engagement in both. Spoiler alert: Thompson's book has minimal, passive markings; in Biko's, the margins come alive with reader response.

What's germane here is the way that Hofmeyr reminds us of the distinctive voluminousness of each book. *The Making* has all the properties of a Victorian novel; its monumentality belies the fragments and evidentiary outcroppings upon which it is built, themselves the products of the social relations they archive. *I Write What I Like* is differently upcycled: it was 'not conceived of as a book and instead comprises a posthumous gathering together of pamphlets, columns, speeches, trial records, and interviews that was produced hastily under conditions of savage political repression', and was often read in pieces, via xeroxed copies (Hofmeyr 2015, 106–107). If *The Making* is more of a closed system and Biko's book is more porous and open-ended, putting them in dialogue reminds us of the power of Isabel Hofmeyr's reading practices – and of the permission they give us to recognise the book as world in itself, while also being fluid and open to all the worlds that endlessly compose and recompose it, no matter where we find it.

NOTE

1   Immeasurable thanks to Renisa Mawani for helping me hone this point.

REFERENCES

Bennett, Jane. 2009. *Vibrant Matter: A Political Ecology of Things*. Durham: Duke University Press.

Biko, Steve. 1978. *I Write What I Like: Selected Writings*. London: Bowerdean Press.

Boehmer, Elleke, ed. 2005. *Scouting for Boys: A Handbook for Instruction in Good Citizenship, by Robert Baden-Powell*. Oxford: Oxford University Press.

Burton, Antoinette and Isabel Hofmeyr. 2014. *Ten Books That Shaped the British Empire: Creating an Imperial Commons*. Durham: Duke University Press.

Gumbs, Alexis Pauline. 2019. 'Being Ocean as Praxis: Depth Humanisms and Dark Sciences'. *Qui Parle: Critical Humanities and Social Sciences* 28 (2): 335–352.

Hofmeyr, Isabel. 2004. *The Portable Bunyan: A Transnational History of 'The Pilgrim's Progress'*. Princeton: Princeton University Press.

———. 2012. 'The Complicating Sea: The Indian Ocean as Method'. *Comparative Studies of South Asia, Africa and the Middle East* 32 (3): 584–590.

———. 2013. *Gandhi's Printing Press: Experiments in Slow Reading*. Cambridge, MA: Harvard University Press.

———. 2015. 'South African Remains: Thompson, Biko, and the Limits of *The Making of the English Working Class*'. *Historical Reflections/Réflexions Historiques* 41 (1): 99–110.

———. 2022. *Dockside Reading: Hydrocolonialism and the Custom House*. Durham: Duke University Press.

Mawani, Renisa. 2018. *Across Oceans of Law: The Komagata Maru and Jurisdiction in the Time of Empire*. Durham: Duke University Press.

Peters, Kimberley and Philip Steinberg. 2019. 'The Ocean in Excess: Towards a More-than-Wet Ontology'. *Dialogues in Human Geography* 9 (3): 293–307.

Sontag, Susan. 1980. *Under the Sign of Saturn*. London and New York: Penguin Books.

Steinberg, Philip and Kimberley Peters. 2015. 'Wet Ontologies, Fluid Spaces: Giving Depth to Volume Through Oceanic Thinking'. *Environment and Planning D: Society and Space* 33 (2): 247–264.

Thompson, Edward Palmer. 1963. *The Making of the English Working Class*. London: Victor Gollancz.

11

Amphibious Form: Southern Print Cultures on Indian Ocean Shores

Meg Samuelson

We begin this excursion into 'amphibious form' by following various fictional figures along a riverbank and into the intertidal zone. The first is a juvenile hippopotamus conveying a soldier, '[e]nthralled and disarmed' (Couto 2019), away from the modernist structures of a post-colonial state consumed by global appetites and civil war. After guiding our soldier along a 'muddy' bank, the 'message-bearing' hippopotamus floats him up a river 'to the land beyond limits' of the imaginative realm, which is also the domain of the ancestors and a place of dreams (Couto 2019).[1] Travelling against the current, it carries also into the interior the skeins of maritime transaction across the Indian Ocean that have, for over a thousand years, been embroidered along the shores of Mozambique, the country in which the story is set.

At the farthest reaches of this ocean, an Aboriginal seafarer likens himself to 'Sinbad the Sailor' as he 'navigates the coastline' (Wright 2006, 334, 333) of his own engulfed country. He comes to land in the wake of a cyclone stirred by the ancestral beings of a world-creating process continuous 'from time immemorial' (7), and which is sometimes translated as 'the Dreaming'. The cyclone has flooded a town established through settler colonialism and shored up with extractive capitalism, and which is named after an imperial circumnavigator. Returning with his grandson, the seafarer, Normal Phantom, turns away from this now deluged 'ghost town' to find his way back 'home', walking 'in mud' to the tune of a 'mass choir of frogs', their 'song wafting off the watery land, singing the country afresh' (336).

Conveying world-making forces at odds with invading and extractive powers, these semi-aquatic and amphibian creatures – a transporting hippopotamus and a chorus of frogs – respectively strike the concluding notes of Mia Couto's short story 'Beyond the River Bend' (1994/2019) and Alexis Wright's epic novel *Carpentaria* (2006). For all the singularity of these works, and the larger oeuvres of the two writers, I propose reading both as exemplary performances of a literary mode that this chapter describes as 'amphibious form'.[2] This reading is motivated by an interest in finding ways of approaching novel forms emanating from the South that inhabit or accommodate more than one cultural biome and that are too often contained in the catch-all category of 'magical realism'. The extent to which this category has come to restrict what Pheng Cheah (2016) helpfully identifies as the 'world-making force' expressed by literatures of the postcolonial South has been widely observed. Not least, as an eminently marketable term, the label of 'magical realism' risks reducing these works to exotic morsels or gold mines of authenticity, making them available through the global circuits of world literature to practices of reading that reiterate the very extractive, appropriative and consuming processes that they challenge.

I am interested in how approaching these forms as *ecotonal* might allow for other ways of thinking with them. An ecological term, 'ecotone' describes a region of transition between biological communities, or biomes. As zones of habitation in which different biomes meet and integrate, ecotones support interaction and adaptation and are therefore often significantly more biodiverse than the individual communities that merge within them. They can, however, also be the signature of disturbance and devastation: a clearing cut into a forest, an abruptly moving shoreline. To approach these fictions as ecotonal, rather than the manifestation of antinomy that is named in 'magical realism', is thus to receive them as zones of enlivening interaction between multiple dimensions of reality, while recognising them also as registers of damage.

Focusing especially on 'amphibious form', this chapter foregrounds zones of interaction between the aquatic and the terrestrial, conceived as both figure and ground or metaphor and materiality. In so doing, it follows a turn to water in the study of Southern print cultures that has been piloted by Isabel Hofmeyr and collaborators.[3] Hofmeyr launched an oceanic turn towards transnational imaginaries and 'multiple inheritances' in southern African scholarship by extending an often land-bound area of enquiry into the fluid domain of an Indian Ocean that she resonantly described as the 'complicating sea' (Hofmeyr 2007, 2012). Her more recent innovation has been to submerge Southern print histories in elemental media studies to investigate 'shore-shaped methods of reading' as she traces the 'hydrocolonial' adventures of the book (Hofmeyr 2022, 15).[4]

This chapter is guided by her signal interventions to consider some of the ways in which forms of textuality that have been generated in the geopolitical and elemental environments of the South might themselves be thought of as 'shore-shaped' or – in the phrasing adopted here – 'amphibious'. It proceeds by bringing the oeuvres of Couto and Wright into contact – not so much in order to add to an already considerable body of scholarship on each as to demonstrate the articulation of a literary mode that is by nature both fluctuant and fractal, and thus to some extent generalisable and iterative across Southern print cultures.[5]

At first blush, the differences between the two writers seem to argue against a reading that not only aspires to comparison but also proposes more boldly to identify an elemental concord between them. This is apposite. One of the things at stake in this chapter is the elaboration of an analytic calibrated to observing the ways in which apparent antinomy blurs into more ambiguous and confounding states – an analytic attuned to inter-elemental dynamics and what we might describe, in a word, as the *muddy*.

The relative positioning of each author is indicative. Defining himself as a 'bridge' who is both 'a white guy and an African', Mia Couto writes from one of the most impoverished countries in the global South under a nom de plume that is received as alternatively female or feline (Couto 2015; Jaggi 2015). Alexis Wright is an Aboriginal woman of the Waanyi nation of the Gulf of Carpentaria, whose ancestry extends into a 'cross-cultural space' that 'stretches' to the Guangdong province of southern China as well as across various species of existence to embrace the living and non-living constituents of Country (Wright 2020, 95).[6] Couto's writing is similarly enlivened by an appreciation of his country as a 'cultural crossroads' in a 'sea of exchanges' (Couto 2015), and by deeply local understandings of the permeability of 'the borders between what is human and not human – what is alive and not alive' (Couto in Jin 2013) – and of the ways in which 'people and things dwell within one indivisible body' (Couto 2015). Writing in a state that is geographically situated in the Southern Hemisphere and enjoys one of the highest living standards in the world, Wright emphasises that although 'Australia, now dominated by its global non-Indigenous population, is included in the economic power division of the Global North', 'Aboriginal people' such as herself share 'more in common with people deemed to be of the Global South geographically and economically' (2020, 97–98).

Couto's and Wright's fictions are also concerned with predicaments that are fundamentally similar and related. For instance, in the novel *Under the Frangipani*, Couto uses the setting of a coastal fort to trace connections between imperial extraction, colonial imprisonment and the jettisoning of the 'guardians' of the 'world of the past' by agents of the postcolonial state who are engaged in an international arms trade that seeds perpetual war (Couto 2001, 53). Wright's magnum opus, in turn, references the fact that First Nations Australians are the most highly incarcerated population on earth and invites readers to think about the relation between these acts of containment and a 'new war on their country' that is displayed in a relentless offshore traffic of 'tankers exchanging mining equipment for mined ore' (Wright 2006, 246, 252). Consuming and befouling what the 'old people' know to be 'sacred country', the alliance that *Carpentaria* exposes between dominant local interests and a multinational mining corporation positions Australia as yet another 'banana state' (260, 255, 267).

It is telling that both Couto and Wright locate these predicaments in coastal settings. Part of the wager of reading them as exemplary practitioners of 'amphibious form' is to propose that they both inhabit and respond to a littoral condition that is to some degree generalisable across the South, even as they evidently write from unique positions within it. In proposing this framework for the study of Southern print cultures, I am inspired by Hofmeyr's (2017) formulation: 'southern by degrees'. This phrasing marks out the Southern Hemisphere as an area of analysis (measured in 'degrees' of latitude). It also implicitly observes a gradated or moderated rather than absolute distinction ('by degrees'). Through this phrasing, then, Hofmeyr helpfully guides the practice of reading from the South out of the conceptually entrapping nature of an absolute North–South binary while still making it possible to register differences that matter.

Two notable material differences that distinguish the South can be located in the littoral. The procedures of imperial invasion, colonial dispossession and global resource extraction that are constitutive of the global South and the war on Indigenous lands alike are, as Hofmeyr has noted, typically 'launched from the littoral' (2019, 12). In addition, a hemispheric difference of oceanic proportions points also to an elemental distinction between North and South: the ratio of sea to land in the Southern Hemisphere is four to one parts, whereas in the Northern Hemisphere it is a mere one-and-a-half to one parts.[7] Engulfed by much vaster bodies of seawater, the land masses of the South are all somewhat littoral in nature.

These two characteristics intersect catastrophically in a climate-changed present in which the populations of the South find themselves increasingly more exposed to storm surges and sea-level rise. This imposed vulnerability is in no small part the result of processes of uneven development that mark a continuity between imperial and global capitalism which has fuelled the complex called the 'Anthropocene': the coastal developments of the South have been expressly designed for the extraction of goods destined to be consumed elsewhere and that return to them disastrously in the form of toxic waste and bad weather.[8]

The fictional town of Desperance in *Carpentaria* has embraced this function while internally reproducing the global division by consigning Aboriginal peoples to the rubbish dump. In something of an 'allegory of the Anthropocene' (see DeLoughrey 2019), the town is ultimately drowned by a cyclone. Accumulating offshore is an island of trash that has been gathered in the backwash and that provides a floating home to the Aboriginal saboteur of a mining enterprise that provoked the force of Country. (Named Will, the saboteur is the son of Norm Phantom and father of the child that Norm delivers back to the 'watery land'.)

Couto's hometown of Beira presents another synecdoche of an all-too-real catastrophe. Providing the unnamed backdrop to 'Beyond the River Bend', Beira is elsewhere described by him as the 'waters of [his] beginning' and credited for inspiring his 'amphibian dreams' (Couto 2015). This city was devastated in 2019 by the arrival of a cyclone that delivered mass destruction and coincided with the publication in English of the collection in which the story appears under the title *Rain and Other Stories*. As with other shores of the global South subsumed in a planetary crisis, Mozambique and its neighbouring states suffered disproportionate loss of life as water swallowed up the hinterland and sucked it out to sea.

These are the improbable and uncanny realities of a time in which fiction seems barely able to keep up with fact, as Amitav Ghosh (2016) has emphasised. This chapter contends that 'amphibious form' provides a literary mode capable of addressing them, and that writers of the South (such as Ghosh himself) are well placed to elaborate its potentialities: whether viewed as planetary position, global periphery and/or structural vulnerability, Southness implies being especially, if not exclusively or exhaustively, concerned with amphibiousness.

Couto and Wright certainly foreground this implication in works derived from their distinct locations. An extraordinary range of terraqueous figures and settings spring from and give shape to their oeuvres. Seashores, islands, rivers, estuaries, lakes, swamps, flood plains and groundwater aquifers abound in these fictions, which are informed by a plethora of amphibious creatures such as fishermen, flamingos, swans and gropers that are said to have walked on land millions of years ago. Narrative duration is often measured in the rhythms of flood and ebb or a seasonal interplay between the Wet and the Dry, while deluge and drought fluctuate between deep time and catastrophic emergencies to author both story and its settings. The most awesome of these forces appears in distinctive but resonant forms in the 'ancient stories' on which Wright and Couto each draw: the ancestral rainbow serpent that describes the amphibious contours of Wright's Gulf Country and the *wamulambo*, or storm snake, that conspires with the guardians of ancient lore against the commerce in arms befouling a land which Couto's fiction presents as a 'balcony' over the Indian Ocean (Couto 2001; Wright 2006).

The action of these prodigious figures in both *Carpentaria* and *Under the Frangipani* is uncannily similar as they wash away the contaminating presence of mines, whether extractive or explosive. (Wright's novel is concerned with the extraction of ore from her country; Couto's with the landmines littering Mozambique, delivering a 'harvest of death' sown by the geopolitics of the Cold War and reactivated in what his subsequent novel, *The Last Flight of the Flamingo*, presents as the deadly circularity of 'the war of business and the business of war' in late capitalist globalism [Couto 2001, 3; 2004, 158]). While both figures are drawn as inherently ambivalent beings that deliver devastation in acts of world-making, their intrusion into the narrative worlds of these creative works also invites reflection on an external reality deranged by the very agents against which they are assembled (Rigby 2015).

The questions towards which I want to direct this enquiry concern the 'affordances' that Southern situations – and particularly those of the Indian Ocean littoral – bring to the 'planetary library' in a context that Ghosh (2016) has evocatively termed 'the great derangement'.[9] Ecological psychologist James Gibson proposed the neologism 'affordance' to name the complementary relation between environment and perceptive creatures, referring specifically to what the environment *provides or furnishes*, either for good or ill' (1986, 127). What, then, does the littoral environment of the South afford the work of creative imagination that Couto and Wright both figure in amphibious beings? And what, in turn, might Southern print cultures afford a planetary imaginary in catastrophic times that cast the earth itself as a littoral writ large, shrinking before the looming spectre of encroaching seas?

These are questions more searching than this short chapter can hope to address. What it ventures are some small and tentative moves towards them. It does so by following the guiding assumption that environment not only translates into Southern print cultures but also actively impresses itself upon the page. Such a conception of the culturally significant and agentive role of what post-Enlightenment thought cast as an external and passive 'nature' is vital across the South, and to Indigenous peoples the world over.[10] This capacity, among others, has enabled cultures of the South and of Indigenous habitation in the North to store and story ways of living with littorals that have been eroded through modernity.

John Gillis points out that the shore has been progressively 'disenchanted' by 'modern notions of linear time and infinite space' that have drawn it as 'edge', thus 'obscur[ing] the reality of its inbetweenness, its ecotonal nature' (2017, 267).[11] This misconception of a fundamentally fluctuant environment has resulted in ruinous coastal developments that are now increasingly vulnerable to surging seas. To use Ghosh's term again, this is a geographic 'derangement' – one closely related to the derangement of print culture that he relates in his study of how the novel form has come to house a rationality that ruinously represses understandings of the dynamic, multidimensional and agentive nature of what it has reduced to an inert 'ground' over which its plots are enacted (Ghosh 2016). His own recent novel, *Gun Island*, draws on the wellspring of 'ancient stories' in search of more responsive and responsible ways of addressing the uncanny realities of these times (Ghosh 2019). Like the narrative of his earlier *The Hungry Tide*, which it revisits and reactivates, *Gun Island* is informed by the dynamism and multidimensionality of littoral environments.

So, too, are the oeuvres of Couto and Wright. Theirs is a form of print culture 'submerge[d] . . . in the realm of orality', and thus able to 'escape the rationality' that inheres in 'the laws of writing', to use the terms Couto employs in describing himself as 'the practitioner of an unbalancing act: to have one foot in each world, that of the text and that of the word' (Couto 2015). Their mode of writing is also, in Wright's resonant words, one that opens to the 'boundless' and 'borderless' condition of the 'imaginative literary mind' while 'counterbalancing' it with responsibility to 'what is going on in your world' (Wright 2020, 92). Transporting the imagination 'beyond the bend in the river', the writings of both Couto and Wright remain alert to the ways in which territorial logics and the currents of global capitalism together shore up particular regions and populations while jettisoning others.

To term this literature 'magical realism' is to deny its capacity to inhabit and describe realities that are inter-elemental and multidimensional, while activating abilities to register and respond to harm.[12] As Couto's and Wright's phrasings suggest, it might be better thought of as ecotonal and amphibious: a writing that is generative of forms adapted to zones of transition – both enlivening and devastated – between the oral and the literate, the oneiric and the rational, the tangible and the intangible, and the visible and invisible. Shaped by the turbulence of non-linear temporalities, it is flooded with the numinous and harbours ontologies that admit permeability between the human and nonhuman, the living and non-living, as well as interior and exterior worlds. As a literary mode that is capable of 'transmitting knowledge' while nourishing 'imaginative possibilities', it extends an ability 'to expand our understanding of how to think through the realities of our future times' (Wright 2019).

This short essay has restricted its focus to the littoral zone, but the more searching enquiry that it proposes into 'amphibious form' would open to broader considerations of the concepts of wetness and dryness that Hofmeyr and her collaborators, Charne Lavery and Sarah Nuttall, have brought into focus in the study of Southern print cultures.[13] Their intervention works to 'resituat[e] the novel in terms of the coming extremities of the Anthropocene, of too little or too much water, conditions exacerbated by the structural conditions of the Global South' (Hofmeyr, Nuttall and Lavery 2022, 318). An enlarged framework of reading for the 'amphibious' might extend from these reflections on Couto's and Wright's fictions to a cultural cartography of the extremities of flood and drought orchestrated in Southern waters by the oscillating systems of El Niño/La Niña and the Indian Ocean Dipole. Like the fluid grounds on which this chapter focuses, these systems structure the terraqueous nature of planetary life in heightened – and now also increasingly deranged – forms while simultaneously marking the contours of an uneven globe.

ACKNOWLEDGEMENT

This chapter contributes to an Australian Research Council–funded project (SR200200704), 'Between Indian and Pacific Oceans: Reframing Australian Literatures'. My thanks to team members Mandy Treagus, Madeleine Seys and Theodora Galanis.

NOTES

1   'Beyond the River Bend'; see also 'The Waters of Time', which opens the collection *Rain and Other Stories* (Couto 2019).
2   See earlier descriptions of this mode as 'coastal form' or an 'amphibian aesthetic' in studies of Couto and Abdulrazak Gurnah that focus specifically on the African Indian Ocean littoral, and my related presentation of 'coastal thought' (Samuelson 2012, 2017, 2020a).
3   See particularly the collaborations with Sarah Nuttall and Charne Lavery (2022) that have produced the special issue on 'Reading for Water' in southern African literatures, and the preparatory reflections on 'Reading in Antarctica' (Hofmeyr and Lavery 2021), along with Hofmeyr's substantial body of work on Indian Ocean print cultures and histories.

4   I use the term 'adventures' advisedly to evoke an etymology of 'arrival': one of Hofmeyr's instructive insights concerns how the colonial custom-house engineers 'dry landings' in order to extend imperial and settler claims to territory.

5   Most of the studies of Couto's fiction have been published in Portuguese, but his oeuvre is also receiving growing recognition in anglophone scholarship. See, inter alia, Hamilton and Huddart (2016), Hofmeyr (2006), Rothwell (2004) and Samuelson (2021). Wright's oeuvre (specifically *Carpentaria*) has received a considerable amount of attention, particularly in Australian literary studies. That which has most informed my reading includes Devlin-Glass (2008), Ng (2018) and Rigby (2015). I want to acknowledge also members of the marvellous cohort of PhD supervisees with whom I have taught and thought about *Carpentaria*: Matthew Couper (who also provided research assistance on the novel), Samuel Cox, Theodora Galanis, Laura Hamilton and Céline Zerna.

6   On the implications of Aboriginal peoples' conceptions of 'Country', see Rose (1996).

7   See Samuelson (2020b); Samuelson and Lavery (2019).

8   See Samuelson (2021) on Couto's Beira, following Ghosh (2016).

9   See Mbembe (2013) on the 'planetary library', along with Spivak's (2003) figure of 'planetarity' as alternative to 'world lit'.

10 See Ghosh (2021).

11 See also Gillis (2012).

12 See also Ghosh's evaluation of the limits of 'magical realism' in addressing the climate crisis: while he welcomes the ways in which 'magical realism' admits the improbable, he concludes that to treat the 'weather events that we are now experiencing . . . as magical . . . would be to rob them of precisely the quality that makes them so urgently compelling – which is that they are actually happening on this earth, at this time' (Ghosh 2016, 27).

13 See Hofmeyr, Nuttall and Lavery (2022); Jones and Lavery (2021); Nuttall (2020).

REFERENCES

Cheah, Pheng. 2016. *What is a World? On Postcolonial Literature as World Literature.* Durham: Duke University Press.

Couto, Mia. 2001. *Under the Frangipani.* Trans. David Brookshaw. London: Serpent's Tail.

———. 2004. *The Last Flight of the Flamingo.* Trans. David Brookshaw. London: Serpent's Tail.

———. 2015. *Pensativities: Selected Essays.* Trans. David Brookshaw. Windsor: Biblioasis. Kindle.

———. 2019. *Rain and Other Stories.* Trans. Eric M.B. Becker. Windsor: Biblioasis. Kindle.

DeLoughrey, Elizabeth. 2019. *Allegories of the Anthropocene.* Durham: Duke University Press.

Devlin-Glass, Frances. 2008. 'A Politics of the Dreamtime: Destructive and Regenerative Rainbows in Alexis Wright's *Carpentaria*'. *Australian Literary Studies* 23 (4): 392–407. https://doi.org/10.20314/als.db10692a2e.

Ghosh, Amitav. 2016. *The Great Derangement: Climate Change and the Unthinkable.* Chicago: University of Chicago Press.

———. 2019. *Gun Island.* London: Hatchette.

———. 2021. *The Nutmeg's Curse: Parables for a Planet in Crisis*. Chicago: University of Chicago Press.

Gibson, James J. 1986. 'Theory of Affordances'. In *The Ecological Approach to Visual Perception*, by James J. Gibson, 127–143. Hillsdale: Lawrence Erlbaum.

Gillis, John R. 2012. *The Human Shore: Seacoasts in History*. Chicago: University of Chicago Press.

———. 2017. 'Afterword: Beyond the Blue Horizon'. In *Coastal Works: Cultures of the Atlantic Edge*, edited by Nicholas Allen, Nick Groom and Jos Smith. Oxford: Oxford University Press.

Hamilton, Grant and David Huddart, eds. 2016. *A Companion to Mia Couto*. London: James Currey.

Hofmeyr, Isabel. 2006. 'Seeing the Familiar: Notes on Mia Couto'. In *Beautiful/Ugly: African and Diaspora Aesthetics*, edited by Sarah Nuttall, 384–391. Durham: Duke University Press.

———. 2007. 'The Black Atlantic Meets the Indian Ocean: Forging New Paradigms of Transnationalism for the Global South – Literary and Cultural Perspectives'. *Social Dynamics* 33 (2): 3–32. https://doi.org/10.1080/02533950708628759.

———. 2012. 'The Complicating Sea: The Indian Ocean as Method'. *Comparative Studies of South Asia, Africa and the Middle East* 32 (3): 584–590. https://doi.org/10.1215/1089201X-1891579.

———. 2017. 'Southern by Degrees: Islands and Empires in the South Atlantic, the Indian Ocean, and the Subantarctic World'. In *The Global South Atlantic*, edited by Kerry Bystrom and Joseph R. Slaughter, 81–96. New York: Fordham University Press.

———. 2019. 'Provisional Notes on Hydrocolonialism'. *English Language Notes* 57 (1): 11–20.

———. 2022. *Dockside Reading: Hydrocolonialism and the Custom House*. Durham: Duke University Press.

Hofmeyr, Isabel and Charne Lavery. 2021. 'Reading in Antarctica'. *Wasafiri* 36 (2): 79–86. https://doi.org/10.1080/02690055.2021.1879501.

Hofmeyr, Isabel, Sarah Nuttall and Charne Lavery, eds. 2022. 'Reading for Water'. Special issue, *Interventions* 24 (3): 303–322.

Jaggi, Maya. 2015. 'Mia Couto: "I am White and African. I Like to Unite Contradictory Worlds"'. *The Guardian*, 15 August.

Jin, Gracie. 2013. 'Q&A with Mia Couto, the Writer Who Just Won the "American Nobel Prize"'. *Mic.com*, 11 April. Accessed 23 November 2019. https://www.mic.com/articles/71373/q-a-with-mia-couto-the-writer-who-just-won-the-american-nobel-prize.

Jones, Stephanie and Charne Lavery. 2021. 'On Water'. *Wasafiri* 36 (2): 1–2. https://doi.org/10.1080/02690055.2021.1879472.

Mbembe, Achille. 2019. 'Thoughts on the Planetary: An Interview with Achille Mbembe'. Interview by Torbjørn Tumyr Nilsen. *Newframe.com*, 5 September. Accessed 13 October 2020. https://www.newframe.com/thoughts-on-the-planetary-an-interview-with-achille-mbembe/.

Ng, Lynda, ed. 2018. *Indigenous Transnationalism: Essays on Carpentaria*. Sydney: Giramondo.

Nuttall, Sarah. 2020. 'Pluvial Time/Wet Form'. *New Literary History* 51 (2): 455–472. https://doi.org/10.1353/nlh.2020.0026.

Rigby, Kate. 2015. *Dancing with Disaster: Environmental Histories, Narratives, and Ethics for Perilous Times*. Charlottesville: University of Virginia Press.

Rose, Deborah Bird. 1996. *Nourishing Terrains: Australian Aboriginal Views of Landscape and Wilderness*. Canberra: Australian Heritage Commission.

Rothwell, Philip. 2004. *A Postmodern Nationalist: Truth, Orality, and Gender in the Work of Mia Couto*. Lewisburg: Bucknell University Press.

Samuelson, Meg. 2012. 'Abdulrazak Gurnah's Fictions of the Swahili Coast: Littoral Locations and Amphibian Aesthetics'. *Social Dynamics* 38 (3): 499–515. http://dx.doi.org/10.1080/02533952.2012.749014.

———. 2017. 'Coastal Form: Amphibian Positions, Wider Worlds and Planetary Horizons on the African Indian Ocean Littoral'. *Comparative Literature* 69 (1): 16–24. http://dx.doi.org/10.1215/00104124-3794569.

———. 2020a. 'Coastal Thought: An Alphabet Spanning the Seas'. *In Borders and Ecotones in the Indian Ocean: Cultural and Literary Perspectives*, edited by Markus Arnold, Corinne Duboin and Judith Misrahi-Barak, 29–52. Montpellier: Presses Universitaires de la Méditerranée. Accessed 23 April 2021. https://books.openedition.org/pulm/6747?lang=en.

———. 2020b. 'The Oceans'. In Handbook of Anglophone World Literatures, edited by Stefan Helgesson, Birgit Neumann and Gabriele Rippl, 375–393. Berlin: De Gruyter. https://doi.org/10.1515/9783110583182-024.

———. 2021. ' "Re-enchanting the World" from Mozambique: The African Anthropocene and Mia Couto's Poetics of the Planet'. In *Transcultural Ecocriticism: Global, Romantic and Decolonial Perspectives*, edited by Stuart Cooke and Peter Denney, 63–81. New York: Bloomsbury Academic. https://dx.doi.org/10.5040/9781350121669.0010.

Samuelson, Meg and Charne Lavery. 2019. 'The Oceanic South'. *English Language Notes* 57 (1): 37–50. https://doi.org/10.1215/00138282-7309666.

Spivak, Gayatri Chakravorty. 2003. 'Planetarity'. In *Death of a Discipline*, by Gayatri Chakravorty Spivak, 71–102. New York: Columbia University Press.

Wright, Alexis. 2006. *Carpentaria*. Sydney: Giramondo. Kindle.

———. 2019. 'The Ancient Library and a Self-Governing Literature'. *Sydney Review of Books*. Accessed 8 July 2019. https://sydneyreviewofbooks.com/essay/the-ancient-library-and-a-self-governing-literature/.

———. 2020. 'A Self-Governing Literature: Who Owns the Map of the World?' *Meanjin* 79 (2): 92–101.

12

Wood and Water:
Resonances from the Indian Ocean

Rimli Bhattacharya

This chapter takes off from some crucial disciplinary break-throughs in Isabel Hofmeyr's work on South Africa and India and the circulation systems of the Indian Ocean world. It also draws on my own experience as a participant in her project Oceanic Humanities for the Global South, particularly a workshop which took place on the Island of Mozambique, or Ilha de Moçambique. I invoke the materiality of the celluloid film; of the tactility of textiles on bodies (and as exchange for human bodies); of ceramics as cargo and ballast, on the ocean floor and as shards washed ashore; and in the signs manifested in the scripts and sounds of vastly different cultures. It is a prelude to putting into words snatches of an ongoing sensorial multimedia project for young people titled Stitching Sails: Rising Oceans.

The intent is 'to factor in this depth of temporalities forged through a longue durée of connection and disconnection, mobility and dislocation' (Hofmeyr 2015, 99), and to take in and act on 'legacies of inequality'

(Hofmeyr 2019b, 2). This precludes a simple reversal of the gaze – from land to sea or from pre-colonial to the colonial-imperial. Wary of distortions caused by templates of 'national literatures', even those from the more 'relational' discipline of comparative literature, the task would be to subsume 'these imaginings' into a 'much longer archive' (Hofmeyr 2015, 99). Perhaps also to fundamentally reconfigure 'the archive', making the arts – songs, dance, installations and cinema – alongside technological developments in satellite imaging and in marine archaeology, more central to our conceptualisation of the movement (and translocation) of plants, people, faiths and technologies, scripts and languages, currency and objects, raw and finished.

My focus is the word – sounded, transcribed, translated, recorded, chanted and sung. I envision the seas and oceans and their enduring but shifting relationship to what are seen as fixed and distinct land masses, across a diachronic and synchronic axis. Beginning with the Bengal Delta, I track the south-eastern maritime path of the Chinese Buddhist pilgrim Fahian.[1] These vignettes are contrapuntally related to the strains of Sufi traditions in Sindh to the west, and thence to Ilha de Moçambique, off the coast of East Africa. In this reflective and exploratory piece, I have sought to articulate new templates of sound, text and image, testing the tension between historical scholarship on print cultures and the myriad microtones of material cultures in movement.[2]

HALF SUBMERGED: IN CELLULOID

We see the face of an adolescent boy – through the intricate patterned openings of a fishing net – yearning to set sail. The boat will move away slowly from his line of vision (figure 12.1). He will not know his father, nor the father him; he has many mothers and yet he has no one. The water calls out to him. One could read this shot from Ritwik Ghatak's (1972) *A River Called Titash* (*Titash Ekti Nadir Naam*; hereafter *Titash*) in multiple ways and not exhaust its resonances within the film and elsewhere.

Figure 12.1: Through the net: a still from Ritwik Ghatak's film *A River Called Titash*. We meet the wide-eyed gaze of the boy (Ananta), his palm outstretched, looking through a fishing net hung up to dry. He is the witness, evoking a recurrent image of boats moving away, their sails unfurled. (© Ritwak Ghatak)

For Ghatak, water is shape-shifting and almost never inseparable from land and vegetation, permeating rituals of fertility, death and regeneration.[3] His student, filmmaker Kumar Shahani, sees Ghatak's ouevre as 'epic-melodramatic', moving between myth and history: capturing and, at crucial moments, swerving away resolutely from naturalistic details into montages of sound and evocation of space (Shahani [1995] 2015). Ghatak's film evolved from the eponymously titled novel by Adwaita Mallaburman ([1956] 1993), recording the slow death of a traditional fishing community.[4] But his black-and-white film bears the aftershocks of the 1947 Partition of the land between independent India and newly created East Pakistan, the unending 'dismemberment and the displacement', and the subsequent fratricidal birth of Bangladesh in 1971.[5]

At the end of *Titash*, the stark shots of a woman stumbling along the dunes of a dried-up river mark a primordial return to digging for that last drop of water before death. Fifty years later, the film becomes an ecological epic of a deltaic region in geomorphic time. The exquisite sensuousness of satellite imagery captures its present precarity (figure 12.2).

Historians remind us there was no political region called 'Bengal' prior to AD 1200. The term *Vanga* indicated the central part of deltaic Bengal as we know it now. And the term *vangasagara* is possibly the oldest indigenous name found in inscriptions for the eastern part of the Indian Ocean (Chakravarti [2002] 2020a).[6] The Gangetic delta, the largest in the world, along with its numerous wayward flooding rivers, all 'oriented' seawards, makes it impossible to separate the coast from the interior, and rivers from the sea (Chakravarti [2002] 2020a, 117). In this fluvial world, deltaic ports of trade rose, flourished and silted up – Tamralipti,[7] Chandraketugarh, Samandar, Saptagram, Chattogram and

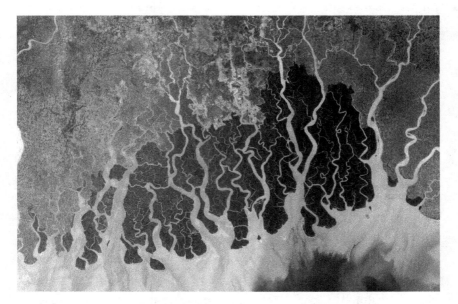

Figure 12.2: Delta, Bay of Bengal, from space. This satellite image reveals the veins and capillaries of the ever-changing riverine world of the delta. (Courtesy of NASA)

others – curving along the Arakan arch of the eastern Indian Ocean (Berthet 2020).[8]

Adding to the region's shifting maritime frontier and course-changing rivers is a rather unique history of sedentarisation. With the coming of Islam from AD 1200, most intriguing is the role of charismatic Sufis (mystics) who initiated a slow eastward and southward movement leading their converted followers to the clearing of forests and the reclamation of land for agriculture, thus creating 'wet-rice cultivating' peasant communities and an 'expanding agrarian frontier' (Eaton [2019] 2020, 363; see also Eaton 1993). This longue durée finds a visionary expression in Akhteruzzaman Elias's ([1996] 2021) novel *Khwabnama* (Narrative of Dreams), which I have elsewhere described as 'a translator's delta', revealing the political undercurrents of undivided Bengal in the 1940s (Bhattacharya 2009, forthcoming).

After centuries of 'being a home to international Buddhism' (Ray [1959] 1994, 578), Bengal became a land of religious heterodoxy with numerous movements against Brahmanical Hinduism, the most significant being Vaishnavism, which had complex overlaps with regional variants of Islam. Both have a rich repertoire of performance practices, of poetry sung with music and even dance constituting worship, practised by wandering minstrels (*bauls* and *fakirs*) in seasonal and annual congregations of fairs and the like, up to our present (Chakraborty 2001).

The literary ecology of the active delta is both fluid and expansive. Instead of classic Western sea fiction 'promoting the romance of maritime manliness' (Hofmeyr 2021, 12), one finds archetypes such as that of *naukadubi* – the bride lost on or immediately after the wedding night, abducted by river pirates from the womb-like hold of the boat covered with planks swaying in the river, as in *Titash*.

The monsoon shimmers across the entire subcontinent, intertwining the sacred and the erotic. The *bhatiali* song (from *bhata*, 'ebbing tide'), with its distinctive 'gait' (*chalan*) and protracted calling out across the water, is probably the most musically evocative of riparian forms.[9] Others, like the *baramasa* or *baramasi* (Dasgupta 2000), are more than a 'peasant calendar', complemented by musical forms in Northern India (Vaudeville 1986).[10] Stylised yet colloquial, they are pierced by the leit-motif of *viraha* (longing in separation, in awaiting the beloved), familiar to us from many strands of medieval *bhakti* (devotional) poetry, as well as in later traditions in which the poet takes on a female persona (Alam 2003). As travellers were dependent on sailing in the direction of the monsoon winds, 'waiting' for the return voyage would be experienced quite differently by the male merchant or slaves, as the case may be.[11]

Enmeshed in words, the writer-scholar-translator stands partly submerged, longing to voyage into the ocean – one of the many rising oceans of our planet.[12]

THREE MOMENTS: FAHIAN'S *BUDDHIST RECORDS OF THE WESTERN WORLD (FO GUO JI)*

It is rare to find an elderly pilgrim-scholar who, for fourteen years, treks across a terrifying desert in Asia, crosses mountain passes and braves dangerous sea voyages before returning home with treasured Buddhist scriptures (Sen 2006). The arc of the Chinese monk Fahian's travels on land and water is wondrous (see figure 12.3).

The voyage out of India and homewards is sea-based and via much-used ports. After visiting and residing in sites and cities sacred to the Buddha, the monk and his companion travel down the River Ganga and come first to Champa. Then, continuing eastward, they arrive at 'the kingdom of Tamralipti', located 'at the sea-mouth'. Fahian stays here for two years, 'writing out copies of the sacred books (*sutras*) and drawing image-pictures'. Then, 'putting to sea, they proceeded in a south-westerly direction, catching the first fair wind of the winter season. They sailed for fourteen days and nights and arrived at the country of the lions (Simhala)' (Beal 1884, lxxi).[13]

Fahian says little about the 'great merchant vessel' he boards or its cargo, unlike some of his fellow monks who later came through the same port (Manguin 2011). Rich epigraphic records compensate for the silence

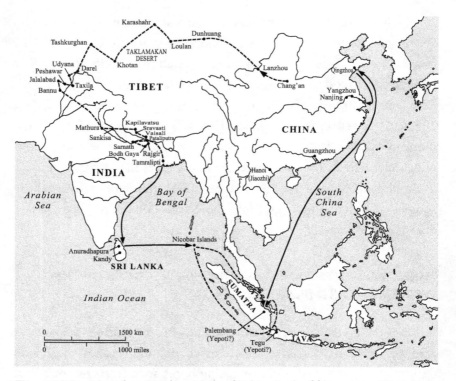

Figure 12.3:   Map showing the travels of Fahian in the fifth century AD. Setting off from Chang'an and trekking across northern China, and then across the Taklamakan Desert and through Central Asia, Fahian enters India from the Hindu Kush mountains into the Buddhist heartland. He leaves the country via the sea route from the delta, following the eastern coast. After a stopover in Ceylon (Sri Lanka), he returns to his homeland through the seas of South Asia. (Courtesy of Tansen Sen)

in the *Records* on this score. Given the 'flourishing agrarian economy' of the region, his ship may have been carrying paddy and/or 'excellent cotton textiles' – the 'Gangetic muslin' unique to the region, noted by Pliny (Chakravarti [2002] 2020a, 119). Chakravati flags another remarkable 'item of transit trade': horses from Central Asia, which travelled down the Ganga from the north-west to 'deltaic Bengal' (120). Horses had double-pronged destinations: 'the Malay peninsula, as also further south to Tamilakam along a coastal voyage'. Bengal's contact with maritime South East Asia grew from 'early medieval times' (Chakravarti [2002] 2020a, 181).

The terracotta seals and sealings excavated in lower Bengal provide evidence in image and in mixed scripts (Kharoshti-Bhrahmi) 'of grains in maritime voyages' depicting stylised paddy stalks on a ship with inscriptions that mention the 'ship in question'; or, more dramatically, the profile of a horse against a masted ship and human figure, probably a handler of Scythian origin (Chakravarti [2002] 2020a, 120, 119). Seals have long been records of trade movement and revenue for goods travelling across land and sea, and 'the very act of sealing, even if for the protection of trade goods, was also a religious act in the old days' (Kosambi [1956] 1975, 79).

Fahian might have sailed along the Arakan coastline and onward to Mallaca, as would I-Jing, who journeyed to India and back to China by sea (Paine 2015);[14] but he chooses to go to Simhala (Ceylon/Sri Lanka), where Theravada Buddhism was already a state religion (Thapar 2013a). Located like a teardrop in the Indian Ocean, Ceylon had long had trade links with West Asia and Africa on the one hand and with East and South East Asia on the other. What Charles Holcombe calls 'the commercial vectors of early Buddhism' were in place (1999, 280). Soon the export of Buddhism would create 'a demand for "holy things" – incense, icons and other religious materials – which exceeded the earlier secular traffic in elite luxury goods' (Holcombe 1999, 281; see also Sen 2006).

In her introduction to *Dockside Reading: Hydrocolonialism and the Custom House*, Hofmeyr (2021) shows, often tongue in cheek, how in the colonial port city 'the hermeneutical practices of the dockside were shaped by an intimate interaction with objects and their accompanying logistic grammars'. There is 'endless correspondence' among customs examiners about objects, and they argue 'endlessly' about 'how they should be defined' and, accordingly, taxed or allowed in or not (Hofmeyr 2021, 6). How might things have been perceived or held (physically and metaphorically) in a much earlier era of sea travel? Might an object be bestowed with a profound significance that neither words nor numbers can encompass?

I highlight three moments in the *Records* that have to do with the multivalence of objects or objectification. Immediately following a detailed glowing account of the hall in Abhaygiri-*vihara* or monastery in Simhala (Thapar 2013a), which has a huge jasper statue of Buddha, comes a rare subjective passage:

> Fa-Hian had now been absent many years from the land of Han . . . *All at once*, as he was standing by the side of this jasper figure, he beheld a merchant present to it as a religious offering a white taffeta fan of Chinese manufacture. *Unwittingly* [Fahian] gave way to his sorrowful feelings, and tears flowing down filled his eyes. (Beal 1884, lxxiii; emphasis added)

He happens to witness an offering – probably also an item of trade – and it triggers the third 'breakdown moment' that Fahian permits himself to record. The first, cited in a highly condensed reference, was when he lost his travelling companion on the overland route to India, at the Pamir Mountains.[15] 'Caressing him', he 'exclaims in piteous voice'; but 'he again exerted himself' to cross over to the south of the range (Beal 1884, xxxvi). The second is when he mourns the absence of Buddha as he visits places that the latter had frequented: he is 'melancholy' but does not weep (xlv).

As a devout Buddhist, Fahian was visiting the homeland of his faith; like other monks, he often referred to China as a 'borderland' indicating its distance from the Buddhist homeland (Sen 2003).[16] Standing beside the jasper Buddha is possibly the only time when the monk acknowledges his intense homesickness, listing some of the more obvious manifestations: the strangeness of people, customs, trees and landscape. Was it not also an aural landscape that he missed, the tonal language, so different from the Pali, Sanskrit and Sinhala (speech and chants) he immersed himself in, and all the innumerable tongues *and* musical modes he must have heard at every stage of his journey?[17] Was it not only the food that was strange, but also the very mode of eating – with chopsticks, not fingers (Sen 2006)? All the spices of the world may not have seduced this monk into forgetting the cuisine, however frugal, he had grown up with. He had already lost, at different stages, his travelling companions. Was it memories of his mother, with whom he had shared a close bond as a young monk? We are left to imagine the tangible manifestations of this trigger. For, immediately after this shot of the weeping monk, the narrator seamlessly takes up again the description of the grand place from where he had left off.

Fahian sets sail again after two years of studying and 'copying' in Simhala. He is a collector par excellence, relentlessly 'obtaining copies in the original language' not only of the *Vinaya-pitaka* (Rules for monks), his primary objective, but of miscellaneous Buddhist texts of diverse schools, still unknown in China (Beal 1884, lxxix–lxxx). Often, when he wants to 'copy down' a discourse that has impressed him, his interlocutor responds: 'This has no scripture-original; I only repeat by word of mouth (what I have learned)' (lxxix). Although there was already a strong scribal tradition among the different schools of Buddhism (Thapar 2013a), the reliance on script as 'record' was different in the subcontinent.

The text as a record of 'the original', and also as a physical object from which translations will be made into Chinese, acquires another dimension in a dramatic event that takes place in a later phase of the punctuated voyage home. Their 'large merchant vessel' (along with a smaller emergency vessel) sets sail from Simhala with the monsoon wind. Sailing eastwards (towards the Straits of Malacca), it runs against a typhoon and, as it springs a leak, a shipwreck is imminent. A fairly common strategy in these circumstances was to jettison the cargo.[18] As the fearful merchants cast away their 'heavy goods', Fahian, too, tosses away the two items that monks were permitted to carry, his ewer and his water pitcher. The real fear is that the merchants will insist on throwing overboard *his* precious cargo – the 'sacred books and images' (icons) (Beal 1884, lxxx). There is no recourse but praying to Guanyin (Perceiver of Sound), who would become a female bodhisattva in Chinese and other Asian forms of Buddhism, from the feminine and compassionate iconography of the male being Avalokitesvara in India.[19] 'As the patron bodhisattva of mariners', Avalokitesvara gave 'the faithful courage to confront the inevitable perils of distant voyages' (Holcombe 1999, 280–281).[20]

A second sea disaster on the last leg of Fahian's journey to China has a group of Brahmins (hostile to Buddhism) marking out the monk himself as 'inauspicious' and threatening to abandon him at 'the next island' (Beal 1884, lxxxi). Was Fahian considered a 'bad omen' for the relics he was carrying? The value given to the relic proposes a different notion of the body and temporality: 'The Buddhist veneration of a bodily relic contrasts with brahminical practice . . . death was a source of impurity . . . Maintaining continuity through an artifact with the person who has died suggests historical continuity, hence the *stupas* [Buddhist shrines containing relics]' (Thapar 2013b, 333).

The concluding sentence of the *Records* suggests that it was written down primarily from memory: 'Having been preserved by divine power . . . he was further induced to commit to writing these records of his travels, desiring that honourable readers might be informed of them as well as himself' (Beal 1884, lxxxiii). Fahian carefully notes even what he has forgotten.

DESERT, SEA AND RIVER: SHAH ABDUL LATIF'S *SURS*

'Stay beside the sailors' anchor cable, woman, in case they raise anchor and leave you, casting your heart into distress' goes the opening verse from the Sufi composer Shah Abdul Latif's *Sur Samundi* (Latif 2018, 131).[21] Part of the monumental *Shah jo Risalo* (the Message of the Shah), *Sur Samundi* in its very title brings together the sailor (*samundi*) and the melody (*sur*). Its birthplace is Sindh, with its long history of maritime commerce and overland invasions; it is also home to Mohenjo-daro, an urban civilisation contemporaneous with Mesopotamia, with whom Sindh had trading ties, as it did with the island of Bahrain (Kosambi [1956] 1975; Pedersen 2015).[22]

The decline of the Indus/Harappan civilisation has now been definitively attributed to migrating monsoons, proof of which has been found in 'tiny single-celled ocean organisms called forminifera' in the bed of the Arabian Sea.[23] The monsoons slowly migrated eastwards, impacting the annual flooding and rich silt deposits that had enabled agriculture. Aridification set in, a process described by contemporary scientists as 'an unprecedented scale of hydroclimatic stress' (Giosan et al. 2012, E1693).

Mohenjo-daro had stood on the bank of the Indus, 'which has also changed its course, due probably to the continued rise of the Himalayas, with slight consequent tilting of the plains' (Kosambi [1956] 1975, 54–55). As to why 'it was the Indus alone that could develop a great urban civilisation when the rest of the country . . . eked out a precarious livelihood by food-gathering', Kosambi observes: 'Clearly, the river by itself does not suffice. The common factor of the earliest riparian urban cultures is that the rivers concerned flow through a desert [so there would be] no heavy forests to clear' (57).

The Indus entered chronological history with Alexander's invasion in 326 BC.[24] Fahian, on his overland entry to India, recorded crossing it twice. Latif is a mystic poet who internalises the terrain – the desert, the sea and the river.[25] *Sriraga* and *Samundi* (Latif 2018) are the two sections in which the maritime world of the region is transformed into the plaint of the thirsting soul. The allusive elements of his spiritual love, articulated as much in words as in the *sur* (with all its microtones), only heightens the elemental quality of the seafaring merchant's travails and triumphs and the intense longing of the woman left behind. The seafarers are called *vanjarin*, loosely translated as 'gypsies' or 'nomads', and used interchangeably for sea and land, reminiscent of the Indonesian term *orang-laut* (the people of the sea) and Kenneth Hall's 'nomads of the Southern Ocean' (2011, 5).

The two sections where land and the 'the deep ocean' are juxtaposed are different in their *sur* and subjective positions. In *Sriraga*, Latif urges his listeners to be forever on alert in traversing the 'turbulent waters', the 'dark whirlpools' and, more graphically, the leaking planks that might destroy the precious cargo of 'cloves, cardamom, fine clothes and lustrous pearls'. There is even a sigh of relief that the merchants 'were not stopped by the customs officers' (Latif 2018, 123). The seafarers and their journey are imagined from the perspective of those left behind: 'After crossing the salty sea, they returned on to the sweet waters of the river' (57). *Samundi* is *viraha*-based, foregrounding through the woman's subjectivity the anguish of separation (from the divine), and the various offerings made to the ocean for the safety of loved ones.

Islam entered Sindh as early as the seventh century but took root much later. Comparing it to Bengal, Richard Eaton argues: 'A similar combination of peasantization and Islamization occurred in the western Punjab, a process that began in the thirteenth century [with the sedentarisation of Jat pastoralists] but not complete until the eighteenth' ([2011] 2020, 366). The slow spread made for a 'tolerant and syncretic population' with unorthodox practices and pre-Islamic beliefs (Sorley 1966, 166). H.T. Sorley notes the immense popularity of shrines dedicated to holy men and the cult of a water god, specifically of the Indus.[26] Latif was influenced by the traditions of wandering yogis and had himself been a great traveller in his youth (Shackle 2018). His compositions absorb the lore of lovers, of passionate women on tragic trysts, celebrated in ballads and other forms that are popular across Punjab. Sindh and Baluchistan are 'identifiable with local geography' (Huang 2022, 179). Latif's heroines are wanderers too, prepared to risk all for love. They celebrate the beauty of the divine that may be found in signs of nature and in the seasons.

Along with this visceral submersion in the topography of a large region, Latif would have internalised at least three distinct and yet overlapping traditions of language and music, emblematised in the three texts that are said to have inspired him: the Quran in Arabic, Rumi's *Masnavi* in Persian, and the verses of his ancestor Shah Karim, composed and subsequently written down in Sindhi (Shackle 2018).[27]

For Latif, the word is fused with *sur*, or melody and tonality. Christopher Shackle (2018) emphasises the prevalence of a literary Persianate culture in the region and the presence of Arabic (from centuries of trade) in which Sindhi poetry grew. Sorley (1966), meanwhile, notes the overlaps with Balochi and other variants such as Siraiki. Pei-Ling Huang makes an impassioned case for 'multilingual *surs*' that live in the *ragi-faquir* as 'performer . . . moving beyond the borders of nation states and connect[ing] the sonic landscapes of Sind and Rajasthan' (2022, 173). She alerts us to the need to move 'between musical lessons and manuscripts' for 'even the non-Sindhi *surs* hint at the historical movements of devotees and musicians' (168).

Latif would sing his verses to the accompaniment of musicians whom he guided (Asani 2003). This mode of transmission is likened to the genre of the *malfuzat* (oral discourses), where records are made by disciplines of the words, actions and sayings of their chosen masters. 'Recording' therefore has many valences in this tradition. Not only were the verses composed at different stages of Latif's lifetime; they are poetry as song and open to variation and improvisation, as is most music in the subcontinent. The movement between desert, sea and river in his songs infuses our definitions of the literary with resonances of the 'vast ocean' – its materiality and its metaphysics.

WOOD, WATER AND PEOPLE: ILHA DA MOÇAMBIQUE

Forts need vantage points. The Fort of São Sebastião, in Stone Town on Ilha de Moçambique, is spectacularly located (see figure 12.4). As we walk up to the huge wooden doorway (though nothing as huge as Akbar's Buland Darwaza in Fatehpur-Sikri), why should I be surprised or excited at the sight of the lotus flowers and elephants carved high above me on the wooden frame?

Figure 12.4: Looking out from the Fort of São Sebastião. The curving grey stone rampart of the fort unfolds to the right, with dense vegetation on the beach below. The tip of the coast extends leftwards into the ocean. (Photo by Rimli Bhattacharya)

We learn that the fort itself was built at the end of the sixteenth century, modelled on Renaissance military fortresses constructed to withstand heavy artillery. The doorway, however, dates to the eighteenth century, and the carvings were made by woodworkers from Portuguese

Goa.[28] The eye soon travels to the columns on the window: they recall traditional Rajasthani/Mughal *jali* work.

The next day, inside the former governor's large mansion, now converted into a museum, I come across a heavy wooden reclining chair, majestic in its proportions, with scenes from the *Ramayana* all along the ornately carved back. (Did the imperial Catholic rulers not worry about the idolatry of the figures? Or did they perhaps see it as simply ornamental?)

The wood for many of the Indian Ocean frigates that sailed between Portugal, India and Mozambique 'came from 3,000 teak trees in the forests of Nagar Avely [Haveli]' (Paine 2000, cited in Duarte 2012, 71).[29] Not all wood came from elsewhere: for example, the timbers from a submerged slave wreck like the *São José* were made of 'extremely rare hardwood only found near Mozambique Island' (Lavery 2020, 272).

The performance that evening took us to a completely different part of the small island that from colonial times had been demarcated for the locals. The terrain is stony and steep, water hard to find: it is called the *macuti* town (Maculuve 2020). I would have to listen and learn more before I could begin to unfold my many responses to the performance by an elderly member of the Rifa'iyya Sufi Order called Maulide Nakira and some of his students (see Maculuve 2020). It was like a stirring, if one may call it that, of wanting to experience and historicise in ways yet unknown to me. So, too, my mixed feelings about the shards of Chinese pottery appearing on the beaches of the Ilha de Moçambique, which the islanders turn into earrings to be sold to us tourists. In the few days that I was on the Ilha, the ocean was transforming from what I could see and feel to what I could sense it has borne through centuries of coming and going, through wind and waves, of people and products.

Pedro Machado's (2004) work on the Gujarati merchants and financiers who were partners with Portuguese buyers of ships (brigs) brings out in different ways the crucial connection between the cotton cloth trade and slavery. The Gujarati merchants and traders 'preferred transporting slaves from the Ilha to the Cape in three weeks rather than the much longer passage to Brazil (90 days)' (Machado 2004, 24). A fair number, captured from the interior of Mozambique, were transported across the waters to western India.[30] The fabric connection continues: specially commissioned fabric for Tufo dancing is still being shipped from India (Arnfred 2004; *Praia Morremone* 2017).

The period mentioned by Machado overlaps with another kind of slavery emerging in the Bay of Bengal. Rila Mukherjee writes about the 'physically active delta and the fluvial changes from the 16th to 18th centuries' (2017, 157) which coincided with the emergence of new land in the form of sandbanks as well as the growth of powerful Portuguese–Arakanese (Magh) slave-raiding networks from the early seventeenth century onwards. All three activities – 'piracy, salt trading and slave sourcing' – were made easier by the numerous inland waterways (165).[31]

Several artists have found ways of seeing the Indian Ocean world and shaping that vision into the distinctive materiality of their métier. Lavanya Mani (2020) finds a quizzical contemplative language through the messy process and the marvellously wrought colours of natural dyes. In her composite titled *Fables* (2007), she uses paint, appliqué and machine embroidery on cotton to lay out in grids the signs and emblems of nature and commerce across waters: each singular within its square. Line drawings contain global histories, as in the blooming cotton flower (figure 12.5).

In Mani's *Traveller's Tales – Vasco Da Gama* (2005), flags, pennants and ensigns, 'participating in the language of the sea' (Hofmeyr 2019a, 4), come alive in the much bigger set of hangings (60" × 65") with rough edges: dense black, fluid orange and warm greens jostle the textured terrain of cloth, intersected by the lines of the compass.

Kumar Shahani has variously invoked the seas as an integral actor in his cinematic compositions, creating with cameraman K.K. Mahajan what has been described as 'free camera choreography': Kelucharan Mohapatra dancing on the Odisha sea coast in *Bhavantarana* (Immanence) (Shahani 1991), and their visit to Konarak, one of the many coastal temples on

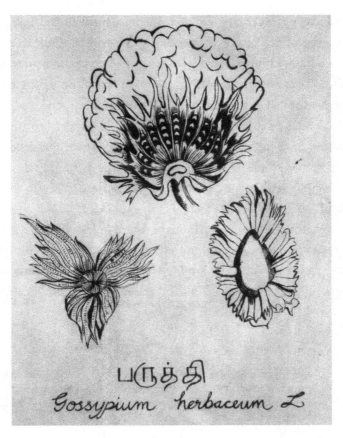

Figure 12.5: The motif and leitmotif of cotton: original artwork by Lavanya Mani. Hand-painted flower, sepal and seed on cotton, using fermented iron mordant on myrobalan tannin, with the inscription *Gossypium herbaceum* (Latin) and the Tamil name *parutti* (in Tamil script). (Courtesy of Lavanya Mani)

India's east coast (Sharma 2015). In *Bansuri* (Bamboo Flute) (Shahani 2000), the ephemeral yet enduring relationship forged between muscle, memory and music pulses in a dynamic sequence of fishermen setting off on a catamaran off the Chennai coast. The microtones of the *raga* played by flautist T. Viswanathan (from sound archives) merge with the fiercely shifting tonalities of waves and sky: the 'haptic eye' (Jayamanne 2015, 187) captures those unique moments in the many millennia of humans fishing in the open seas.[32]

In the early twenty-first century, in the seabed of the Indian Ocean off the coast of Sri Lanka, a wreck was discovered. Quite fittingly, two fishermen had fathomed it. Subsequently known as the Godavaya wreck (Carlson, Koyagasioglu and Willis 2015), radiocarbon dating places it at the first century BC or the first century AD, making it the oldest known shipwreck in the Indian Ocean. Of the objects resting on the sea floor, most fascinating for me were the four stone querns and several 'cylindrical grinding stones'. A saddle quern had been found in each house of the ancient settlement of Mohenjo-daro, presumably to grind flour (Kosambi [1956] 1975, 59).

As for cylindrical grinding stones: they are not mysterious at all. I, too, have used one, although I am not as adept as were my grandmothers at grinding spices and cereals. We are yet to fathom how many stories of our planet lie beneath the waters and the invisible skeins that link them to our everyday life.

ACKNOWLEDGEMENTS

I am grateful to all who made this article possible in different ways: the editors of this volume, Adrienne van Eeden-Wharton, Anibal Goth, Kumar Shahani, Lavanya Mani, Tansen Sen, Taposhi Ghoshal, Tazeen Ali, Uttara Shahani, and Isabel Hofmeyr, who invited me to be part of her Indian Ocean world.

NOTES

1   Although 'China did not belong, at least geographically, to the Indian Ocean World, her links with South and West Asia had to be maintained via South-East Asia' (Chakravarti [2002] 2020a, 162). Fahian is a pioneering Buddhist monk taking the maritime route home to China, anticipating the synergic relationship between trade and religion that would affect subsequent and diverse trade and migration histories of this region. Pierre-Yves Manguin has recorded 'the linguistic ground of common seafaring technology' between the South East Asian and the Bay of Bengal traditions (2011, 609–610).

In recent decades, the soft-power appeals of cultural icons and versions of history have become crucial in the competing geostrategic interests of nation states in the Indian Ocean world. China has deployed Buddhism across a range of media, monuments and institutions (Ramachandran 2019). Sri Lanka has deployed Buddhism to buttress ethno-nationalism in policies and films (Silva 2022). State-supported corporate/neo-colonial 'interests' of both China and India across Africa need little elaboration.

2   To summarise the methodology underlining these sections: Following Fernand Braudel (1972), historians of other regions make a strong case for the dynamic inter-action between the land and the sea. In riverine regions, they propose a compara-tive study of 'ancient ports, whether located near or on the coast or situated in the interior on the banks of rivers' (Chakravarti [2002] 2020a, 143).

3   The immersion (*visarjan*) of the mother goddess Durga after celebrating her annual return to her 'natal home' often takes place with the idol poised between two boats that slowly move away from one another. In Bombay, the idol of Ganesha is submerged in the sea. In her article on Durban, Isabel Hofmeyr describes the waters around the port being filled with 'the remains of ritual paraphernalia from religious festivals' of many different faiths brought to South Africa by indentured labourers and other immigrants (2019a, 10–11). I was struck by the ritual 'immersion' of the Muharram *taziya* in Durban, given that in most parts of India, select parts of the *taziya* are given a symbolic burial (Khalid Fayaz, personal com-munication) while most of it is stored for the next year (Arjumand Ara, personal communication).

4   *A River Called Titash* is one of many riverine novels in Bangla. Two other classics include *The Boatman of the Padma* (Bandyopadhyay [1936] 2012) and *Restless Waters of the Ichhamati* (Bandyopadhyay [1950] 2018).

5   'Ghatak . . . enacted the tearing sensation of schism formally . . . in his radical use of music and sound . . . in his rigorous, ultramodern editing style' (Martin 2013). He made a cinematic departure in creating a 'third space' between sound and the visual (Stubblefield 2006).

6   Later, the Arabs would call it the *bahr Harkal* (or Harkand), derived from Harikela, located in south-eastern present-day Bangladesh. Written and often illustrated Arab accounts (fantastic tales, geographical treatises and travelogues) abound from the tenth century onwards (Chakravarti [2002] 2020a).

7   Tamralipti, also known as Tamralipta, is now called Tamluk and has moved about 90 km inland; Chattogram was known as Chittagong in British India.

8   Berthet holds that the triad of three mighty rivers, the Ganga–Brahmaputra–Meghna (GBM), 'represents arguably the widest river navigable system in the world accessible from a delta' (2020, 267). Elsewhere, Berthet has argued that 'the northern Bay of Bengal as a nodal region where networks across the Indian Ocean and from Central Asia to China congregate seems the most appropriate for studying its trade and shipbuilding' (2015, 180).

9   For a collection of *bhatiali* songs by one of its most eminent exponents, Hemango Biswas (1912–1987), see https://www.youtube.com/watch?v=uiIUfgWovXs (accessed 17 July 2022). Many boating and fishing castes were accomplished performers of drums and wind instruments (*shanai*) (Berthet 2020).

10 *Baramasa/Baramasi* is the name of the genre and literally means 'twelve months'; the verses refer to the changing season and vegetation of each month of the year.

11 Travellers have written about slaves imprisoned in 'the slave yards' on the island being permitted to 'dance in the evenings' as they waited for the 'right wind' before being shipped to their destinations (Maculuve 2020, 265–266).

12 See https://www.facebook.com/bbcnews/videos/the-sinking-islands-of-sundarbans/543650633716261/ (accessed 18 November 2021).

13　Fahian's own accounts of his travels, translated by George Beal (1884), were written in the third person.

14　I-Jing (635–713) features as a protagonist in a recent Chinese state-sponsored docuseries to establish China's antecedents as a maritime power across the globe: 'Tales from the Silk Road of the Sea' (CGTN 2019, Episode 1). Episode 5 spotlights Chinese businessmen in Madagascar 'clothing the natives' (22:00–26).

15　See Andy Isaacson, 'Pamir Mountains, the Crossroads of History', *New York Times*, 17 December 2009.

16　On 'the borderland complex', see (Sen 2006, 30).

17　Shall we call it 'language sickness'? I experienced it most acutely as student of Mandarin Chinese in Taiwan during my sojourn of about a year in the mid-1980s (no internet). I had no access to Bangla, Hindi or Asomiya – the Indian languages I had grown up with.

18　John Keay (2005) cites an instance, from an account by a ninth-century Persian sea captain of a fleet of three large ships with 1 200 men, where nothing could be saved because they waited too long to jettison the cargo.

19　As the author of a comprehensive study on Guanyin writes, 'I was interested in how an imported Buddhist savior succeeded in becoming one of the most important Chinese deities, and also in how he was domesticated and transformed into the "Goddess of Mercy"' (Yü 2010, ix).

20　My chapter has focused on the peripatetic, the sailor and the nomad-turned-peasant. Fahian was a free agent in many ways: he had not been conscripted or bought and sold; neither had he set off for 'Buddhist lands' under royal decree, nor had he been forced to migrate for economic or political reasons, as would indentured labourers in colonial times.

21　A moving rendering of *Sur Samundi*, accessible to listeners who cannot attend/partici-pate in musical concerts at Shah Abdul Latif's shrine, is by Abida Parveen (2019b), the Sindhi singer from Pakistan. (For another rendering, see Parveen [2019a]).

22　'Indian copper was taken by sea to the island of Bahrein (Tilmun) for exchange with commodities brought by a special group of traders' (Kosambi [1956] 1975, 59–60). Seals from Mesopotamia and Harappa were found in Bahrain (Pedersen 2015).

23　See 'Why Did an Entire Civilisation Vanish?', a BBC Reel (2019) by Elise Hugus and Daniel Cajanu. ('Die out' might be more appropriate than 'vanish'.)

24　Alexander had hoped to sail back from Sindh, although ultimately that did not happen. According to Strabo, 'Alexander's fleet was built of Himalayan timber floated down the Beas river' (cited in Kosambi [1956] 1975, 67).

25　In the section called 'Dahar', Latif laments 'the old riverbed' where once there was a prosperous habitation (2018, 575).

26　Sorley mentions the cult of Khwajo Khizr, also known as the Zinda Pir or living saint, who is regarded as 'the patron saint of waters in general but regarded as the god of the river Indus' (1966, 169).

27　The Sindhi language has had as many as thirteen script systems over the course of centuries, with distinctive cursive hands being confined to specific religious and or trading castes (Asani 2003). Shah Latif's verses were written down in the Perso-Arabic script. After Independence/Partition, Sindhis who came to India chose Devanagari. Kosambi makes the interesting observation that 'in later India, not only every part of the country, but every century developed its own characteristic script, whereas the Indus script shows no variation from the earliest to the latest discovered strata' ([1956] 1975, 66).

28   Ricardo T. Duarte, Ilha da Moçambique, voice recording by the author on 14 June 2019.

29   Now a union territory between the states of Gujarat and Maharashtra.

30   A 1938 Gujarati novel, Gunvantrai Acharya's *Dariyalal* (the local name for the Indian Ocean) is a rare text from India that fictionalises this history. The presence of African slaves in India is held to be as early as the third century AD, 'shipped' by Arab traders to India (Campbell 2008).

31   Records (rather, impressions) of the maritime activities of other European powers are found in unlikely places, such as images of Dutch ships (and cannons) on the panels of terracotta temples in Bengal (Chakravarti 2020b).

32   Shahani has long nurtured a film he described in 'The Cotton Project: Proposal for a Cinematic Exploration' ([1992] 2015). He was awarded a grant from the UNESCO World Decade for Cultural Development (1994) and the Jawaharlal Nehru Fellowship (1993–1995). He continues to work on it, as he awaits funding to realise a six-part film whose 'location' stretches across continents and oceans.

REFERENCES

Alam, Muzaffar. 2003. 'The Culture and Politics of Persian in Precolonial Hindustan'. In *Literary Cultures in History: Reconstructions from South Asia*, edited by Sheldon Pollock, 131–198. Berkeley: University of California Press.

Arnfred, Signe. 2004. 'Tufo Dancing: Muslim Women's Culture in Northern Mozambique'. *Lusotopie* 2004 (11): 39–65. Accessed 5 July 2021. https://www.persee.fr/doc/luso_1257-0273_2004_num_11_1_1588.

Asani, Ali S. 2003. 'At the Crossroads of Indic and Iranian Civilizations: Sindhi Literary Culture'. In *Literary Cultures in History: Reconstructions from South Asia*, edited by Sheldon Pollock, 612–646. Berkeley: University of California Press.

Bandyopadhyay, Manik. [1936] 2012. *The Boatman of the Padma*. Trans. Ratan K. Chattopadhyay. Hyderabad: Orient Blackswan.

———. [1950] 2018. *Restless Waters of the Ichhamati*. Trans. Rimli Bhattacharya. New Delhi: Rupa.

BBC. 2019. 'Why Did an Entire Civilization Vanish?' Elise Hugus and Daniel Cajanu. BBC Reel, 03:51. Accessed 15 July 2021. https://www.bbc.com/reel/video/p077x0m7/why-did-an-entire-civilisation-vanish-.

Beal, Samuel, trans. 1884. *Si-Yu-Ki: Buddhist Records of the Western World: Translated from the Chinese of Hiuen Tsiang (A.D. 629)*, vol. 1. London: Trübner.

Berthet, Samuel. 2015. 'Boat Technology and Culture in Chittagong'. In 'Canal Through Time: A Technological Answer to Socio-Environmental Variability? Application to Constraining Environments'. Special issue, *Water History* 7 (2): 179–197.

———. 2020. 'Sailing Across Topology: Vessels of the North-Odisha-Bengal-Arakan Arch'. *Journal of Bengal Art* 25: 267–285.

Bhattacharya, Rimli. 2009. 'On the Track and Off: Fragment, Resonance and Fact'. Unpublished paper, Leverhume Translation Project (International), Jawaharlal Nehru University, New Delhi, 6 January.

———. Forthcoming. 'Subject Nature Divination'. *In Assured Self, Restive Self: Encounters with Crisis, edited by Prasanta Chakravarty*. New Delhi: Bloomsbury.

Braudel, Fernand. 1972. *The Mediterranean and the Mediterranean World in the Age of Philip II*. Trans. Siân Reynolds. London: Fantana.

Campbell, Gwyn. 2008. 'Slave Trades and the Indian Ocean World'. In *India in Africa, Africa in India: Indian Ocean Cosmopolitanisms*, edited by John C. Hawley, 17–51. Bloomington: Indiana University Press.

Carlson, Deborah, Orkan Koyagasioglu and Staci Willis. 2015. 'The Ancient Shipwreck Excavation at Godavaya, Sri Lanka: Finds from the Oldest Shipwreck in the Indian Ocean'. *INA Quarterly* 42 (2): 15–19. Accessed 25 April 2020. https://www.academia.edu/38065354/The_Ancient_Shipwreck_Excavation_at_Godavaya_Sri_Lanka.

CGTN. 2019. 'Tales from the Silk Road of the Sea'. Accessed 9–16 October 2020. Episode 1: https://www.youtube.com/watch?v=M3UPj7NmWTI. Episode 5: https://www.youtube.com/watch?v=uCqd2JQAC0Q.

Chakraborty, Sudhir. 2001. *Baul Fakir Katha*. Kolkata: Ananda Publishers.

Chakravarti, Ranabir. [2002] 2020a. *Trade and Traders in Early Indian Society*. 3rd ed. New Delhi: Manohar Publishers.

———. 2020b. 'Coasts and Interiors of India: Early Modern Indo-Dutch Cross-Cultural Exchanges'. In *The Pull Towards the Coast and Other Essays: The Indian Ocean History and the Subcontinent before 1500 CE*, edited by Ranabir Chakravarti, 93–115. Delhi: Primus Books.

Dasgupta, Subha Chakraborty. 2000. 'Towards an Understanding of the Baromasi and Aspects of Lyric Poetry in Bengal'. In *The Renewal of Song: Renovation in Lyric Conception and Practice*, edited by Earl Miner and Amiya Dev, 88–103. Calcutta: Seagull Books.

Duarte, Ricardo T. 2012. 'Maritime History in Mozambique and East Africa: The Urgent Need for the Proper Study and Preservation of Endangered Underwater Cultural Heritage'. *Journal of Maritime Archaeology* 7 (1): 63–86. https://doi.org/10.1007/s11457-012-9089-6.

Eaton, Richard M. 1993. *The Rise of Islam and the Bengal Frontier 1204–1760*. Berkeley: University of California Press.

———. [2019] 2020. *India in the Persianate Age: 1000–1765*. Delhi: Penguin Books.

Elias, Akhteruzzaman. [1996] 2021. *Khwabnama*. Trans. Arunava Sinha. Delhi: Penguin.

Ghatak, Ritwik, dir. 1972. *Titash ekti nadir naam* (A river called Titash). Introduced by Kumar Shahani. Criterion Collection.

Giosan, Liviu, Peter D. Clift, Mark G. Macklin et al. 2012. 'Fluvial Landscapes of the Harappan Civilization'. *PNAS*, 29 May. https://www.pnas.org/doi/pdf/10.1073/pnas.1112743109.

Hall, Kenneth R. 2011. *A History of Early Southeast Asia: Maritime Trade and Societal Development, 100–1500*. Plymouth: Rowman & Littlefield.

Hofmeyr, Isabel. 2015. 'Styling Multilateralism: Indian Ocean Cultural Futures'. *Journal of the Indian Ocean Region* 11 (1): 98–109. https://doi.org/10.1080/19480881.2014.993565.

———. 2019a. 'Imperialism Above and Below the Water Line: Making Space Up (and Down) in a Colonial Port City'. *Interventions* 22 (8): 1–13. https://doi.org/10.1080/1369801X.2019.1659172.

———. 2019b. 'Literary Ecologies of the Indian Ocean'. *English Studies in Africa* 62 (1): 1–7. https://doi.org/10.1080/00138398.2019.1629677.

———. 2021. *Dockside Reading: Hydrocolonialism and the Custom House*. Durham: Duke University Press.

Holcombe, Charles. 1999. 'Trade-Buddhism: Maritime Trade, Immigration, and the Buddhist Landfall in Early Japan'. *Journal of the American Oriental Society* 119 (2): 280–292. Accessed 23 March 2019. http://www.jstor.org/stable/606111.

Huang, Pei-Ling. 2022. 'A Meshwork of Melodies: *Des*-making Through the Singing and Wayfaring of Shah Abdul Latif's Devotees'. *Philological Encounters* 7 (1–2): 161–196.

Jayamanne, Laleen. 2015. *The Epic Cinema of Kumar Shahani*. Bloomington: Indiana University Press.

Keay, John. 2005. *The Spice Route: A History*. London: John Murray.

Kosambi, Damodar D. [1956] 1975. *An Introduction to the Study of Indian History*. Bombay: Popular Prakashan.

Latif, Shah Abdul. 2018. *Risalo*. Trans. and ed. Christopher Shackle. Cambridge, MA: Harvard University Press.

Lavery, Charne. 2020. 'Diving into the Slave Wreck: The *São José Paquete d'Africa* and Yvette Christianse's *Imprendehora*'. *Eastern African Literary and Cultural Studies* 6 (4): 269–283. https://doi.org/10.1080/23277408.2020.1799706.

Machado, Pedro. 2004. 'A Forgotten Corner of the Indian Ocean: Gujarati Merchants, Portuguese India and the Mozambique Slave-Trade, c. 1730–1830'. In *The Structure of Slavery in Indian Africa and Asia*, edited by Gwyn Campbell, 17–27. London and Portland: Frank Cass.

Maculuve, Rufus. 2020. 'Soundscapes of Omuhipiti'. *Eastern African Literary and Cultural Studies* 6 (4): 258–268. https://doi.org/10.1080/23277408.2020.1809612.

Mallabarman, Adwaita. [1956] 1993. *A River Called Titash*. Trans. Kalpana Bardhan. Berkeley: University of California Press.

Manguin, Pierre-Yves. 2011. 'Asian Ship-Building Tradition'. In *The Trading World of the Indian Ocean, 1500–1800*, edited by Om Prakash, 597–629. Vol. 3, Part 7, of *History of Science, Philosophy and Culture in Indian Civilization*, edited by Debi Prasad Chattopadhyaya. Delhi: Pearson.

Mani, Lavanya. 2020. 'Lavanya Mani in Conversation with Art Historian Sylvia Houghteling'. Uploaded 16 December 2020. Accessed 17 July 2021. https://youtu.be/rfatxS568OA.

Martin, Adrian. 2013. 'A River Called Titas: River of No Return'. Criterion Collection, 12 December. Accessed 28 June 2020. https://www.criterion.com/current/posts/2990-a-river-called-titas-river-of-no-return.

Mukherjee, Rila. 2017. 'Accidental Ports: The Bengal Delta in the Sixteenth–Seventeenth Centuries'. In *Subversive Sovereigns Across the Seas: Indian Ocean Ports-of-Trade from Early Historic Times to Late Colonialism*, edited by Kenneth R. Hall, Rila Mukherjee and Suchandra Ghosh, 146–175. Kolkata: The Asiatic Society.

Paine, Lincoln. 2015. 'The Indian Ocean in the Seventh and Eighth Centuries'. In *Maritime Contacts of the Past: Deciphering Connections Amongst Communities*, edited by Sila Tripati, 37–53. New Delhi: Delta Book World.

Parveen, Abida. 2019a. 'Ayal Karyan Kian – Sur Samoondi'. Uploaded 24 February 2019. Sur Ji Dunya. Accessed 13 December 2020. https://www.youtube.com/watch?v=o7Dq15N15IM&ab_channel=SurJiDunya.

———. 2019b. 'Shah jo raag – Sur Samundi'. Uploaded 22 July 2019. Indus Point. Accessed 13 December 2020. https://www.youtube.com/watch?v=wI1ZeBWSGu4.

Pedersen, Ralph K. 2015. 'A Survey for Shipwrecks, Submerged Settlements and Seafaring Technology in Bahrain'. In *Shipwrecks Around the World: Revelations of the Past*, edited by Sila Tripathi, 1–20. Accessed 17 November 2020. https://www.academia.edu/10962892/A_survey_for_shipwrecks_submerged_settlements_and_seafaring_technology_in_Bahrain.

Praia Morremone 1. 2017. Filmed at Vila de Pebane, Mozambique, 23 October 2017. Uploaded by Ellen Hebden, 25 February 2019. Accessed 17 October 2020. https://www.youtube.com/watch?v=m30-k9qXN-Q&ab_channel=EllenHebden.

Ramachandran, Sudha. 2019. 'Rivalries and Relics: Examining China's Buddhist Public Diplomacy'. *China Brief* 19 (5). Accessed 20 October 2020. https://jamestown.org/program/rivalries-and-relics-examining-chinas-buddhist-public-diplomacy/.

Ray, Niharranjan. [1959] 1994. *History of the Bengali People*. Trans. John W. Hood. Calcutta: Orient Longman.

Sen, Tansen. 2003. *Buddhism, Diplomacy, and Trade: The Realignment of Sino-Indian Relations, 600–1400*. Honolulu: University of Hawai'i Press.

———. 2006. 'The Travel Records of Chinese Pilgrims Faxian, Xuanzang, and Yijing: Sources for Cross-Cultural Encounters Between Ancient China and Ancient India'. *Education About Asia* 11 (3): 24–33. Accessed 27 July 2020. https://www.asianstudies.org/publications/eaa/archives/the-travel-records-of-chinese-pilgrims-faxian-xuanzang-and-yijing-sources-for-cross-cultural-encounters-between-ancient-china-and-ancient-india/.

Shackle, Christopher, ed. 2018. 'Introduction'. In *Risalo*, edited by Christopher Shackle. Cambridge, MA: Harvard University Press.

Shahani, Kumar, dir. 1991. *Bhavantarana*/Immanence (Oriya and Sanskrit). Ministry of External Affairs and Kumar Shahani.

———. [1992] 2015. 'The Cotton Project: Proposal for a Cinematic Exploration'. In *The Shock of Desire and Other Essays*, edited and introduced by Ashish Rajadhyaksha, 336–343. New Delhi: Tulika Books.

———. [1995] 2015. 'Ritwik'. In *The Shock of Desire and Other Essays*, edited and introduced by Ashish Rajadhyaksha, 250–257. New Delhi: Tulika Books.

———, dir. 2000. *Bansuri*/Bamboo Flute (Hindi and Tamil). Ministry of External Affairs and Kumar Shahani.

Sharma, Aparna. 2015. *Documentary Films in India: Critical Aesthetics at Work*. London: Palgrave Macmillan.

Silva, Neluka. 2022. 'A Crisis of Nationhood: Post-War Sri Lankan Cinema and Revisiting of History'. In *South Asian Ways of Seeing: Contemporary Visual Cultures*, edited by Samarth Singhal and Amrita Ajay, 89–110. New Delhi: Primus Books.

Sorley, H.T. 1966. *Shāh Abdul Latif of Bhit: His Poetry, Life, and Times: A Study of Literary, Social and Economic Conditions in Eighteenth Century Sind*. Karachi: Oxford University Press.

Stubblefield, Thomas. 2006. 'Ritwik Ghatak and the Role of Sound in Representing Post-Partition Bengal'. *PostScript*. 25 (3): 17–29. Accessed 20 November 2020. https://www.academia.edu/3854196/Ritwik_Ghatak_and_the_Role_of_Sound_in_Representing_Post_Partition_Bengal.

Thapar, Romila. 2013a. 'The Buddhist Tradition: Monks as Historians'. In *The Past Before Us: Historical Traditions of Early North India*, edited by Romila Thapar, 381–413. Ranikhet: Permanent Black.

———. 2013b. 'Early Inscriptions as Historical Statements (Up to c. the Sixth Century AD)'. In *The Past Before Us: Historical Traditions of Early North India*, edited by Romila Thapar, 319–352. Ranikhet: Permanent Black.

Vaudeville, Charlotte. 1986. *Barahmasa in Indian Literatures: Songs of the Twelve Months in Indo-Aryan Literatures*. Delhi: Motilal Banarasidass.

Yü, Chün-fang. 2001. *Kuan-yin: The Chinese Transformation of Avalokitesvara*. New York: Columbia University Press.

PART 4

CLOSING REFLECTIONS

13

Travel Disruptions: Irritability and Canonisation

Danai S. Mupotsa and Pumla Dineo Gqola

> The broken tongue is displaced on and through and traverses
> multiple registers: the linguistic, the kinaesthetic, the aural, the
> alimentary, the symbolic, and the socio-political.
> — Xin Liu (Mupotsa and Xin Liu 2019, 128)

*This offering is a brief entry into some of the ways we think together –
and, more specifically, a playful reanimation of a recent telephone
conversation during which we recounted the manner in which Isabel
Hofmeyr's person, process and work have animated our own. Hofmeyr has
been a colleague to us both. Explored here are what those relations leave
imprinted in our experiences, and the means whereby they steadily hold
each of us in the grounds of our own encounters with scholarly production. It is also an experiment with form – simultaneously taken seriously
and remaining under question – as we continue to play and work with
questions of attachment and method in Hofmeyr's scholarship. In differently
accented yet shared idiom, we reflect on the value of circuits, circulations*

and pathways of ideas in Hofmeyr's work. To write together, intentionally and lovingly dialogic, filling the pages with the anxieties created within the differences or distinctions in our narrative registers; the fear of being misunderstood or misrecognised, even with the intimacy between us – this gap or space generates what is also our experience of our relationship to Hofmeyr and her work. We turn over the connections between her illumination of how ideas migrate in productive and/or troubling ways across space and time in a reading of a moment of cinematic difficulty, as well as in our own ongoing work on slavery and questions of power.

In 'Stammering Tongue' (Mupotsa and Xin Liu 2019), Danai writes with another of her beloved thinkers, Xin Liu, about the generative potentiality in those gaps, the stammering tongue offered as a governing metaphor and a modality put to use in practices of reading and writing. Practices of reading and writing are woven pursuits and intentions in Hofmeyr's work. We relish her productive irritability and how it reveals the gaps in field constitution or canonisation, such as we discuss here in her early critique of what becomes taken for granted under the banner 'South African literature' (Hofmeyr 1996). This is where we both meet her and her work – this commitment to move in and through disciplinary formations, in and through the registers of their languages, and also often against them in trying to find forms of theorising that can better accommodate our ethical commitments.

Danai: I remember a time when I was away for a conference in Germany and preparing to talk about a film that has perhaps preoccupied me too much, Ntshavheni waLuruli's *Elelwani* (2012). The film's co-producer, Jyoti Mistry, views the film as framing its narrative, conceptual and temporal territory in the mode of *translation*, with Venda as a 'rich cultural landscape' and 'community informed by a long tradition of royal lineage and a vibrant history woven with incredible legends of sacred forests and lakes' (Mistry 2015, 118). Since both the original novel by Titus N. Maumela (1972) and the film script are written entirely in Tshivenda, this translation is one related to the visual, the oral and the aural. It is translation of the lifeworlds and cosmological structure of the language, conscripted to the assumption that language is culture, which was key to the making of a white South Africa and the creation of black 'homelands' intended as surplus labour pools and repositories of 'tradition'. This is translation mediating the oral and the written by a mission-educated cultural organiser and teacher negotiating the tensions of the past and the present while in the process of inventing tradition, and becoming laden with didactic orientations as well as complex and often contradictory deployments of tradition and modernity. The film's narrative arc rests on the place of women, with democracy temporally located in the space/time of modernity. The category of freedom, articulated through the concept of the sovereign or autological subject, is placed under strain by what Elizabeth Povinelli (2006) offers in juxtaposition: a genealogical society. While sitting at the conference in Germany, I emailed Hofmeyr, asking for her advice on how to read one of the scenes of this film. It's the very long wedding scene, in which the titular protagonist crosses various thresholds, performing a liminal phase – one that I would offer is filled with narrative disruptions and refusals of closure that mirror the film's attempt to decentre an easy sense of the attachment between democracy and individual freedom as provisional points of entry into intimate modernity. This scene is soundscaped with Zim Ngqawana's dirge as Elelwani moves from one position to another, lying on a mat on the ground under a veil, her body organised around multiple territorial and temporal wishes, around an oral, performative and visual elegy, as the madman Madzwara repeats 'We are exterminated' while Elelwani's father calls out her clan names. This dirge is a song of sorrow, with marriage a threshold of life and death where neither operates in oppositional status against the other, a circular, recitative process, half-spoken and half-sung, the music of a life cycle.

In my email I asked Hofmeyr for something to help me understand the oral structure of the elegy. She referred me to Ruth Finnegan's ([1970] 2012) *Oral Literature in Africa*, which of course has canonical status. I felt a bit silly for asking, perhaps from the kind of misrecognition you and I both anxiously hold or anticipate when we think and attempt to write together. And perhaps even more meaningful to me is Hofmeyr's *'We Spend Our Years as a Tale That is Told': Oral Historical Narrative in a South African Chiefdom* (1993), which I came across in a second-hand bookshop, with 'Margaret Daymond, 1994' inscribed in blue pen on the first page and filled with Daymond's annotations.[1] This book, now suffused with my own annotations, is really dear to me. In it, Hofmeyr engages historical narrative, story, history, literacy, time, form, telling and the very relation to intimate modernity I continue to grapple with; and she sets out her intentions from the gaps elicited in Finnegan's study. The book, a gift, one that becomes a love object, the object of circulation and translation in Hofmeyr's work – this becomes an attachment and method. Circulation, the commodity and the gift at the interface in much of Hofmeyr's work, takes on new resonance.

Pumla: Circulation and circuits appear as unrelenting curiosity in Hofmeyr's work, and the relationship of texts to place is one way in which she revisits this set of enduring interests. Academic disciplines socialise us into precise conceptions of this association of text and place as always more than context, but as peculiar 'ways of seeing' in the John Berger (1972) sense. Although the borders between these traditions are porous, academics largely accept that to read sociologically is something distinct from how a historian might make meaning. In the discipline of English literature, *place* is the world that produces a sensibility, and although the 'eight periods of English literature' model has lost some of its burnish, its logics are still everywhere in how we read in literary scholarly ways. All of this is part of Hofmeyr's inheritance (and mine). And yet, tracing her intellectual patterns morphs into a dance with the generative work of exceeding these discipline-bound logics. At different stages of her career, circuits and circulations are treated with an irritable restlessness, and as a joyful experiment. I see both in her early co-edited collection, *LIP from Southern African Women* (Brown, Hofmeyr and Rosenberg 1983), which has now disappeared from public view, and was an experiment with form as much as space.

(This aesthetic play and seriousness found in the titles of all her books should be no surprise. She is a writer and a literary scholar, after all. Still, it is a delight.)

Texts and spaces interact in mutually constitutive ways, shadowed by the question, what happens to this mutuality under conditions of loss? Hofmeyr's appreciation of texts 'made across time and space' in *The Portable Bunyan: A Transnational History of 'The Pilgrim's Progress'* (2004), where she plots the corridors of Bunyan's *Pilgrim's Progress* across centuries, continents and traditions, is another instance of what I have in mind. For instance, in the first chapter of this work, she queries how Bunyan, quintessentially 'an intellectual of the world with a transnational circulation, is remembered only as a national writer with a local presence' (2) in English literary canon formation.

Inevitably, what she illuminates here – as she does in *'We Spend Our Years as a Tale That is Told'*, when she expresses irritation at how comfortably the South African literary academy can draw boundaries around the category 'South African literature' – is something about canonisation. We already know much about the enmeshments of power, selection, empire, nation and taste in the making of literary and religious canons. But there is a granularity that her work exposes to this schema for me. A theorisation. For example, I was thinking through Hofmeyr as I returned as an older reader interested in slavery and the literary imagination to William Blake's illustrations to his *Songs of Innocence* (1789), and later to his *Songs of Innocence and Experience* (1794); and again when I was rereading Thomas Pringle (1819, 1828), dubbed 'the first South African poet'.[2] Both Blake and Pringle had been the standard stuff of my high school and undergraduate English literature education, taught in ways that spoke of moral and environmental degradation that came with the Industrial Revolution, and in ways that excised any mention of slavery. This part of canonisation that Hofmeyr is unhappy to leave explained as simply the work of empire or even as conceptually paradoxical – like Bunyan's transnationalism somehow being squeezable into small, ill-fitting national English literary sensibility – is not a world away from the processes that insist on the canonisation of two prominent abolitionists while completely erasing references to slavery conceptually or even in the illustrations Blake himself made for the first edition of *Songs*.

Of course, Hofmeyr's generative circulatory reading strategies make her particular texts – oral or in book form – compelling. Additionally, in my view, hers are such generative conceptual and reading orientations that they travel in disruptive ways to sites far outside of her interest.

Danai: The irritation, as you describe it, is one of the things I enjoy most. It is sharp. And present. And I suppose that through it we glean some of our own disciplinary and methodological tendencies. Hofmeyr's attention to oral history operates on so many levels – for instance, in relation to gender and genre; or to time, where a quest for purity often not only implies a gendered subject who transfers the story but also designates a language of narrative closures and monolingual and mono-humanist 1:1 translation. I would love to think of the irritation with regard to the practice of oral history, and with the assumptive approach to method that repeats on the level of form, as something that is in communion with what Keguro Macharia (2019) describes as 'frottage'. The latter is bodily, sensational, a relation of proximity, an aesthetic and libidinal. We could think here of Hofmeyr's provocations in 'Not the Magic Talisman: Rethinking Oral Literature in Southern Africa' (1996) as putting a strain on modes of reading oral narrative. Macharia describes frottage another way, as 'an awkward term, one that hinted at strangers rubbing themselves against others in public spaces' (2019, 5). I am thinking Hofmeyr and Macharia in frottage, perhaps because Hofmeyr's irritation in form and method offers insight into another term Macharia (2020) plays with: belated/belatedness.

I have been thinking about belatedness, what it means to be marked as absent or delayed or not yet ready or undeveloped or illiterate or primitive. Or as child or woman or black or blackened. Or African. I have been thinking about what this belatedness means for politics and thinking, for theory and coalition, for genealogies of knowledge and pedagogical practice, for co-imagining freedom and co-building a different world.

Belatedness operates at the level of power/knowledge because it has produced modes of doing research that separate the authority of the interpreter (the one who receives the translation and then interprets it; the one with the ability to abstract from the story to the extent that it becomes theory) from the authority of the one who collects the story. This relies on a belated relation to oral narrative, pure and unmediated. This reading feeds my heart, as I have sat with field, the field, fieldwork, fieldworker. The potential in belatedness is also another threshold, congestion, a swollenness that feeds the assemblage of circulation, the gift, commodity, territorial scales between 'a local' and otherwises, the making of the sovereign subject, the relation to speech, writing and authority, and how in oral and written forms, authoring and authority take on a polyphonic register, so to speak.

Pumla: Yes, I am reminded of Edward Said (1983) on travelling theory: its mobility and capacity to simultaneously multi-root and intervene in vastly different material geographies, altering how we see what it touches, like a commodity, a book, but also more. 'What made this particular text so translatable?' is a question Hofmeyr asks about Bunyan's book. Such a necessary question when we are thinking about how to constantly orient ourselves to reading creative, political and cultural production.

Although so much of her work is about voyaging and what such movements enact, it is also about holding. The languaging of her work is also about making place: a portal, a portable text, but also a conceptual capacity to hold more than one set of ideas in place.

As we necessarily fixate on memory and archive in southern Africa (and beyond), the guiding questions in Hofmeyr's '*We Spend Our Years as a Tale that is Told*' (1993) are taking on a new – or maybe just additional – saliency. Maybe just 'again'. I have in mind her dissatisfaction with the connections between oral narrative and territorialised memory as fixed. Revisiting that text when we are thinking about land, materiality and place in South Africa allows me to see something in her insistence of the imaginative capacity of mutating and transfiguring oral narrative, first, and the corrosive, dislodging violence of forced removal, second, as actually two intertwined possibilities.

Again, while teaching us much about the oral and written interpretative text traditions treated with such ingenuity by Hofmeyr, I am now seduced by the possibility of reading the local/transnational or the oral/book form in integrated ways, as an older re-reader of her 1993 text. I do not think it is because I did not understand it when I first read it the year after its initial publication, only half-interested as I was in 'oral literature'. I am not necessarily more interested in the study of oral literature now, but Hofmeyr's is a text that speaks to temporally and spatially changed times in differently generative ways.

NOTES

1   Margaret Daymond (1940–2021) was nationally and internationally recognised as a leading scholar on the writings of southern African women. She retired from the University of Natal (now the University of KwaZulu-Natal) as an emeritus professor and a fellow.
2   See also Pringle's preface to Prince (1831).

REFERENCES

Berger, John. 1972. *Ways of Seeing*. London: Penguin.

Blake, William. 1789. *Songs of Innocence*. London: W. Blake.

———. 1794. *Songs of Innocence and Experience: Shewing the Two Contract States of the Human Soul*. London: W. Blake.

Brown, Susan, Isabel Hofmeyr and Susan Rosenberg, eds. 1983. *LIP from South African Women*. Johannesburg: Ravan Press.

Finnegan, Ruth. [1970] 2012. *Oral Literature in Africa*. Cambridge: Open Book Publishers.

Hofmeyr, Isabel. 1993. *'We Spend Our Years as a Tale That is Told': Oral Historical Narrative in a South African Chiefdom*. Johannesburg: Wits University Press.

———. 1996. 'Not the Magic Talisman: Rethinking Oral Literature in Southern Africa'. *World Literature Today* 70 (1): 88–92.

———. 2004. *The Portable Bunyan: A Transnational History of 'The Pilgrim's Progress'*. Johannesburg: Wits University Press.

Macharia, Keguro. 2019. *Frottage: Frictions of Intimacy Across the Black Diaspora*. New York: New York University Press.

———. 2020. 'belated: interruption'. *GLQ* 26 (3): 561–573.

Maumela, Titus N. 1972. *Elelwani*. Johannesburg: Van Schaik.

Mistry, Jyoti. 2015. 'Filmmaking at the Margins of a Community: On Co-producing *Elelwani*'. In *Gaze Regimes: Film and Feminisms in Africa*, edited by Jyoti Mistry and Antje Schuhmann, 118–132. Johannesburg: Wits University Press.

Mupotsa, Danai S. and Xin Liu. 2019. 'Stammering Tongue'. *Tydskrif vir Letterkunde* 56 (1): 127–142.

Povinelli, Elizabeth. 2006. *The Empire of Love: Toward a Theory of Intimacy, Genealogy, and Carnality*. Durham: Duke University Press.

Prince, Mary. 1831. *The History of Mary Prince, a West Indian Slave: Related by Herself*. London: F. Westley and A.H. Davis.

Pringle, Thomas. 1819. *The Autumnal Excursions; or, Sketches in Teviotdale*. Edinburgh: Archibald Constable and Co.

———. 1828. *Ephemerides; or, Occasional Poems: Written in Scotland and South Africa*. London: Smith, Elder and Co.

Said, Edward. 1983. *The World, the Text, and the Critic*. Cambridge, MA: Harvard University Press.

Proximate

Gabeba Baderoon

Sea-bidden,
wind-coursed,
you yourself

are dorsal,
surging –

mast and compass,
element and strait,
at once.

On quests
and their making, books
and their making and seas,

your making leaves
a lucent trail.
Ever questing, else-

bound, but bearing
transverse,
you yourself

are liquid,
liminal,
limitless.

Wake-
borne, we
conjure you

proximate,
infinite,
here.

Sunil Amrith is the Renu and Anand Dhawan Professor of History at Yale University, New Haven, Connecticut. His research focuses on the movements of people and the ecological processes that have connected South and South East Asia. Amrith's areas of particular interest include environmental history, the history of migration and the history of public health. His most recent book is *Unruly Waters* (2018), a history of the struggle to understand and control the monsoon in modern South Asia. He is also the author of *Crossing the Bay of Bengal: The Furies of Nature and the Fortunes of Migrants* (2013) and of *Migration and Diaspora in Modern Asia* (2011).

Gabeba Baderoon is a poet and scholar. She is the author of several poetry collections, including *The Dream in the Next Body* (2005), *A Hundred Silences* (2006) and *The History of Intimacy* (2018), and the monograph *Regarding Muslims: From Slavery to Post-apartheid* (2014). She co-edited, with Desiree Lewis, the essay collection *Surfacing: On Being Black and Feminist in South Africa* (2021). Baderoon co-directs the African Feminist Initiative at Penn State University, Philadelphia, and is the 2023 Sarah Baartman Senior Fellow at the University of Cape Town.

Karin Barber is Emeritus Professor of African Cultural Anthropology at the University of Birmingham and Visiting Professor of Anthropology at the London School of Economics. She obtained her PhD at the University of Ifẹ̀, Nigeria (now Ọbáfẹ́mi Awólọ́wọ̀ University). Her research focuses on Yorùbá oral literature, popular theatre and print culture in Nigeria. She has also done comparative work on popular culture and textual production across Africa. Her publications include *The Anthropology of Texts, Persons and Publics* (2007), *Print Culture and the First Yorùbá Novel* (2012) and *A History of African Popular Culture* (2018). In 2019 Barber received the President's Lifetime Achievement Award of the Royal Anthropological Institute. She was appointed a DBE in 2021.

Rimli Bhattacharya trained in Comparative Literature at Jadavpur University (Kolkata, India) and Brown University (Providence, Rhode Island). She works in the fields of gender and performance, children's literature and primary education, with an emphasis on visual culture. Recent publications include *'The Dancing Poet': Rabindranath Tagore and Choreographies of Participation* (2019), *Public Women in British India* (2018) and a translation of Bibhutibhushan Bandyopadhyay's novel *Restless Waters of the Ichhamati* (2018). She is involved in Stitching Sails: Rising Oceans, an ongoing multimedia project for young people on the Indian Ocean.

Antoinette Burton is Professor of History at the University of Illinois, Urbana-Champaign. Her work has focused on women, gender, sexuality, race and empire history. She collaborated with Isabel Hofmeyr on *Ten Books That Shaped the British Empire: Creating the Imperial Commons* (2014). She is the co-editor, with Renisa Mawani, of *Animalia: An Anti-Imperial Bestiary for Our Times* (2020), which features Isabel Hofmeyr's 'J is for Jackal'.

Pumla Dineo Gqola is Professor of Literary and Cultural Studies and South African Research Chair in African Feminist Imagination at Nelson Mandela University. Author of five books, including *Rape: A South African Nightmare* (2015) and *Female Fear Factory* (2021), she also edited

Miriam Tlali: Writing Freedom (2021). She has been Professor in African Literature at the University of the Witwatersrand, Johannesburg, and Chief Research Specialist in Society, Culture and Identities at the Human Sciences Research Council.

Carolyn Hamilton is the South African Research Chair in Archive and Public Culture at the University of Cape Town. Her work, ranging across the early history of southern Africa, the production of history, and the nature of archive and of public deliberative processes, deals with the mutual shaping and reshaping across time of archive and historical discourse. She is the author of *Terrific Majesty* (1998) and co-editor of *Refiguring the Archive* (2002), *The Cambridge History of South Africa* (2010) and *Babel Unbound* (2020).

Madhumita Lahiri is the author of *Imperfect Solidarities: Tagore, Gandhi, Du Bois, and the Global Anglophone* (2020). Previously a postdoctoral fellow at the Centre for Indian Studies in Africa at the University of the Witwatersrand, Johannesburg, she is currently Associate Professor at the University of Michigan, Ann Arbor. Her research engages the interlinked trajectories of South Asian, southern African and African American literature, with occasional forays into film and media studies.

Charne Lavery is Senior Lecturer in the Department of English at the University of Pretoria and Co-director of the Oceanic Humanities for the Global South Project based at the Wits Institute for Social and Economic Research (WiSER), University of the Witwatersrand, Johannesburg. She researches literary and cultural representations of the Indian Ocean, the Southern Ocean and the Antarctic seas, and explores ocean writing of the global South in a time of environmental change. She is a South African Humanities and Social Sciences delegate to the international Scientific Committee on Antarctic Research, co-editor of the Palgrave series Maritime Literature and Culture and board member of the journal *Global Nineteenth-Century Studies*. Her monograph *Writing Ocean Worlds: Indian Ocean Fiction in English* was published in 2021.

Khwezi Mkhize received his PhD in Africana Studies from the University of Pennsylvania, Philadelphia. He is currently Lecturer in the Department of African Literature at the University of the Witwatersrand, Johannesburg, and co-editor of the journal *African Studies*. He is the author of numerous essays and co-editor of *Foundational African Writers: Peter Abrahams, Noni Jabavu, Sibusiso Nyembezi and Es'kia Mphahlele* (2022).

Danai S. Mupotsa teaches in the Department of African Literature at the University of the Witwatersrand, Johannesburg. She recently co-edited a special issue of *Agenda*, titled 'Covid-19: The Intimacies of Pandemics' (2021), with Moshibudi Motimele, and the special issue of *GLQ* titled 'Time Out of Joint: The Queer and the Customary in Africa' (2020) with Neville Hoad and Kirk Fiereck. In 2018 she published her first collection of poetry, *feeling and ugly*. The Portuguese translation, *feio e ugly*, was published in 2020.

Sarah Nuttall is Professor of Literary and Cultural Studies and Director of the Wits Institute for Social and Economic Research (WiSER) at the University of the Witwatersrand, Johannesburg. She has published numerous books on South African and African literatures, art, cities and cultures, including *Entanglement: Literary and Cultural Reflections on Postapartheid* (2009) and *Johannesburg: The Elusive Metropolis* (2008). In 2022 she co-edited, with Isabel Hofmeyr and Charne Lavery, a special issue of *Interventions* on 'Reading for Water' in southern African literatures. Most recently she has written *Your History with Me: The Films of Penny Siopis* and co-edited the collection *Hinterlands: Extraction, Abandonment, Care*.

James Ogude is the Director of the Centre for the Advancement of Scholarship at the University of Pretoria. He is Professor of African Literature and Cultures, with a special focus on memory and postcolonial literatures, popular culture and, more recently, Ubuntu and African ecologies. He recently concluded a five-year project on the southern African philosophical concept of Ubuntu (funded by the Templeton World Charity Foundation) and is currently leading a Mellon-funded supra-national project on African urbanities. He is also the Director of the African Observatory for Environmental Humanities located at the Centre for the Advancement of Scholarship at the University of Pretoria. His most recent edited volume is *Ubuntu and the Reconstitution of Community* (2019).

Christopher E.W. Ouma is an Associate Professor in the Department of English at the University of Cape Town. His research and teaching interests include the broader field of contemporary African and African diasporic literary and cultural production. He has held fellowships at the Open University Milton Keynes, the University of Johannesburg and, recently, the Mandela Fellowship at Harvard University. Ouma is the author of *Childhood in Contemporary Diasporic African Literature: Memories and Futures Past* (2020). He co-edited *The Spoken Word Project: Stories Travelling Through Africa* (2014). He is currently co-editor of the journal *Social Dynamics: A Journal of African Studies*.

Ranka Primorac is an Associate Professor in the Department of English at the University of Southampton, United Kingdom. Her research interests centre on the literatures and cultures of southern Africa. Her first monograph, *The Place of Tears* (2006), is a bench-mark analysis of the anglophone Zimbabwean novel under Robert Mugabe. Her second, in the making, is provisionally titled *Queues of Limitless Hope*, and would not be thinkable without Isabel Hofmeyr's *The Portable Bunyan*. Ranka co-edits the Boydell & Brewer mono-graph series African Articulations.

Meg Samuelson is Associate Professor in the Department of English and Creative Writing at the University of Adelaide and Associate Professor Extraordinaire at Stellenbosch University. She has published widely in (South/ern) African, (Indian) Ocean, (global) South and Anthropocene studies, with a focus on literature, photography and film. She co-edits the Palgrave series Maritime Literature and Culture and is currently lead researcher on the Australian Research Council–funded project titled Between Indian and Pacific Oceans: Reframing Australian Literatures.

Lakshmi Subramanian is Research Professor at the Centre for Studies in Social Sciences in Calcutta, India. She has authored several major books on the economic and cultural history of India, her special subfields of interest being trade and social networks in the Indian Ocean, histories of predation and the social history of music in modern south India. Major publications include *Three Merchants of Bombay* (2012) and *A History of India 1707–1857* (2010).

INDEX

Page numbers in italics indicate figures.